Western Civilization
A Concise History
VOLUME I
From Early Societies to the Reformation

Western Civilization
A Concise History
VOLUME I

From Early Societies to the Reformation

Glenn Blackburn
Clinch Valley College of the University of Virginia

St. Martin's Press
New York

Senior editor: Don Reisman
Development editor: Bruce Glassman
Project editor: Elise Bauman
Production supervisor: Alan Fischer
Text design: Leon Bolognese & Associates, Inc.
Graphics: G&H Soho, Inc., Dolores Bego
Photo researcher: Tara Dooley
Cover design: Jeanette Jacobs Design
Cover photo: Encyclopedia of Hrabanus Maurus, Codex of 1028, folio 527, book XXII, Abbey Library, Montecassino. Scala/Art Resource.

Library of Congress Catalog Card Number: 89-63886

Copyright © 1991 by St. Martin's Press, Inc.
All rights reserved. No part of this book may be reproduced, stored in a retrieval system, or transmitted by any form or by any means, electronic, mechanical, photocopying, recording, or otherwise, except as may be expressly permitted by the applicable copyright statutes or in writing by the Publisher.

Manufactured in the United States of America.
54321
fedcba

For information, write:
St. Martin's Press, Inc.
175 Fifth Avenue
New York, NY 10010

ISBN: 0-312-01861-4

ACKNOWLEDGMENTS

Page 200, from *The Complete Poems of Thomas Hardy*, edited by James Gibson (New York: Macmillan, 1978).

To the many colleagues and students
of Clinch Valley College
of the University of Virginia
who helped make this work possible.

Preface

In *Western Civilization: A Concise History,* I attempt to present the text in ways that are appealing and useful to both instructors and students. First, I strive to tell the story of Western Civilization *concisely.* Second, I integrate many themes into Western history that allow examination of Western Civilization in a global context. Third, analyses of Western technology appear throughout the text in an effort to demonstrate its powerful influence on the course of Western history. Finally, I emphasize the impact of religious beliefs and philosophical ideas on both Western and "non-Western" history.

A concise text can be valuable to both instructors and students because it presents the major themes and basic facts of Western history without overwhelming the student. Highly detailed texts often tempt students to perceive the study of history as an exercise in memorization of data, whereas a concise text encourages students to concentrate on the most important themes and facts. To be more precise, a concise text allows instructors to teach Western history in one semester or one quarter, since the major themes of that history are crisply presented. For two-semester courses (using either the two-volume edition or the combined edition), a concise text is short enough to allow instructors the opportunity to develop other assignments for students—supplementary readings from other sources or library work, for example—while using the text as the core reading.

Integration of non-Western influences on Western history allows discussion of several important topics, such as the beliefs and impact of the major world religions and an understanding of the various technologies that the West has adopted from other civilizations. Another significant question, why the West eventually became wealthier and more powerful than other societies and civilizations, is analyzed in some detail in Chapter 14.

The influence of technology on Western history is demonstrated both in the primary text and, more specifically, in the **Technology boxes** that are included in most chapters. These special illustrated sections contain discussions of new technologies that became important in a particular period and integrate the prevailing attitudes that encouraged the interest in, and the development of, technology. Examples of technologies discussed include the development of irrigation, the Indian (arabic) numeral system, new types of plows, the windmill, gunpowder, the printing press, the log cabin, the railroad, the steam engine, and modern military weapons.

The study of religious beliefs and philosophical ideas is intrinsically important to the text, for it is through religion and philosophy that humans define and express their understanding of their world. The text frequently turns to discussion of religious and philosophical trends throughout history because these themes often reveal the most fundamental desires and goals of people.

In addition, *Western Civilization: A Concise History* includes **timelines** that serve to introduce each chapter, numerous **maps** and **illustrations,** and an *Instructor's Manual.*

ACKNOWLEDGMENTS

In preparing the manuscript, I received assistance and encouragement from many people and institutions. I learned a great deal during my twenty years of teaching, from my students and colleagues at Clinch Valley College of the University of Virginia, and particularly from the members of the Department of History and Philosophy: Stanley Willis, E. L. Henson, William F. Maxwell, David Rouse, and Robert Dise. The library staffs of Clinch Valley College and Wake Forest University were especially helpful, as was Professor George Munro of Virginia Commonwealth University. Always resourceful were the able people at St. Martin's Press, including Don Reisman, Bruce Glassman, and Elise Bauman. I am also grateful to those colleagues who reviewed the various drafts of this manuscript and offered me their valuable insights in shaping the text: Douglas D. Alder, Dixie College; Erving E. Beauregard, University of Dayton; Gerald P. Bodet, University of New Orleans; Werner Braatz, University of Wisconsin, Oshkosh; Edward A. Cole, Grand Valley State College; Patrick Foley, Tarrant County Junior College; Richard M. Golden, Clemson University; Louise E. Hoffman, Penn State University, Harrisburg; Jerry A. Pattengale, Azusa Pacific University; William C. Reynolds, Mercer County Community College; Barry Rothaus, University of Northern Colorado; Thomas Turley, Santa Clara University; and Charles W. Webber, Wheaton College.

Finally, my wife, Jere, and my mother, Margaret Blackburn, were very supportive and patient during the years in which I was writing this text. I thank them both.

Glenn Blackburn
Wise, Virginia

To the Student

Cynics sometimes say that history is "one damn thing after another," the implication being that history is just a chronicle of facts. But history is much more than a series of facts. Most historians try to present facts as part of an interpretation in which events fit together in an overall pattern. In this way, historians seek to make sense of the past, to find some coherence in historical events.

This book emphasizes the impact of science and technology on Western civilization. Science—the attempt to understand the natural world—and technology—the development of tools to manipulate the natural world for human use—have been developed by many societies and civilizations but have been particularly prominent in Western Civilization. This prominence is well illustrated by two mythical stories. One is the story of Prometheus, a deity in ancient Greek mythology who stole fire, a symbol of creativity, from the gods and gave it to humans. In doing this, Prometheus became a symbol embodying the human ability to create. The second is the story of a sixteenth-century German astrologer named Faust, who according to legend sold his soul to the devil in exchange for forbidden knowledge. Thus, both Faust and Prometheus symbolize the human quest for knowledge and power as well as the human willingness to suffer in order to attain knowledge. Historians and others sometimes refer to Western Civilization as "Promethean" or "Faustian," meaning that the West was particularly driven to use science and technology to understand and manipulate nature for human purposes.

The first eleven chapters of this book (Vol. 1) tell the story of Western Civilization from our prehistoric ancestors to the seventeenth century A.D. The Western desire to understand nature began in prehistoric times, but it first became clearly defined by the ancient Hebrews and ancient Greeks. The Hebrews created a unique religion (the source of Christianity, in particular) in which God was considered to be *transcendent*, a spirit separate from nature. This notion of a transcendent God implied that nature is an inanimate thing that could and should be used by humans. The Greeks contributed the idea that the universe is a rational place governed by orderly laws that are comprehensible to humans. These two concepts—the Hebrew idea of a transcendent God and the Greek idea of a rational universe—eventually became the theoretical underpinning of what we call modern science.

The Hebrew-Greek influence was passed on to the Romans who, in turn, passed it on to the Germans—peoples who settled in Europe and were the ancestors of modern Europeans and many North Americans. During the early Middle Ages (A.D. 500–1000), the Germanic peoples created a powerful technological tradition. They developed new farming techniques, windmills, and watermills as sources of nonhuman energy. Certainly peoples in other places also developed new tools and technologies, but by the end of the Middle Ages it was the Europeans who were particularly innovative.

Chapters 12 through 22 of this book (Vol. 2 of the two-volume edition) cover the period from the seventeenth century to the present. During this time, science and technology began to support each other. Science in the form of astronomy, for example, helped create the knowledge and navigational expertise that allowed European sailors to find the sea routes to North and South America and to Asia. Technology in the form of telescopes helped astronomers to peer into the heavens and in the process initiate a scientific revolution. By the eighteenth century, science and technology, in addition to certain political and social developments, helped to produce an industrial revolution. The Industrial Revolution, a new way of producing goods, slowly made Western Civilization wealthier and more powerful than any other civilization on earth. In the nineteenth century, Western Civilization dominated the world. By the twentieth century, that domination began to dissipate, as many Western nations became embroiled in wars that weakened European power. Furthermore, the use of technology began to have many undesirable consequences, such as the despoliation of the environment.

It should already be obvious, from the preceding paragraphs, that science and technology are central elements in the story of Western Civilization. Certainly, other things—political developments, intellectual and artistic achievements, the lives of the common people—are also important, and they are studied in this book as well. But particular emphasis is given to the role of science and technology, for that role is a unique aspect of Western history.

Contents

Preface vii
To the Student ix

1 The Beginning of the Human Story to 800 B.C. 1
  The Paleolithic Era 2
    Human Thought and Religion during the Paleolithic Era 3
    The Last Millennia of the Paleolithic Era 6
  The Neolithic Era 6
    Neolithic Religion 8
    The Impact of Neolithic Society 9
  The Development of Civilization 9
  TECHNOLOGY: The Paradox of Technological Advance 11
    Mesopotamian Civilizations 12
    Egyptian Civilization 16
  Other Early Civilizations 19
    Indus Valley 19
    Minoan 20
    Phoenician 20
    Shang 21
    Mesoamerican 22
  The Decline of the Early Civilizations 22
  Conclusion 23
  Things You Should Know 24
  Suggested Readings 24
  Notes 25

2 A Spiritual and Intellectual Transformation, 800 to 200 B.C. 27
  General Characteristics of the Axial Period 28
    Causes of the Axial Revolution 29

xi

China 30
   Confucianism 30
TECHNOLOGY: The Alphabet 31
   Taoism 33
   The Impact of Religion on Chinese History 34
India 34
   Hinduism 35
   Buddhism 36
   Jainism 37
   The Spread of Buddhism 38
   The Impact of Religion on Indian History 38
Persia 39
   Zoroastrianism 39
The Hebrews and the Greeks 39
   Judaism 40
   Greek Thought 41
The Significance of the Axial Period 41
   Conclusion 43
   Things You Should Know 45
   Suggested Readings 45
   Notes 45

3 The Hebrews, 2000 to 1000 B.C. 47
The Book of Genesis 48
The Origins of Hebrew Religion 49
   Abraham 49
TECHNOLOGY: The Consequences of the Book of Genesis 51
   Moses 52
The Establishment of a Hebrew State 52
The Prophetic Movement 56
Judaism after the Prophets 60
   Conclusion 61
   Things You Should Know 62
   Suggested Readings 62
   Notes 62

4 The Greeks, 1200 to 30 B.C. 63
The Homeric Age 64

Ionia and the Discovery of the "Mind" 66
  Thales and Other Ionians 68
Sparta 69
Athens 71
  Political Evolution 72
  The Position of Women and Slaves 74
  The Persian Threat 75
  Intellectual and Artistic Creativity 75
  Athenian Society 78
  The Peloponnesian War 79
  The Great Philosophers 80
The Hellenistic Era 82
  Hellenistic Creativity 83
Conclusion 84
TECHNOLOGY: Hellenistic Inventions 85
Things You Should Know 86
Suggested Readings 86
Notes 87

5 Rome and the Birth of Christianity, 800 B.C. to A.D. 400 89

Early Roman History 90
The Roman Republic 91
  The Conquest of Italy 93
  The Punic Wars 94
How the Roman Conquests Changed Rome 94
A Century of Turmoil and the End of the Republic 96
The Roman Empire 98
  Augustus, the First Emperor 98
The Grandeur and Degradation of Roman Society 100
TECHNOLOGY: Roman Roads 101
  First-Century Emperors 102
  The Five Good Emperors 103
  Chaos in the Third Century 104
The Origins and Growth of Christianity 104
  The Teachings of Jesus 104
  Jesus' Followers 105
  The Christian Message 107
  Christian Institutions 107
  Christianity in the Early Roman Empire 108

The Political Transformation of the Roman Empire 109
   Militarization 109
   Centralization of Power 109
   Christianization 110

The Spiritual Transformation of the Roman Empire 111

Conclusion *113*
Things You Should Know *113*
Suggested Readings *113*
Notes *114*

6 The Great Migrations, Byzantine Civilization, and Islamic Civilization, A.D. 400 to 700 115

Civilization and Nomad Invaders across Eurasia 116
   Consequences of the Nomad Invasions 118

TECHNOLOGY: A Better System of Numbers 119

The Germanic Peoples and the End of Rome in the West 120
   Western Europe after the Fall of Rome 121

The Eastern Roman, or Byzantine, Empire 124
   Justinian 124
   Byzantine Christianity 125
   External and Internal Conflict 127
   The End of the Byzantine Empire 128

Islam 129
   Muhammad 130
   The Islamic Faith 130
   Islam Expands 133
   Islamic Society and Culture 134

Conclusion *136*
Things You Should Know *136*
Suggested Readings *136*
Notes *137*

7 The Early Middle Ages: A Dynamic Frontier, 500 to 1000 139

The Sixth to Eighth Centuries 140

Contributions of Monks and Nuns 141
   The Benedictine Rule 142

The Peasants Create an Agricultural Revolution 145

TECHNOLOGY: The Moldboard Plow 147

The Carolingian Empire 149
Another Wave of Invasions 151
The Vikings 151
Feudalism and Manorialism 154
The Feudal Relationships 154
Serfdom and Manorialism 157

Conclusion *157*
Things You Should Know *158*
Suggested Readings *158*
Notes *159*

8 The High Middle Ages, 1000 to 1300 161
Towns, Technology, and Trade 162
Towns 163
Technology 164
TECHNOLOGY: The Water Mill and Windmill 165
Trade 166
The Church 168
The Papacy 168
Monasticism 170
The Common People's Christianity 170
Romanesque and Gothic Architecture 171
The Jews 174
The Rise of National Monarchies 175
England 175
France 178
Germany 179
Eastern Europe 181
The Significance of Medieval Political History 182
European Expansion: The Crusading Spirit 182
Crusades to the Holy Land 183
Crusades in Europe 184
Social Change 185
Aristocratic Ideals 185
The Status of Women 186
Growing Individualism 187
Intellectual Debate and Creativity 188
The University and Scholasticism 188
Abelard 189
St. Thomas Aquinas 190
William of Occam 190

Conclusion *192*
Things You Should Know *193*
Suggested Readings *193*
Notes *193*

9 The Countryside and the City, 1200 to 1700 **195**

The Peasant's Life-Style **197**
Material Conditions of Peasant Life *197*
Villages *198*
Customs and Attitudes *200*

Times of Famine **202**

Peasant Rebellions **204**

Changes in Peasant Life **206**
Peasant Standard of Living *206*
The Manorial System Declines in Western Europe *207*
Serfdom Expands in Eastern Europe *208*

The Aristocracy **209**

The Culture of the City **211**

TECHNOLOGY: The Chimney **212**

Crime, Punishment, and Death **215**

Conclusion *216*
Things You Should Know *216*
Suggested Readings *217*
Notes *217*

10 The Renaissance and the European Discovery of the Americas, 1300 to 1600 **219**

Famine, Plague, and War **220**
The Black Death *220*
The Hundred Years' War *222*
The War of the Roses *223*
Reactions to the Calamities *224*

Pax Mongolica and the Growth of Capitalism in Italy **224**
European Trade with the East *225*
Capitalism *225*

The Renaissance **226**
Italy during the Renaissance *226*

TECHNOLOGY: The Printing Press **227**
The Northern Renaissance *234*

Science and Magic during the Renaissance   236

The Conquest of the Oceans by Portugal and Spain   **238**
The Portuguese Voyages   239
The Spanish Discoveries   240

TECHNOLOGY: Improvements in Navigation   **241**
The Spanish in the Americas   242

Conclusion   243
Things You Should Know   244
Suggested Readings   244
Notes   244

11 The Reformation and Subsequent Conflicts, 1500 to 1715   247

The Protestant and Catholic Reformations   **248**
Martin Luther and the Reformation in Germany   249
John Calvin and the Reformation in Switzerland   252
The Reformation in England   253
The Catholic Reformation   254
Art during the Reformation   255
Consequences of the Reformation   256

The Emergence of Strong Monarchical States   **257**

European Wars of the Sixteenth and Seventeenth Centuries   **258**
Spain and the Netherlands   258

TECHNOLOGY: Weaponry   **259**
The Thirty Years' War in the Germanies   262
The English Civil War and the Glorious Revolution   263
The Wars of Louis XIV   264

Conclusion   265
Things You Should Know   266
Suggested Readings   266
Notes   266

Index   267

List of Maps

The First Civilization, 3500–1500 B.C. *7*
Religions and Philosophies of the Axial Age *40*
Ancient Israel, 800 B.C. *57*
Ancient Greece *70*
The Empire of Alexander the Great *83*
The Expansion of Rome, 264 B.C.–A.D. 120 *97*
Barbarian Invasions and the Division of the Roman Empire *122*
The Spread of Islam, A.D. 622–945 *134*
Charlemagne's Empire and Invasions by the Vikings, Magyars, and Muslims, A.D. 800–950 *152*
Medieval Europe, 1200 *163*
Trade Centers in Medieval Europe *167*
The Known World, 1000–1500 *221*
The Old World, 1225–1400 *228*
The Religious Division of Europe, 1517–1648 *252*
Lands Ruled by Charles V, 1514 *254*

Western Civilization

A Concise History

VOLUME I

From Early Societies to the Reformation

1
The Beginning of the Human Story to 800 B.C.

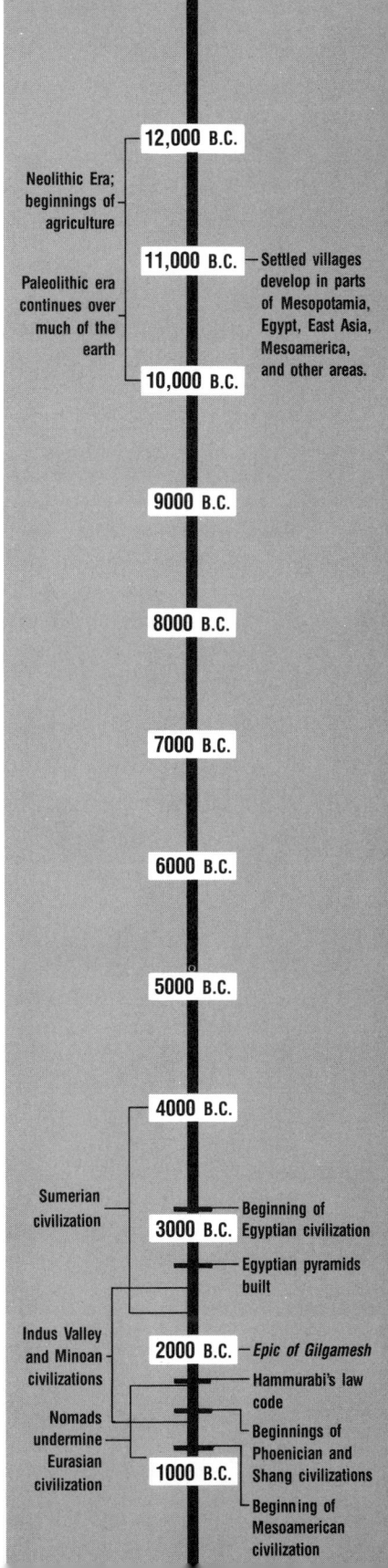

The planet Earth is four to five billion years old, but the human story only began a little more than one million years ago. A million years is a very long time, of course, but it is only a small part of the history of our planet. There was no precise moment at which humans first appeared, for our ancestors evolved human characteristics slowly (such as standing upright) and gradually "became" human. The drama of becoming human may have occurred first in east Africa, but it is possible that humans originated in two or three separate places across the wide tropical belt in Africa and Asia.

Scholars differ on the question of whether life was easy or hard for our oldest ancestors. Some argue that early humans "worked" only a few hours a day and had plenty of leisure time, that life was somewhat like that described in the Garden of Eden story in the Old Testament. Others contend that early humans endured a violent struggle for survival, that life was "nasty, brutish, and short" in the words of the seventeenth-century philosopher Thomas Hobbes.

We do not know what early humans thought about their lives. They had not developed the art of writing and could not communicate their thoughts and feelings with the written word to people of later ages. As a result, our knowledge of early history is fragmentary and inexact, based on fossil records painstakingly gathered and analyzed by archaeologists and anthropologists.

THE PALEOLITHIC ERA

The first era in the human story is known as the *Paleolithic Era* or "Old Stone" Age because early humans used chipped stones for tools and weapons. They survived at first by gathering food and scavenging for whatever plants or animals could be eaten raw. Most people died before the age of thirty, so they produced relatively few children. Consequently, during the Paleolithic Era, which lasted over a million years, down to 12,000–10,000 B.C.,* probably no more than half a million humans were alive at any one time.

That early humans survived at all was due in part to certain advantageous biological traits. They had large, well-developed brains and, therefore, great mental capacity. They could walk upright, so their arms and hands were not brawny instruments used primarily for locomotion. Instead, hands became nimble tools capable of grasping and manipulating things. The brain and the hands gradually became co-workers—what the brain could conceive (a stone turned into a tool, for

---

*The method used in this text for dating years is based on a Christian system that centers around the presumed date of the birth of Jesus Christ. Those years before his birth are designated as B.C. ("before Christ"); those years after Christ's birth are designated as A.D. (from the Latin *anno Domini,* or "in the year of the Lord").

example) the hands could make. Another biological advantage was a special kind of vision: the eyes of early humans were capable of seeing in color and in three dimensions. Humans also had a well-developed larynx, which made them capable of developing speech and language.

These biological traits were typical of all humans, regardless of differences in body appearance or skin color. Racial differentiation occurred as humans developed genetic differences and adapted to different environments around the world. (Differences in skin color, for example, evolved to protect the skin against different intensities of sunlight. Since sunlight intensity is greatest in tropical areas, darker skin colors evolved to protect the body by filtering out some of the sun's rays. Lighter skin colors prevailed in colder climates where sun rays are less intense.) Eventually, different racial groups became associated with particular parts of the world—the Caucasoid in Europe and the Middle East, the Negroid in sub-Saharan Africa, the Australoid in Australia and Southeast Asia, and the Mongoloid in East Asia and the Americas.

In addition to biological advantages, early humans survived because of their ability to adapt culturally. One important aspect of this cultural adaptation was social cooperation. Early humans lived together in groups, or tribes, which protected them from danger and enabled them to gather food more efficiently. These tribal groups were composed of several dozen interrelated people and were egalitarian in nature, with men and women working together and participating in making important decisions. The tribes were also nomadic, constantly on the move in search of food.

Another aspect that made these tribes culturally adaptive was their development of language. No one knows exactly when or how language evolved, but the development of linguistic ability during Paleolithic times greatly expanded human capacities. For example, language allowed small groups of men to cooperate in hunting large animals, thus enabling them to become hunters as well as gatherers.

Hunting brought a degree of specialization to Paleolithic society. Mature men tended to concentrate on the hunt, while women stayed at the camp to care for the children, to collect berries and wild fruits, and to keep the home fires burning. Some scholars believe that the development of hunting may have destroyed Paleolithic egalitarianism by leading to male dominance over women. Others argue that, since hunting was only occasionally successful, women remained equal to men because they were the more reliable providers of food.

Human Thought and Religion during the Paleolithic Era

The development of language was one of the most important episodes of the Paleolithic Era, not only because it made hunting easier but also

Paleolithic and Neolithic Tools The ability to make tools was one of the most distinctive traits of early humans. Paleolithic tools *(top)* were made by striking flakes off a small stone to give it an edge. Neolithic tools *(bottom)*, more finely ground or polished stones, were used in farming communities. (American Museum of Natural History)

because it revealed the fundamental source of human strength—the ability to think. Words, after all, are simply sounds that express externally the concepts or feelings we have inside ourselves. Early humans were "thinkers," seeking to understand the world in which they lived. In particular, they sought to understand the sources of important natural events, such as rain, heat, and sunlight.

Paleolithic religion was *animistic*, meaning that early humans believed that all natural objects had souls or spirits within them. With no source of knowledge but their own experiences, early humans tended to compare everything to themselves. They knew that they were alive and also that nature was full of life, that plants grew, rivers flowed, and animals searched for food. From this they concluded that all things in the world were to some degree alike and shared a common existence. Thus they attributed their own inner feelings or "souls" to other things in the world. Just as a person did something because he wanted to, so the river flowed because it wanted to and the cloud gave rain because it wanted to.

For early humans, nature and humanity were not separate; rather, they were together a reality akin to human life. Since nature was alive, any natural event was seen as a form of intentional action (the river wanted to flow) and any accounting of a natural event was told in the form of a story or myth. The myths of early humans described dramatic actions and explained events in nature. A typical myth, for example, would explain the creation of the world by comparing it to human birth. A primeval couple—the earth and sky—would be portrayed as parents of all that exists. Myths explained such things as how the world originated, who controlled it, and how the world operated. Thus, early humans were engaged in an early form of *cosmology*, a study of the structure and nature of the universe.

The early human's animistic conception of nature gradually developed into a religion of *polytheism*—a belief in many gods—in which the sun, the rain, the soil, and other things important to humans were deified (worshipped as gods). These gods, or spirits, were not considered omnipotent; rather, each had power only in a particular sphere. Thus the rain-god controlled rain and the sun-god controlled the sun. Further, the gods were presumed to have power only in the area occupied by a tribal group, for different tribes had different gods.

Early humans believed that they could influence these gods of nature. Assuming that anything that affects a person is real, ancient peoples made no distinction between what we call subjective processes—dreams and ideas, for example—and external realities. They assumed that what was in the mind was just as real as any physical reality. Thus, they came to believe that by acting out what was in the mind they could influence the course of natural events. When they wanted rain, they acted out this idea through a rain dance, communicating their wishes to the rain-god. Often, these rituals seemed to provide the desired consequences. The ritual to encourage the return of warm weather, usually performed at the end of a cold winter, for example, appeared, rather consistently, to cause spring weather to soon follow. After this happened for several years, it became an accepted fact that the ritual had to be performed to help ensure the coming of spring. Early humans were not foolish enough to think that they alone controlled the forces of nature. They knew that some other force controlled the sequence of the seasons and that their rituals alone did not produce the arrival of spring. Correct performance of the rituals, they believed, was only one of the factors necessary to produce the desired result.

Obviously, the commonly held beliefs and religion of our ancient ancestors were different from those of the modern day. In fact, it is easy to contrast primitive animistic thought with modern scientific thought and imply that Paleolithic humans were ignorant and childish. But this limited view denigrates our ancestors. Given the extent of their knowledge and experiences, animistic religion was a logical and reasonable response to the world in which they lived. After all, if one assumes that nature is alive in the same way as humans, then it is reasonable to conclude that natural objects have spirits or gods within them. Paleolithic religion reveals that people were capable of thinking logically, reasoning coherently from one thought to another.

The Last Millennia of the Paleolithic Era

The Paleolithic Era was the longest period in human history. During this time tribes migrated over much of the earth. They crossed into the Americas by way of a land bridge from Asia to present-day Alaska. They learned how to make tools, how to speak, how to live together in social groups, how to dance and create music (in rituals), and how to draw (cave art). Most of this learning occurred slowly over thousands of years, but near the end of the Paleolithic Era human development advanced rapidly.

Between 30,000 and 10,000 B.C., a people we call the Cro-Magnon inhabited much of the earth. The Cro-Magnon ate better than their predecessors, in large part because they invented a spearthrower that made hunting more fruitful. As a result, the Cro-Magnon were better nourished and their numbers multiplied. They were also artists of considerable skill, drawing animals on cave walls and decorating some of their dwelling places with tiny statuettes. The Cro-Magnon people were more intelligent and skilled than their ancestors, and were, in a sense, at the pinnacle of Paleolithic achievement.

THE NEOLITHIC ERA

For thousands of years humans lived as nomads, constantly moving to follow the animal herds and to find new sources of food. This nomadic way of life began to change between 12,000–10,000 B.C., the beginnings of the *Neolithic Era* or the "New Stone" Age. The primary characteristics of the Neolithic Era were the creation of more sophisticated tools formed by grinding and polishing stones, the discovery of agriculture, and the transformation of growing numbers of people from hunters into peasant farmers.

Why did the Neolithic revolution occur? One reason was overpopulation in some areas that encouraged searching for new sources of food. Another was a gradually warming climate that made farming more rewarding. The most recent ice ages ended around 10,000 B.C., and the glaciers that melted in North America and Eurasia left more land available for farming. But the change from hunting to farming was a slow process, occurring at different times in different places. In hunting societies, where women usually stayed at the camp while men were on

THE NEOLITHIC ERA

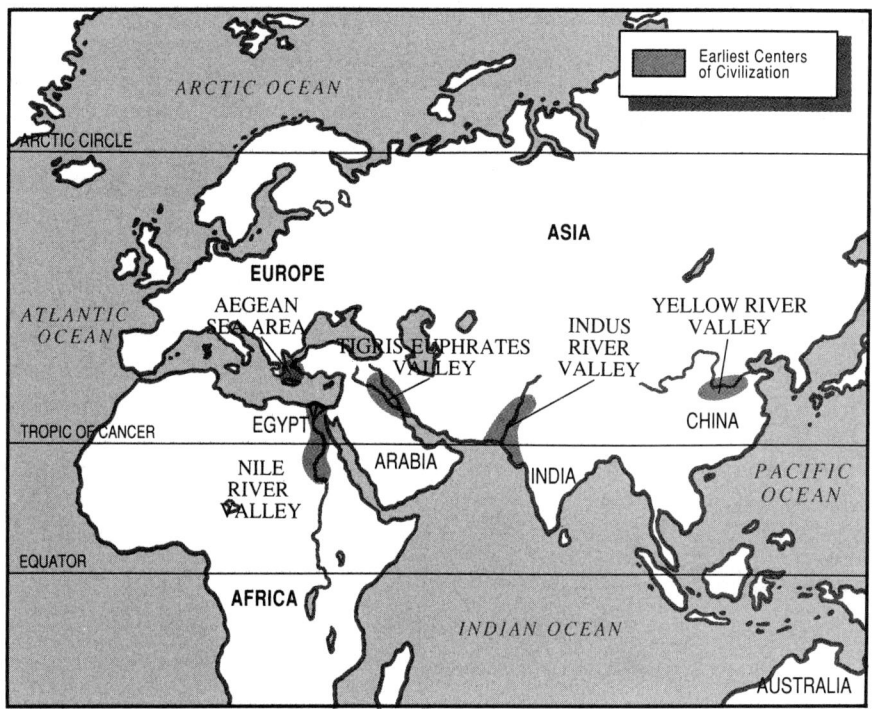

Figure 1.1 The First Civilizations, 3500–1500 B.C.

the hunt, it was probably women who invented agriculture by learning that wild plants could be domesticated and cultivated. As women started to grow small crops, men began to remain at home in order to expand the fields and do the heavy work of plowing and harvesting. Gradually, over dozens of generations, the men in a particular area became farmers instead of hunters, sedentary dwellers instead of nomads.

The discovery of agriculture occurred independently in several areas of the world. It happened first around 12,000–10,000 B.C. in the western end of Asia—between the eastern end of the Mediterranean Sea and the deserts of Central Asia—where some people learned how to grow wheat and barley. By 7000 B.C., yams and rice were being grown in East and Southeast Asia, and beans, potatoes, and corn were cultivated in Mesoamerica (central America and Peru). It wasn't until 2000 B.C., however, that crops were cultivated in sub-Saharan Africa. Agricultural gains were slow there partly because debilitating diseases such as yellow fever and malaria hindered human development, and partly because the drying up of the Sahara desert restricted African communication with the rest of the world.

Life changed dramatically for those who settled in farming villages. Most farmers were less free than hunters, in the sense that they could not move about as they pleased but had to remain near their land. Also, in contrast to hunting societies which had little social structure, farming villages were often tightly organized so as to ensure cooperation. A small group of elders usually controlled the important decision making—such as how to plant and how to parcel out land. Farmers lost a certain degree of freedom but gained a slightly improved standard of living. Their food supply from crops was more regular and secure than in the hunting days, and they could build permanent homes. In their homes, they could accumulate items to make life more comfortable: rough pieces of furniture, more tools and cooking utensils, and pottery for cooking and storing grain and beer.

Permanent homes and the accumulation of goods brought some problems, though. Permanent homes meant that human and animal wastes were collected in one area, making diseases and epidemics common in Neolithic villages. Accumulation of goods and food tempted nearby nomads to steal. Organized warfare originated in Neolithic times, as the nomads raided the villages and the villagers formed or supported military forces for protection.

Neolithic Religion

The Neolithic Era also witnessed modified religious beliefs and practices. The primary concern of farmers was ensuring the fertility of the soil. Since they perceived a connection between human fertility and soil fertility, the primary deity in Neolithic religion was usually an earth goddess that symbolized fertility, and the primary rituals were sexual in nature. Some modern scholars contend that the superiority of the feminine principle in Neolithic religion indicates that some Neolithic societies were matriarchal (governed by women); others refute this idea because it has not been proven.

The most common Neolithic religious myth told of a mother goddess who was impregnated each year by a masculine god of vegetation or rain, thereby ensuring the renewed fertility of the soil. The masculine god, which disappeared or died during the winter, was revived in the spring to be reunited with the mother goddess. The farmers often reenacted this separation and reunion of the gods in symbolic dramas, including sexual acts of various kinds performed by sexually active young people. Here was the origin of many sexually oriented rituals in early societies— orgies, sacred prostitution, and the emasculation of men who were to be priests to the goddess. The farmers believed that correct performance of the rituals, as well as their own labor and adequate rainfall, was essential to producing good crops. Thus, those who participated in the rituals were honored.

The Impact of Neolithic Society

The farming way of life gradually came to dominate most human societies during the New Stone Age, as all but a few hunting tribes slowly disappeared. The farming life-style was one of unchanging conservatism; farmers lived in accordance with the enduring rhythms of nature, planting and harvesting the same way at the same time every year. Whatever political, social, or intellectual changes occurred in Neolithic societies were usually accomplished by small, privileged, groups—elites—who lived off the agricultural surplus produced by farmers. This kind of social organization, in which small elite groups controlled large masses of villagers, continued to dominate most human societies until the eighteenth or nineteenth century A.D. At this time, political revolution and industrialization in Europe led to the creation of industrial societies.

THE DEVELOPMENT OF CIVILIZATION

During the fourth millennium (4000 to 3000) B.C., two village societies in areas dominated by river valleys—Mesopotamia and Egypt—evolved into *civilizations*. Other civilizations, also centered in river valleys, developed later in the Indus valley (modern Pakistan), China, Mesoamerica, and around the eastern end of the Mediterranean.

The development of civilization brought a more complex way of life, including the formation of an elaborate political structure. The political leaders of the time were usually priests thought to have influence with the gods. Gradually, the chief priest became recognized as a "king" with political powers. Civilization also meant the growth of cities, the elaboration of formal laws and a system of taxation, the creation of the art of writing, the development of economic specialization, the division of people into social classes based on their economic and political status, the organization of permanent military forces for protection, and the encouragement of the arts and large-scale architecture. Not all of these characteristics were present in every early civilization—writing, for example, had not yet developed in parts of Mesoamerica.

The term *civilization* implies a value judgment, the connotation being that "civilized" peoples are more advanced and somehow superior to noncivilized peoples. In some respects, civilized life was an improvement, for life in farming villages was often harsh (because of crop failure and famine) and dangerous (because of attacks by nomadic robbers). But whether the rise of civilization marked an overall advance or decline in human fortunes remains an interesting question. On the positive side, the early civilizations provided law and order and protection from nomad attacks. They also provided greater economic security, since they were better able than villages to accumulate and store agricultural surpluses as a hedge against famine. Furthermore, economic and artistic opportunities were more abundant in cities, so life for some was more stimulating and colorful. However, early civilizations also introduced large-scale slavery and warfare to the world. Many formerly free farmers were enslaved to support the needs of the governing classes, while others remained technically free but oppressed by heavy taxes. Women lost the equal status they had enjoyed in many Paleolithic and Neolithic societies, for most early civilizations prevented women from participating in public life and relegated them to the home. At the same time, the scope of warfare was enlarged, because early civilizations often sought to conquer more land and because small societies were tempting targets for nomad invaders. Furthermore, more extensive social organization allowed for the creation of larger fighting forces.

"Civilization" was a mixed blessing for those involved, but modern historians regard it as the great breakthrough that triggered the development of written records. These records enable us to know a great deal more about the past and have, in particular, taught us more about the early civilizations of the third and fourth millennia than about Paleolithic and Neolithic societies. One of the first questions that written records help to clarify is: What caused the rise of civilizations?

The answer seems to be that civilization arose from an interaction of several factors, all of them results of human creativity. Population increases required greater agricultural production, so farming societies in some river valleys began to construct irrigation systems to improve soil fertility. Governments gradually evolved to organize the labor forces necessary to enlarge and maintain the irrigation systems. Another factor that contributed to the rise of civilization was new technology. In particular, the plow—originally just a sapling with a sharp point—and the wheeled cart slowly made agriculture more productive, and helped to produce a surplus that could be taxed and used to support an upper class of governing officials. A third element in the creation of civilization was growth of trade, caused in part by the invention of the sail. It was much easier and more efficient to transport goods by water than by pack animals on land, and the resulting increase in commerce created wealth that could be used to construct cities and support governments. Commerce also encouraged interchange of ideas and technologies between different societies and thus facilitated the spread of civilization. Finally, a fourth factor that advanced civilization was the invention of bronze, which was used to fashion weapons for the armies that were formed to protect the new civilizations. These factors, developed slowly over several centuries, reinforced one another and encouraged many farming societies to evolve into civilizations. This evolutionary process occurred first in Mesopotamia.

TECHNOLOGY
The Paradox of Technological Advance

The creation of civilization resulted in part from the development of several new technologies, the most fundamental being irrigation. Little rainfall occurred in Mesopotamia, for example, but irrigation from the Tigris and Euphrates rivers brought moisture and soil-enriching silt to the nearby lands. Irrigation created problems, however. A major problem was caused by silt, which kept clogging up the irrigation canals. To battle this, gangs of slaves had to be continually employed in clearing the canals.

Civilization lasted in Mesopotamia as long as the canals could be kept relatively free of silt, but after several thousand years of irrigating, the canals were so clogged that large-scale civilization gradually disappeared from the area and the desert sands slowly covered the ruins of old cities. The creation of civilization is, therefore, an early example of how technology can lead to great human achievement but also despoil the natural environment, in many ways cancelling out the gains of the same achievement.

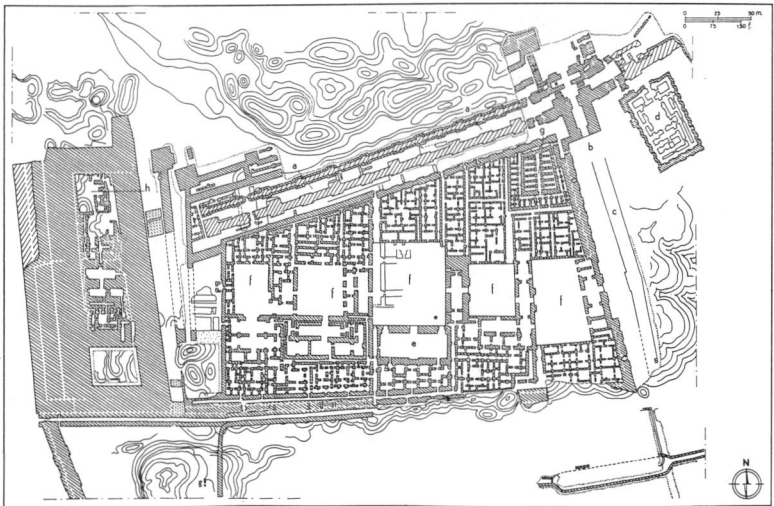

Plan of the Southern Fortress at Babylon, alongside the Euphrates River   *The layout is typical of early cities in Mesopotamia. City walls and a fortress* (left) *protected the royal palace, the temples, and the residences of the most powerful people. Outside the city were the farmlands, irrigation canals, and huts of farmers. (The Granger Collection)*

Mesopotamian Civilizations

Mesopotamia means "between two rivers," and it carries that name because it is the land between the Tigris and Euphrates rivers, which both flow into the Persian Gulf. For centuries Mesopotamia had been a site of human settlement, since it contained fertile land and was in the middle of a huge plains area that nomads regularly crossed. By the fourth millennium B.C., the farming villages in the area came under the domination of a people known as the *Sumerians* (named after their city, Sumer). The Sumerians probably came from present-day Iran or southern Russia to conquer the native Mesopotamian peoples, and the first civilization arose out of the political and social interchange between these conquerors and their new subjects.

Sumerian civilization evolved slowly as a result of many of the economic factors previously mentioned: the need to organize people to build irrigation systems and growing urbanization and trade. The leaders of this "civilizing" effort were probably the Sumerian priests, who were thought to represent divine will. Consequently, the first government was a *theocracy*—government by the gods or by representatives of the gods. This early priest-run government gradually turned into a *monarchy*, and by the late fourth millennium kings embodied divine power and were governing Sumer. The first fully developed civilization was in place.

The Sumerians were never able to form a fully centralized government. Their civilization consisted of a collection of semi-independent city-states scattered around Mesopotamia. These city-states, each dominated by a monarch, had populations of less than fifty thousand and contained masses of peasant huts centered around a few large religious shrines and royal palaces. (Peasants were farmers of low social status.) Outside the city walls were the fields where the peasants grew beans, peas, dates, and especially barley, which they ate as bread and drank as beer. Most of the fields were temple lands, believed to be owned by the gods, so the peasants were considered to be serfs or servants of the gods. In reality, they were controlled by the priests.

The Sumerians were extraordinarily creative. They were the first to accomplish the political breakthrough of forming a government based on laws and administration rather than on kinship ties. They also developed a mathematical system to keep commercial accounts and used early astronomical data to keep a calendar. The Sumerians invented a writing system to record government actions and to glorify human deeds and beliefs in literature. Writing was done in the cuneiform system (*cuneus* means wedge), in which symbols composed of various combinations of wedge shapes represented different objects or ideas. They built the first schools in an effort to pass these skills on to later generations. They also held the first political congress, around 3000 B.C. On that occasion, a monarch called some of the upper-class citizens to an assembly to

Winged Lion From an Assyrian royal palace of the ninth century B.C., this statue of a winged lion represents the Assyrians' admiration of masculine military prowess and suggests a sense of power and sternness. (Metropolitan Museum of Art, NY)

consider a question of war and peace, thus marking a first in the history of political representation.

Despite their creativity, though, the Sumerians were not an optimistic people. The Tigris and Euphrates rivers often flooded at irregular intervals and destroyed their crops. The Mesopotamian climate was harsh, with extreme heat and dust storms from the desert in the summer months and extreme cold from the northern mountains in the winter. Occasionally, torrential rains turned the entire area into a mud sea. It was during these times that the Sumerians developed a strong sense of human weakness and frailty and tended to assume that the gods were cruel and capricious.

The Sumerians conceived of their gods as being human-like in form but immortal and with superhuman qualities. The gods personified the various powers of nature and, since nature was harsh, the gods were believed to be harsh. For example, the god Enlil represented the essence of storms, as is expressed in the following ancient verse.

> Enlil called the storm.
>   The people mourn.
> Exhilarating winds he took from the land.
>   The people mourn.
> Good winds he took away from Sumer.
>   The people mourn.
> He summoned evil winds.
>   The people mourn.[1]

Even though they were cruel, the gods were the source of life. The god Enki personified the power of water that was the source of life in the desert. His actions are celebrated in the following words.

> To clear the pure mouths of the Tigris and Euphrates, to make verdure plentiful,
> Make dense the clouds, grant water in abundance to all ploughlands,
> To make corn lift its head in furrows and to make pasture abundant in the desert,
> To make young saplings in plantations and in orchards sprout.[2]

The gods had absolute control over the universe and human beings. (The world as the Sumerians knew it was quite small, extending only from modern Armenia in the north to the Persian Gulf in the south and from Iran in the east to the Mediterranean in the west.) The Sumerians believed that they were servants to the gods in life and at death descended to a dark, shadowy world of spirits. They sometimes wished wistfully that life could be better. Like other peoples, they had a myth about a Golden Age in their past.

> Once upon a time, there was no snake, there was no scorpion,
> There was no hyena, there was no lion,

There was no wild dog, no wolf,
There was no fear, no terror,
Man had no rival.³

But they knew better than to expect a Golden Age in reality, particularly in an area so susceptible to bad weather and nomad attacks from without.

It was probably nomad invasions that eventually destroyed the Sumerians. Late in the third millennium B.C., the Akkadians, led by their great king Sargon I, conquered all of southern Mesopotamia. The Akkadian Empire lasted from approximately 2360 to 2180 B.C., when it was destroyed by another wave of invaders. Soon thereafter, a people known as the Babylonians established a new empire in Mesopotamia that lasted about four hundred years.

The Babylonian Empire produced at least one great monarch, Hammurabi, who ruled from 1792 to 1750 B.C. Hammurabi's reign revealed a new human awareness—that people were more than just the playthings of the gods, as the Sumerians had believed. The instrument of this new awareness was Hammurabi's law code, which implied that people were entitled to justice as a right rather than as a favor from the gods. Previously, justice was conceived as being whatever the gods deemed it to be. Although Hammurabi's code still portrayed laws as being received from the gods, it was based on the principle of "an eye for an eye, and a tooth for a tooth." The code defined justice as a system of standardized rules that provided a degree of fair treatment to people. Fairness, of course, was most readily available to the upper classes; slaves were always punished more harshly than nobles, and women were regarded as legally inferior to men, although widows had certain specified rights.

Another Mesopotamian example of the increased awareness humans had of themselves as independent of the gods is illustrated in the *Epic of Gilgamesh*. An *epic* is a long poem usually about great heroes in a peoples' past. Epics were often memorized, recomposed, and recited orally by bards for several generations before they were written down. The *Epic of Gilgamesh*, originating in Sumerian culture, was written in its final form sometime around 2000 B.C. The story of a heroic human figure, Gilgamesh, and his adventures, the poem is unlike others of its time because it does not focus on the gods. Rather, it focuses on emotional and spiritual questions important to people, such as the need for friendship, the love of adventure, and the fear of death.

The *Epic of Gilgamesh* is one of the last great creations of the first wave of civilization in Mesopotamia. Sumerian culture was the basis of Mesopotamian life for more than a thousand years (including the times of the Akkadian and Babylonian empires), but it died out during the first half of the second millennium B.C. The first Babylonian Empire also died when, around 1595 B.C., another wave of invaders—the Kassites—overran Mesopotamia.

Egyptian Civilization

Ancient Egypt was dominated by the Nile River. Unlike the unpredictable rivers in Mesopotamia, the Nile flooded at regular intervals and brought soil-enriching silt to the land alongside the river. Thus was created in the midst of a desert a green belt of fertile land from five to twelve miles wide, the demarcation between the two being so sharp that in some places a person could stand with one foot in the desert and the other on cultivated soil. It is no wonder that the Egyptians sang hymns to the river: "Hail to Thee, O Nile, that gushest forth from the earth and comest to nourish Egypt."[4]

Peasant villages existed along the Nile through much of the Neolithic Era. Beginning around 3100 B.C., these villages were gradually united into a centralized state by the first pharaohs, or kings. The impetus for centralization was much the same as in Mesopotamia: the need for an irrigation system, population pressures, and new technologies. The pharaohs who led the centralization effort probably evolved out of either the priestly caste or the merchant class, both of which were natural sources of leadership in farming societies. As creators of a new way of life, the pharaohs were thought to embody the divine gift of creation and thus were assumed to be gods. More precisely, they were thought to be gods descended to earth in human form.

The unification of the peasant villages occurred gradually between 3100 and 2700 B.C., during what historians call the Protodynastic stage of Egyptian history. During the next five hundred years, down to about 2160 B.C., Egypt enjoyed a long period of stability and prosperity known as the Old Kingdom. During the era of the Old Kingdom, the Egyptians developed a unique perspective on life. The Egyptian world was dominated by regularities—the Nile flooding at the same times every year, the sun (rarely interrupted by rainfall) rising and setting every day, and the deserts protecting Egypt from sudden changes brought by foreign interference or invasion. Thus, the Egyptian worldview stressed stability, the assumption being that life was generally good and the goal of life was to be tranquil and in harmony with nature and the gods. Unlike the pessimistic view of the Mesopotamians, the cheerful Egyptians sang happy, optimistic songs:

> The Earth-god has implanted his beauty in every body.
> The Creator has done this with his two hands as balm to his heart.
> The channels are filled with water anew
> And the land is flooded with his love.[5]

Compared to other peoples of their time, the Egyptians lived relatively well. Most favored among them was the pharaoh, but it was his duty to see that the entire land was favored. As a god, a pharaoh was expected to ensure that crops were good and Egypt was protected from invaders. However, the pharaohs did little actual governing, leaving the day-to-day decisions to a large bureaucracy staffed by the upper classes. Upper-class people were often educated and well-off materially, living in large houses that sometimes had rudimentary bathrooms and were constructed to be naturally cool in summer and warm in winter. The great majority of Egyptians were peasants or slaves who toiled in the fields. The peasants lived in crude huts with their animals and endured a hard life, but they were no worse off than peasants elsewhere and their rural life-style was slow and tranquil. Although some slaves were allowed to rent and cultivate land, most were required to work on large construction projects, such as the pyramids.

Life expectancy through most of ancient Egypt was around thirty-six years, about the average for other civilizations of that epoch. And life, though short, was relatively good for many, since Egypt had great resources. The land produced wheat, figs, grapes, melons, lettuces, beans, and peas. Wine and beer were common, and there were herds of sheep, pigs, and goats.

Many Egyptians loved life and came to believe they could extend its pleasures after death. At first, only the pharaoh was believed to live eternally, but gradually the promise of eternal life was thought to be available to more and more people. This belief in eternity led to construction of the great pyramids, the most famous monuments in ancient Egypt. The pyramids were tombs for pharaohs, built early in the Old Kingdom. Politically they were construction projects for which the pharaohs organized peasant and slave labor and thus asserted their authority. Spiritually, the construction of the pyramids was a way for peasants to serve the gods, in this case by building resting places for the divine pharaohs before they ascended to eternity.

The pyramids reveal an Egyptian confidence in human power: they represent an attempt to overcome nature by overcoming death. The historian James Breasted once said:

> The Great Pyramid of Gizeh is thus a document in the history of the human mind. It clearly discloses man's sense of sovereign power in his triumph over material forces. . . . The pharaoh's engineer was achieving the conquest of immortality by sheer command of material forces.[6]

Another example of the Egyptian sense of human power is the sphinxes, colossal statues of a human head on an animal body. According to the nineteenth-century philosopher G. W. F. Hegel, the sphinxes express an

Pyramids at Giza, Egypt The Egyptian pyramids were built as tombs for the pharaohs. The pyramids represent the human desire for power over nature and immortality. They also represent the power of people to control others, for thousands of farmers and slaves were forced to work for many years to build these enormous structures. (Trans World Airlines)

awareness of the human world emerging out of the natural, animalistic world. The Egyptian affinity for gigantic architecture is thus comparable to the creation of the *Epic of Gilgamesh* in Mesopotamia. Both the Egyptians and the Mesopotamians were celebrating human creativity, a creativity that they knew enabled them to build a new way of life—civilization.

The era of the Old Kingdom in Egypt declined in the middle of the twenty-second century B.C. Local rulers weakened the centralizing power of the pharaohs, and for nearly fifty years Egypt endured a period of political instability and economic decline. In about 2135 B.C., central authority was restored and the Middle Kingdom began, lasting about three hundred years. In 1786 B.C. another period of chaos ensued, when Egypt was invaded by Asians whom the Egyptians called "Hyksos." For the first time, Egypt was burdened by external intervention, and it was more than a century before the Egyptians drove the intruders out. Around 1575 B.C., the New Kingdom was established by a succession of pharaohs, and it lasted nearly five hundred years (until c. 1087 B.C.). That kingdom was followed by the Late Period, which extended from 1087 to 332 B.C., when Alexander the Great conquered Egypt.

OTHER EARLY CIVILIZATIONS

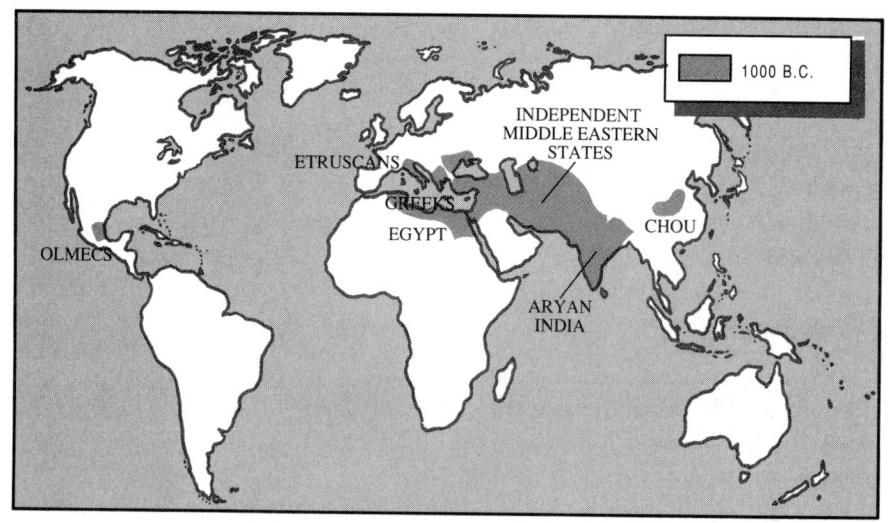

Figure 1.2 World Civilizations, 1000 B.C.

Egyptian attitudes changed dramatically during the New Kingdom and the Late Period. The confident, optimistic days of the Old Kingdom were gone. The pyramids were already regarded as ancient monuments to be visited by sightseers. The Egyptians now constantly feared foreign attack, first from the Hyksos, then in succession from the Hittites, the so-called "Sea Peoples," the Libyans, and the Assyrians. Fear led them to stress the need for national security rather than individual happiness. It also led them to regard humans as helplessly dependent on the gods and unable to control their own destiny. With this loss of confidence, the Egyptians became a superstitious people, turning for solace to oracles, horoscopes, and magical spells.

The most impressive feature of ancient Egyptian civilization is its endurance. By the first millennium B.C., it was already an ancient civilization that fascinated other peoples with its architectural marvels. Its energy and creativity were gone, however, and Egypt was a somnolent land of toiling peasants and slaves and a small, indolent upper class.

OTHER EARLY CIVILIZATIONS

Indus Valley

Early civilizations developed in several other areas of the world. Some of these civilizations were stimulated by contact with the Mesopotamians or the Egyptians whereas others evolved independently. The Indus valley civilization (located in modern Pakistan) originated around 2500 B.C.

and lasted for nearly a thousand years. Because Indus writing has not yet been deciphered, little is known about Indus civilization. It was similar to Mesopotamian and Egyptian civilizations in that it centered around a river valley where irrigation systems were organized to increase agricultural production. It carried on some commerce with the Mesopotamians through the Persian Gulf and was a thriving society for a time. Eventually, it collapsed due to invasions by external enemies and the silting up of the irrigation system.

Minoan

In the eastern Mediterranean on the Greek island of Crete, a civilization known as Minoan emerged sometime between 2500 and 2000 B.C. It lasted until about 1400 B.C., when it was destroyed either by foreign attack or by some kind of natural disaster. This early Greek civilization was probably stimulated by contact with the Egyptians, and the Minoans quickly became a powerful, creative people. In particular, they were great engineers and architects, constructing paved streets, aqueducts, and sewer systems. The Minoans were also enterprising sailors, dominating the eastern Mediterranean between 1600 and 1400 B.C. During that time they colonized much of Greece and their culture became one of the bases of later Greek civilization.

One interesting aspect of Minoan civilization is that women appear to have been much more powerful than their counterparts in other civilizations, sometimes participating in political decisions and usually controlling religious rituals. Minoan religion, like Neolithic religion, centered on mother goddesses who symbolized fertility. Also interesting is the particular reverence that the Minoans extended to bulls. In one religious performance, young men seized the horns of a charging bull and leaped over its back. (Modern Spanish bullfighting may be descended from this ancient ritual.) Bulls were also celebrated in legend. One legend told of a Minotaur, a monster with the body of a man and the head of a bull; the Minotaur inhabited the center of a labyrinth from which no one could escape until a young hero left a trail of thread to follow back after he had killed the monster. A final note about the Minoans is the gaiety and gracefulness expressed in the art displayed on pottery and wall paintings. This art suggests that the Minoans enjoyed and appreciated life on this earth.

Phoenician

Close to the Minoans (in present-day Lebanon), a people known as the Phoenicians organized a civilization during the second millennium B.C. Originally farmers who practiced a brutal religion that included human sacrifices, the Phoenicians became sailors and merchants of the entire

OTHER EARLY CIVILIZATIONS

Minoan Snake Goddess Only three inches in height, this statuette symbolizes several aspects of Minoan culture: the importance of females in Minoan religion and society; the association of snakes with the divine (snakes were considered friendly creatures that protected Minoans from other, harmful creatures); and the style of dress for upper-class Minoan women. The Minoans were a fun-loving people who encouraged open sexuality, and women sometimes dressed so as to expose their bare breasts in public. (Museum of Fine Arts, Boston)

Mediterranean region from 1000 to 500 B.C. Some even sailed into the Atlantic Ocean, a risky venture at that time.

The Phoenicians gradually established colonies around the shores of the Mediterranean, and as they did so they proliferated the use of one of their greatest discoveries—the alphabet. The Phoenician alphabet, probably derived from the ideas of other peoples as well as their own, was one of the Phoenicians' greatest achievements and an important breakthrough in human history, providing a much simpler form of writing than the earlier picture-writing system of cuneiform (see the Technology Box in Chapter 2).

Shang

On the other end of the Eurasian landmass, the Shang civilization arose in the Yellow River area of northern China around 1500 B.C. The Shang were nomads who may have had some contact with the peoples of Mesopotamia or the Indus valley and, thus, were exposed to some civilized arts—such as writing and the wheel—when they conquered peasant villages along the Yellow River. But Shang civilization was not wholly derivative. It was unique in its emphasis on rice cultivation, its manufacture of fine silk cloth, and its development of ancestor worship in its religion.

The Shang dynasty disappeared around 1000 B.C., when the Chou dynasty assumed power. However, agricultural prosperity continued around the Yellow River and Chinese civilization retained many of the features introduced by the Shang, such as ancestor worship and silk manufacturing.

Mesoamerican

Unlike the Indus, Minoan, Phoenician, and Shang civilizations, which were stimulated partly through contact with older civilizations, Mesoamerica (Middle America) was an elaborate civilization that developed independently around 1200 B.C. During that time, a people known as the Olmecs lived in present-day Mexico, and they created the foundation for what would later become Mesoamerican civilization. The Olmecs established an agricultural society based on peasant slavery, an authoritarian political structure, and a fertility-based religion, all of which remained basic components of the Mesoamerican heritage. By 300 B.C. in southern Mexico, Mayan civilization evolved out of what the Olmecs had created. The Mayans were eventually succeeded by the Toltec (800–1200 A.D.) and Aztec (1200–1520 A.D.) civilizations. The Aztecs were still flourishing when the Spanish came to the New World in the sixteenth century A.D.

Another early American civilization emerged around 1100 A.D. in present-day Peru. This was the Inca Empire which at its height extended from the mountains of Peru down the Pacific coast into present-day Chile. The Incas were farmers who developed engineering skills to hold their empire together. An elaborate road and bridge system facilitated transportation and communication within their empire, and some Inca cities were so elaborately planned and constructed (often out of rock) that they still inspire awe in the twentieth century. The Inca Empire lasted until the Spanish came to the Americas and conquered it in 1532–33.

THE DECLINE OF THE EARLY CIVILIZATIONS

During the second millennium B.C., many ancient civilizations either collapsed or just barely survived as a result of nomad warriors who surged across Eurasia and attacked everything in their way. The nomads were in search of food and were probably threatened by famine. Two new developments gave the nomads a military advantage over their civilized opponents. One was the domestication of the horse, which the nomads attached to war chariots. The other was iron, used to forge weapons more powerful than those previously made. Thus, the second millennium B.C. marks the beginning of what historians call the Iron Age.

There were two waves of nomad attacks. The first occurred from 1700 to 1500 B.C. As noted earlier, the Kassites, a Semitic tribe from the deserts, conquered Mesopotamia. In addition, the Hyksos invaded Egypt, and other nomads destroyed the Indus civilization. The second wave of nomad attacks followed soon after and lasted until 1100 B.C. An obscure group of nomads known only as the "Sea Peoples" threatened Egypt and may have destroyed Minoan civilization as well. Farther east, Mongols (from Mongolia, an area north of China) destroyed the Shang dynasty in China. As a result of these nomad attacks, most ancient civilizations were either gravely weakened or disappeared altogether. In many areas, population declined and organized society was reduced to localized farming units.

The lands around the eastern end of the Mediterranean began to recover sometime after 900 B.C. Iron, first worked by the Hittites of Asia Minor (modern Turkey), became a source of improved farm implements. The development of the Phoenician alphabet further stimulated economic activity. Although small kingdoms gradually arose (such as the Hebrew state of Israel), most of them were soon conquered by a series of large empires centered in Mesopotamia. The first of these was the Assyrian Empire, which lasted from the mid-eighth century to 612 B.C. The Assyrians established peace and orderly government for their subjects, but they had a reputation for extreme cruelty. One Assyrian king, Ashurbanipal, boasted that after defeating an enemy army he ". . . caught the survivors and impaled them on stakes in front of their towns."[7]

The Assyrians were defeated by a new Babylonian Empire established by a people known as the Chaldeans, but that empire lasted only a few decades. The most famous of the Chaldean rulers was Nebuchadnezzar (reigned 604–562 B.C.), builder of the legendary Hanging Gardens, an elaborate roof garden constructed for a Persian concubine who was tired of the flat Mesopotamian landscape. In 550 B.C., Babylon was conquered by the Persians, the most successful empire-builders of that time. The Persian Empire, which lasted about two hundred years (until 333 B.C.), extended from the Iranian plateau eastward almost to India and westward to Greece and Egypt. The Persians, more tolerant than the Assyrians and Babylonians, allowed their subjects to retain their own local governments and religious traditions. It was for this reason that the Persians gained a reputation for fair, honest government.

CONCLUSION

By the first millennium B.C., ancient peoples had developed various ways of living. The Paleolithic hunters of nomadic tribes wandered in search of animals to kill in some parts of the world. Neolithic farmers lived in small villages in other areas. And large-scale civilizations existed in a few places. Common to all these different ways of life was the belief, shared by almost all people, in some form of animistic religion. Animistic beliefs would begin to change, however, with the spiritual and intellectual transformation that occurred in several parts of the world during the first millennium B.C. This transformation is the subject of the following chapter.

THINGS YOU SHOULD KNOW

The biological and cultural advantages of humans
Paleolithic thought and religion
Cro-Magnon people
Neolithic thought and religion
Characteristics and significance of "civilization"
Sumerians
Irrigation technology in ancient Mesopotamia
Hammurabi
Epic of Gilgamesh

Ancient Egyptian civilization
Significance of the pyramids
Indus valley civilization
Minoan civilization
Phoenician civilization
Shang civilization
Mesoamerican civilization
Why many of the early civilizations were undermined in the second millennium B.C.

SUGGESTED READINGS

Two good introductions to the development of prehistoric humans are Robert J. Braidwood, *Prehistoric Man* (Chicago: Scott Foresman, 1957) and Richard Leakey and Roger Lewin, *Origins* (New York: 1977). On the Sumerian and Egyptian civilizations, see Samuel N. Kramer, *History Begins at Sumer* (New York: Univ. of Pennsylvania Press, 1956) and Cyril Aldred, *The Egyptians* (New York: Praeger, 1961). An old but still valuable analysis of the thoughts and beliefs of early humans is H. A. Frankfort, John A. Wilson, and Thorkild Jacobsen, *Before Philosophy: The Intellectual Adventure of Ancient Man* (Baltimore: Penguin, 1946). For an introduction to the status of women in ancient societies as well as in later ages, see Elizabeth Fox-Genovese and Susan Mosher Stuard (eds.), *Restoring Women to History: Materials for Western Civilization I* (Bloomington: Univ. of Indiana Press, 1983). Also important is Frances Dahlberg (ed.), *Woman the Gatherer* (Yale: Yale Univ. Press, 1981). A good examination of how early civilizations (and later ones as well) used and often destroyed agricultural land is Vernon Gill Carter and Tom Dale, *Topsoil and Civilization* (Norman, Okla.: Univ. of Oklahoma Press, 1974). Arthur Ferrill analyzes the early history of warfare in *The Origins of War* (New York: Thames and Hudson, 1985).

NOTES

[1] Quoted in Thorkild Jacobsen, "Mesopotamia," in *Before Philosophy: The Intellectual Adventure of Ancient Man*, rev. ed. H. A. Frankfort et al. (New York: Penguin, 1959), p. 154.

[2] Ibid., p. 161.

[3] Ibid., p. 255.

[4] Quoted in Sabatino Moscati, *The Face of the Ancient Orient* (New York: Anchor, 1960), p. 101.

[5] Quoted in Cyril Aldred, *The Egyptians* (New York: Praeger 1961), p. 139.

[6] James Breasted, quoted in John A. Wilson, "Egypt," in *Before Philosophy: The Intellectual Adventure of Ancient Man*, rev. ed. H. A. Frankfort et al. (New York: Penguin, 1959), p. 105.

2

A Spiritual and Intellectual Transformation, 800 to 200 B.C.

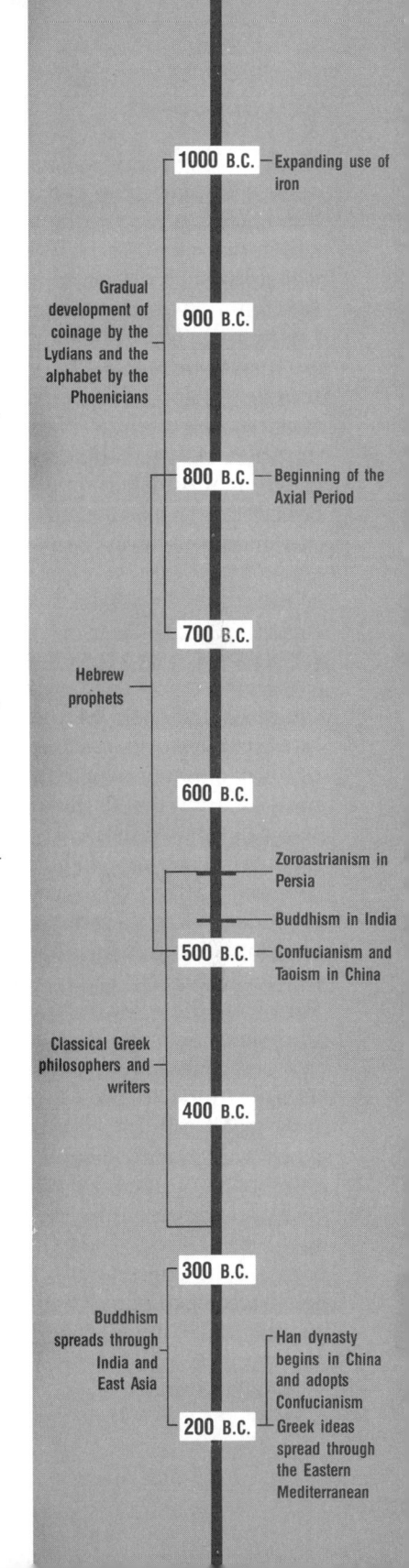

1000 B.C.	Expanding use of iron
900 B.C.	Gradual development of coinage by the Lydians and the alphabet by the Phoenicians
800 B.C.	Beginning of the Axial Period
700 B.C.	Hebrew prophets
600 B.C.	
500 B.C.	Zoroastrianism in Persia; Buddhism in India; Confucianism and Taoism in China
400 B.C.	Classical Greek philosophers and writers
300 B.C.	
200 B.C.	Buddhism spreads through India and East Asia; Han dynasty begins in China and adopts Confucianism; Greek ideas spread through the Eastern Mediterranean

In *The Origin and Goal of History,* the German philosopher Karl Jaspers defines the time span of 800–200 B.C. as the *Axial Period of* world history. This period is, according to Jaspers, the axis—the central point around which world history revolves—because a spiritual and intellectual transformation occurred in several parts of the world during this time.[1] In China, two new religions appeared—Confucianism (founded by Confucius) and Taoism (founded by Lao-tzu). In India, the Buddha created Buddhism, a new religion with roots grounded in the older Indian religion of Hinduism. In Persia, Zoroaster taught another new religion that became known as Zoroastrianism. In Israel, the Hebrew prophets changed the ancient Hebrew religion into the fully developed religion of Judaism, the ancestor of Christianity and Islam. And, in Greece, a succession of intellectual figures created what is referred to as rational thought and philosophy.

GENERAL CHARACTERISTICS OF THE AXIAL PERIOD

The great teachers of the Axial Period transformed the spiritual and intellectual world and were, therefore, far more influential than any military conqueror or political leader. Except for some Taoist teachers, they all repudiated the polytheistic religions that deified nature and sought instead a more universal, more spiritual conception of the divine. In the process, they helped to create most of the modern world's major religions. Most Axial teachers also repudiated the magic and ritual associated with the polytheistic religions, and the new moral codes that they introduced defined many of the ideals and rules that have motivated people ever since. The historian Herbert J. Muller believes that the Axial Period is "the most extraordinary creative era in man's history between the rise of civilization and the rise of modern science."[2]

The spiritual revolution of the Axial Period was limited to five areas—China, India, Persia, Israel, and Greece—and at first involved only small minorities within them. Many people in other parts of the world were not affected; the few people who remained food gatherers and hunters continued to follow Paleolithic religious practices, and the peasants, representing the majority of the world's population, continued to follow agricultural religions based primarily on analogies between human and soil fertility. The adherents of these old religious practices may have been happy with their way of life, but they would not play the leading roles on the stage of world history. Those roles would be filled by the Axial peoples, those who experienced the spiritual breakthrough of the Axial period.

Causes of the Axial Revolution

Why some peoples and not others participated in the Axial revolution remains a mystery. It is difficult if not impossible to determine the ultimate source of spiritual and intellectual creativity. It is significant, though, that the five Axial areas were in or near regions where one or more of the early civilizations developed. The Chinese religions emerged in areas close to where Shang civilization had existed, Buddhism flourished in areas near the old sites of Indus civilization, Zoroastrianism developed in an area of Persia close to the old center of Mesopotamian civilization, and both the Hebrews and Greeks lived in close proximity to Mesopotamian and Egyptian civilizations. The old civilizations had disappeared or were declining by the time of the Axial Period and they did not share in the spiritual revolution. However, they contributed to it by passing on their knowledge and ideas to the Axial peoples. Furthermore, the end of the old civilizations produced a political and spiritual crisis in the first millennium B.C. The old beliefs and ideas were questioned, leading to a search for the new. This search was a major stimulus of the spiritual revolution.

Another cause of the Axial revolution was technological development, which fostered social as well as spiritual change. The growing availability of iron, a cheap metal used to produce better plows, tools, and weapons, resulted in a growing agricultural prosperity and became the economic base for cities where spiritual, intellectual, and political debate could be pursued. The invention of coinage, developed in the eastern Mediterranean area by the Lydians (who lived in Anatolia or present-day Turkey) also encouraged the Axial revolution. Before coinage, bars of metal were used for monetary exchange. The bars were bulky and difficult to transport over long distances. They also represented only large monetary values, making trade among local merchants and farmers difficult. The development of coinage alleviated these difficulties, stimulated trade over wider areas, and even encouraged exchange of ideas among trading peoples. Finally, there was the important invention of the Phoenician alphabet, which affected primarily those people in the eastern Mediterranean. The alphabet allowed more people to become literate and, therefore, better able to study and discuss spiritual and intellectual issues.

The various causes of the Axial revolution affected each of the five Axial areas in a different way. Although Zoroastrianism influenced Judaism and Buddhism influenced the Chinese religions, for the most part the five areas had little contact with each other and developed independently.

CHINA

The first Chinese civilization—the Shang—was overthrown around 1000 B.C., by a new group of rulers known as the Chou. The Chou dynasty governed most of China for over two centuries, but invading nomads in the eighth century B.C. forced the Chou to move eastward. Now known as the Eastern Chou, the same dynasty ruled eastern parts of China until the fifth century B.C. In reality, however, Chou control was precarious. Through much of the first millennium B.C., local princes ignored the Chou emperors and fought each other in local wars, while nomads occasionally invaded and conquered parts of China. This political upheaval was short-lived, though, and Chinese social structure changed very little.

Chinese society was conservative, stable, and hierarchical, in part because of the nature of the agricultural system. The main crop was rice, which requires a great deal of water. Consequently, large irrigation systems and water conservancy projects had to be built and maintained, and these public works were managed by strong, local governments that enforced social cooperation and social order. In theory, every person regardless of wealth had an assigned place in the social hierarchy; in practice, though, Chinese rural life was dominated by a landowning elite.

The hierarchical social structure was intertwined with a worldview that stressed "quiet" virtues, such as living in harmony with nature and accepting one's position in life. The Chinese traditionally interpreted everything in ecological terms, in the sense that all things in nature and human society were considered parts of one interconnected reality and, therefore, people were expected to live harmoniously within the whole.

Confucianism

The great Chinese teacher Confucius (c. 551–479 B.C.), was born into a world of social stability interrupted periodically by political upheaval. He was a wandering intellectual who spent much of his life as a schoolteacher and tutor to princes. After his death, his students collected his words and ideas into a book known as the *Analects*.

The goal of Confucius's teachings was to show people how to live in a harmonious social order. Thus, he was a conservative, speaking for the traditional Chinese worldview. He was also a humanist, teaching a "this-world" religion that focused on humanity rather than on gods. Confucius rarely mentioned gods or any other kind of supernatural realm, and he opposed magical practices derived from the Shang civilization, like the sacrifice of young women to the gods of the Yellow River. Confucius used the word *heaven* not to refer to someplace beyond the earth but to refer to a spiritual and moral order that he regarded as immanent in everyday life.

TECHNOLOGY
The Alphabet

Most early civilizations used some form of picture-writing: the Mesopotamians developed the cuneiform system, the Egyptians created a system known as hieroglyphics, and the Chinese evolved their own type of writing in symbols. Since at least several hundred symbols, often several thousand, were needed to express an entire language in writing, only a few professional scribes had the time and training to be literate. In most early civilizations, these scribes controlled the means of communication.

In contrast, the Phoenician alphabet formed words out of only twenty-two consonants, leaving the reader to add vowel sounds. The Greeks improved the Phoenician system by adding five vowel signs. Later the Romans and still later the Europeans evolved alphabetic systems based on the Greek model.

The alphabetic system made it easier for people to become literate and gain access to knowledge. Certainly, most poor people remained illiterate, and many parts of the world—China, for example—retained their picture-writing systems for many centuries. But the alphabetic system gradually came to dominate the Mediterranean area that gave birth to Western Civilization. Since education is one of the prerequisites for technological development, the creation of the alphabet was one of the major steps in the history of Western technology.

Egyptian Hieroglyphics *This funerary papyrus from the eleventh century B.C. is an example of hieroglyphic writing, which required a greater number of more complicated symbols to communicate than does the alphabet system. (Metropolitan Museum of Art, NY)*

Confucius (551–479 B.C.)
A 1734 ink rubbing that portrays the traditional conception of Chinese philosopher K'ung Ch'iu, known as Confucius. Dedicated to a life of government reform and teaching, Confucius became the most revered person in Chinese history. His teachings on ethics, happiness, and family have provided the cornerstone for much Chinese thought through the ages. (The Granger Collection)

Confucius taught that a person must cultivate his inner self in order to learn how to live in harmony with the spiritual and moral order of the world. In practice, self-cultivation meant studying the ancient Chinese classics, including *The Classic of History* (also known as *The Book of Documents*) and *The Classic of Change* (also known as *I Ching*). By so doing, a person could deepen his self-awareness, develop his understanding of the "good" and the "beautiful," and gradually become a "good man." By studying the classics, a person would learn that "goodness" meant performing one's assigned duties in life. The first duty was within the family, for being a good man required being a good son. According to Confucius:

> Filial piety is the root of all virtue, and the stem out of which grows all moral teaching. It commences with the service of parents; it proceeds to the service of the ruler. . . .[3]

Having become a good son and later a good father, the good man, as Confucius asserted, should strive further to become a good citizen. In practice, this meant serving the state. Confucius believed that harmony within the state was produced by the same virtues that brought harmony within the family—self-awareness and diligence in performing duties.

At its best, Confucianism taught the Chinese to cultivate those moral and aesthetic qualities that are most distinctively human, so its practice was more conscious of the human spirit than were the traditional animistic religions. At its weakest, however, Confucianism emphasized harmony and duty to such a degree that it tended to undermine the spirit of adventure and experimentation. It also tended to limit the highest human goal—the sustained cultivation of human character—to an elite few. It clearly favored men and the leisured upper classes, who had the time and energy to study the ancient classics.

Taoism

Taoism, another Chinese religion created during the Axial Period, was founded by the renowned figure Lao-tzu, who lived at about the same time as Confucius. Whereas Confucianism stressed living in harmony within society, Taoism emphasized living in harmony with nature. The Taoist conception of nature was philosophical rather than scientific. The Taoists did not seek to understand how nature operated but to comprehend the underlying order and meaning of nature. They were mystics who often withdrew from society so they could meditate on the *Tao*, or "the Way." *Tao* was the rational principle found in nature, the basic order of the universe. Sometimes this order was expressed in the terms *yin* and *yang*. The yin-yang concept held that everything in the universe could be explained in terms of contrasting pairs (female–male, weak–strong, cold–hot).

For Taoists, the good life consisted of identifying themselves with the order of nature. In practice, this meant living a simple life by limiting desires and disregarding the artificial rules and customs of organized society. Lao-tzu described the Taoist conception of utopia as follows:

> There are no books; the people have no use for any form of record save knotted ropes. They relish the simplest form of food, have no desire for fine clothing, take pleasure in their rustic tasks, are content to remain in their home. The next village might be so close that one could hear the cocks crowing in it, the dogs barking, but the people would grow old and die without ever having been there.[4]

Taoism was first followed by a few self-disciplined mystics but gradually became popular among ordinary Chinese. When it was adopted by the lower classes, Taoism came to include belief in several supernatural deities and forces and even in witchcraft. Thus, the popularized version of Taoism did not repudiate polytheism, as did most of the other religions of the Axial Period.

The Impact of Religion on Chinese History

Both Confucianism and Taoism envisioned the attainment of harmony as the supreme goal of life; the Confucians stressed social harmony and the Taoists stressed harmony with nature. This common goal meant that Chinese religions were not "exclusive" but that a person could follow several religious traditions. For example, a Chinese individual might be married in a Buddhist ceremony (after that Indian religion came to China in the first century A.D.), adopt a Taoist attitude of calmness when facing adversity, and adhere to Confucian practices in family and social life.

Chinese religion discouraged interest in science and the actual workings of nature. Certainly, China produced notable scientists and a scientific tradition over the centuries, but the study of science never became a dominant force in Chinese society. The Confucians were primarily concerned with human society and had little interest in nature, while the Taoists wanted only to live in a kind of mystic harmony with nature and made no attempt to investigate it by any scientific means.

In terms of China's political history, Confucianism had a great influence. Around 202 B.C., the Han dynasty imposed political order on most of China and established a centralized empire that lasted until A.D. 220. (The Han Empire flourished at the same time as the late Roman Republic and the early Roman Empire.) The Han rulers adopted Confucianism as the official state religion, using it to impose ideological unity in China. The Han required, for instance, civil service exams (and, hence, access to government employment) to be based on knowledge of the Confucian classics. This practice became a tradition, and for much of the next two thousand years Chinese bureaucrats were trained in Confucian teachings. The Confucians welcomed this practice, believing that their teachings would humanize politics by training government officials to behave humanely. In reality, though, Chinese rulers usually used Confucianism as a means of training docile, conservative bureaucrats who would loyally serve royal purposes.

The religious and cultural influences of Confucianism eventually extended beyond China to Korea, Japan, and other East Asian societies. As we will see later in the chapter, Buddhism (after it came to China) also spread into those smaller Asian countries. Thus, Chinese and Indian philosophies permeated all of East Asia.

INDIA

After the decline of Indus civilization during the second millennium B.C., India remained politically chaotic and divided into separate kingdoms for most of the next thousand years. Political disunity did not, however, prevent the growth of cultural and religious unity throughout much of the Indian subcontinent. For example, several intellectual figures wrote the *Vedas,* a collection of religious and philosophical poems that expressed the religious beliefs held by many Indians. Others produced the *Upanishads,* another series of philosophical poems. From these sources Indians derived a worldview that stressed tolerance and the need to understand differing points of view.

The Indians tended to assume that all religions attempt to understand the same divine reality but through different perspectives. This attitude is supported by an old Indian parable about several blind men and an elephant. One blind man feels the elephant's trunk and says it is a snake, another feels a leg and calls it a tree, and a third feels the tail and calls it a rope. The point, of course, is that each man "saw" only a part of the elephant and not the entire reality.[5]

Hinduism

The Indians derived from their ancient scriptures a system of beliefs known as Hinduism. Hinduism distinguished sharply between ultimate reality and the material reality of this world. Ultimate reality is the *Brahman* (or "world-soul"), the undefinable spiritual reality that underlies and transcends the material world. It is like an ocean on which the material reality floats. The material world is just an "appearance," a manifestation of the basic reality, and as such it is an inferior, essentially meaningless form of existence. For the Hindu, the goal of life is to achieve *moksha* ("release") from this world and sink back into the ocean of divine reality. Most people cannot achieve this goal, however. They are enticed by worldly desires (such as the desire for wealth or fame) that have the *karma* ("consequence") of tying them to this world. So, when they die they are reborn into this world in accordance with the laws of *karma.* Those who lived by the rules appropriate to their place in society might attain rebirth to a higher status, whereas those who were cruel or unjust might be reborn as a wild beast. Only those who are able to give up worldly desires can attain release from the endless cycle of rebirths and return to divine reality.

Obviously, Hindu beliefs were closely intertwined with a hierarchical social structure that prescribed for each person a well-defined social status. In fact, a caste system was probably brought to India by Aryan invaders, who imposed the system on the native Indians they conquered. (The Aryans were Indo-European nomads, who conquered much of Iran and northern India during the late second millennium B.C. and early first millennium B.C. It may have been the Aryans who destroyed the Indus civilization.)

A *caste* was a social group into which a person was born and from which there was virtually no escape. A person spent his or her entire life in a caste, performing the occupations and living by the rules appropriate to that caste. Originally, there were three upper castes, populated mostly by the Aryans: the priests *(Brahmins)*, the warrior rulers *(Kshatriya)*, and the merchants *(Vaisya)*. These castes were sharply distinguished from the two lower castes, which contained most of the Indian natives conquered by the Aryans: the laboring caste *(Sudra)* and the "untouchables" *(pariahs)*. The untouchables were considered "polluted" because they were descended from backward tribes and because their occupations involved "dirty" work, such as the taking of animal life (butchers and fishermen, for example).

Hinduism and the caste system clearly complemented each other. According to Hindu teachings, a person was born into a caste in accordance with the *karma* achieved in a previous existence. Furthermore, depending on whether people adhered to the rules of their caste, they would after death be reborn into a higher or lower caste. A higher rebirth was very desirable, since Hindus believed that only members of the Brahmin caste could attain *moksha*, release from this world.

Buddhism

Many Indians resented the Brahminic assertion that only they could achieve *moksha*. As a result, Buddhism took hold in the sixth century B.C. as a more egalitarian religion, teaching that "release" was available to everyone. At the time, the Ganges River valley in northern India was enjoying a wave of prosperity. The use of iron to make farm implements and the domestication of the horse produced agricultural growth and led to the expansion of cities where commerce thrived. Prosperous commercial and farming classes emerged, which in turn supported the rise of Buddhism that taught that *moksha* was available to them as well as to Brahmins.

Buddhism was founded by Siddārtha Gautama Sakyamuni (c. 563–483 B.C.), a minor Indian prince who eventually acquired the name "Buddha" or "the enlightened one." As a young man, he renounced his wealth, left his home and family, and began to travel around India in search of spiritual enlightenment. Having found it, he then began to teach others. His religion was completely humanistic—he did not teach about gods but focused solely on people's ability to achieve a form of salvation through their own efforts.

According to the Buddha, human life is characterized by pain, sorrow, and meaninglessness. It is meaningless because people cannot attain any kind of salvation from ordinary ways of living; it is full of pain and sorrow because people constantly experience physical and emotional pain. The ultimate cause of all this evil is human desire, because desire for things (such as wealth or fame) creates a kind of restless striving for more that leaves people constantly anxious and frustrated. Thus, without those desires people could free themselves of the sources of anxiety and

Buddha (563–483 B.C.) From the second or third century A.D., this statue of the Buddha was created at a time when he was thought of as a god. Siddhārtha Gautama, known as the Buddha, was the founder of Buddhism, a belief system that advocates meditation, austerity, and a rejection of material things as a means of attaining spiritual happiness. (Seattle Art Museum)

pain. In the Buddha's words, "The fire of life must be put out. For everything in the world is on fire with the fire of desire, the fire of hate, and the fire of illusion."[6] One could escape desire through detachment, by renouncing all passions and ambitions. A person could do this by following the "Eightfold Noble Path"—right beliefs, aspirations, speech, conduct, living, efforts, thoughts, and contemplation. By following this path, a person could attain *nirvana,* a state of being in which desire and hate are extinguished and life (on earth, not in heaven) is detached, enlightened, filled with compassion and love for others.

Jainism

Originating in the sixth century B.C., Jainism was similar to Hinduism and Buddhism in its teachings that the chief goal for humans was release from earthly life. Jainism was unique, however, in its emphasis on nonviolence, extending to a refusal to kill even the smallest creature. Nonviolence became a fundamental belief of many Indians. A notable example of Jainist influence is the life and teachings of Mohandas

Gandhi, the great Indian political leader who used a philosophy of nonviolence during the Indian struggle for independence from Britain during the twentieth century A.D.

The Spread of Buddhism

The number of Buddhist adherents remained relatively small during the first decades after the founding of the new religion, largely because Buddhist teachings were so demanding that only a few ascetics who withdrew from everyday life could hope to follow them. Buddhism began to expand when Mahayana ("Great Vehicle [of salvation]") Buddhism evolved out of the Buddha's original teachings. Mahayana Buddhism was developed by those Buddhists who wanted to make the new religion available and comprehensible to ordinary people. In so doing, the Mahayana teachers gradually began to portray the Buddha as a god—an object of religious devotion—rather than as just a teacher. Soon, likenesses of the Buddha, who never claimed to be a god, began to appear in much Indian art and architecture.

By the third century B.C., Buddhism had spread over much of India. At that time most of India was ruled by the Mauryan Empire, which lasted from 321 to 181 B.C. The most famous Mauryan ruler, Aśoka (274–237 B.C.), converted to Buddhism. He encouraged Buddhists to send out missionaries, and over the next few centuries Buddhism spread to China, Korea, and Japan. Although it thrived for a time, after A.D. 700 Buddhism began to decline. In India it all but disappeared, as it was either reabsorbed into Hinduism or replaced by Islam, which was then spreading to India from the west. Outside of India, it survived as a significant force in China, Japan, and Southeast Asia.

The Impact of Religion on Indian History

The reabsorption of Buddhism into Hinduism was easy in India. Those two traditions, as well as Jainism, shared a common worldview that earthly life was ultimately unimportant and was something to be escaped. That attitude had certain implications. One was a tendency for Indians to accept the realities of earthly life and not to be overly concerned about political, social, or economic change. Certainly, Indian history includes many individual political figures who sought to accomplish political change, and many merchants who sought to amass wealth. But these figures rarely dominated Indian society because Indian religion taught Indians to accept the caste system, not to seek social reform or material wealth. Another implication of seeing earthly life as unimportant was the assumption that physical nature is of little significance, so there was little reason to explore and understand the workings of the natural world. Religion was not the only force inhibiting the growth of Indian science, but it was a powerful one.

The strength of Indian religion was its ability to teach people how to achieve spiritual and emotional contentment. Its weakness was its indifference to social change and the development of science.

PERSIA

Zoroastrianism

The Persians, who had lived quietly on the Iranian plateau for centuries, created a powerful empire in the middle of the sixth century B.C. (see the last section of Chapter 1). They also developed a new religion—Zoroastrianism—that was named after its chief prophet, Zoroaster (sometimes called Zarathustra). Zoroaster taught that the universe is controlled by two divine forces, one good and the other evil. The god of light and justice—Ahura-Mazda—was believed to wage eternal combat with, and seek victory over, Ahriman, the god of darkness and evil. Humans, according to Zoroaster, could choose sides. They could support Ahura-Mazda by following the appropriate rules of moral goodness. In this case, they would be rewarded with entry into paradise (a Persian word) after death. However, if they ignored the moral commandments and supported the god of darkness, then they were believed to be condemned to eternal damnation.

Zoroastrianism captured the allegiance of the Persian upper classes and gradually eliminated some of the superstitions and magical rites practiced by ordinary Persians. It became the dominant religion in Persia only in the first centuries A.D., but after A.D. 700 it was supplanted by Islam (see Chapter 6). From that time on, only a handful of adherents in India continued to follow Zoroaster's teachings.

Even though Zoroastrianism did not survive as an independent force, some scholars believe that it endured through its impact on Judaism and Christianity. As we will see in Chapter 3, the ancient Hebrews were ruled by the Persians for a time (the sixth and fifth centuries B.C.) and probably adapted some of Zoroaster's teachings into their faith. Specifically, they probably absorbed the concepts of paradise and hell. The ancient Hebrews had only vague concepts of an afterlife at first, but under Zoroastrian influence they began to believe in a clearly defined heaven for the virtuous and a hell for those who were evil. These beliefs they later passed on to Christianity.

THE HEBREWS AND THE GREEKS

The Hebrews and the Greeks were the spiritual and intellectual cofounders of Western Civilization and, therefore, are studied in greater detail in Chapters 3 and 4. At this point a brief summary of the Hebrew and Greek

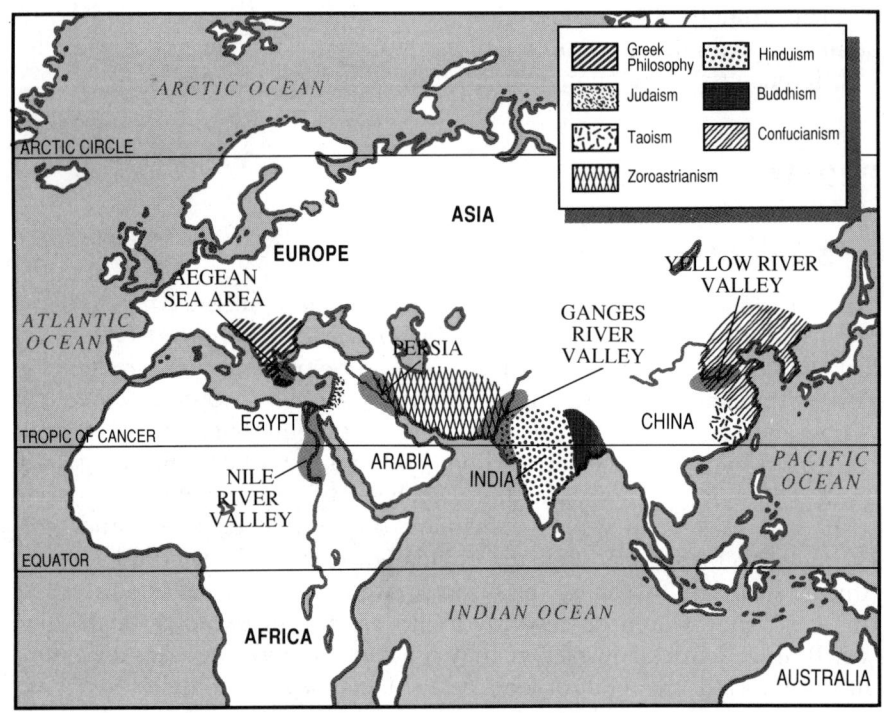

Figure 2.1 Religions and Philosophies of the Axial Age

spiritual breakthroughs of the Axial Period is needed, so that these breakthroughs may be compared with those of China, India, and Persia.

Judaism

The Hebrews were a semi-nomadic people who eventually settled in Israel, along the eastern shore of the Mediterranean. Over a thousand years or more, they developed a religion—Judaism—that is the original source of both Christianity and Islam.

Hebrew religion was different from polytheistic religions in a number of ways:

1. It was monotheistic, repudiating the chaotic variety of polytheism (gods scattered throughout nature) and eventually insisting that only one God created and ruled the entire universe. Actually, Hebrew monotheism evolved slowly over the centuries. The Hebrews originally conceived of their god as ruler only of Hebrews and made no attempt to deny the existence of other gods for other peoples. Not until the rise of the Hebrew prophets during the eighth to sixth centuries B.C. did the Hebrews begin to become pure monotheists, followers of only one God.

2. The Hebrews conceived of their god as transcendent, separate from, and superior to, the material world. God revealed himself through historical events, not in nature as the adherents of animistic religions believed. God was pure spirit and nature in the Hebrew conception was a separate earthly reality, created by God. This separation of God from nature would have far-reaching implications, some of which are discussed in the final section of this chapter.
3. The Hebrews also believed that God demanded moral behavior rather than the performance of rituals from humans. They gradually developed a moral code that was relatively humane and included demands for social justice for the poor and oppressed. In addition, they opposed the rituals—fertility rites or human sacrifices, for example—associated with the polytheistic religions.

Greek Thought

The Greeks lived around the Aegean Sea and were the cultural heirs of Minoan civilization. They accomplished a spiritual breakthrough that was more intellectual and philosophical than religious. A number of Greek intellectuals sought to use the reasoning abilities of the human mind to understand the world in which they lived. As a result, during the eighth to sixth centuries B.C., they began to define rational thought ("rational" in the sense of using the human mind to think logically from one point to another). These intellectuals came to think of the world as a *cosmos* ("world order"), an orderly whole that operated according to laws that humans could discover and understand. They repudiated the polytheistic assumption that the world was a chaotic place where different gods controlled different things. The philosophical concept of an orderly nature governed by laws was accompanied by the development of a political concept of human society as also governed by law. Hence, the Greeks created what would later be termed "constitutional government," government by laws agreed upon by rational people rather than government by monarchical decrees. This new conception of human government and society was elucidated by a number of brilliant Greek poets, philosophers, dramatists, and artists.

Even though the Hebrews and the Greeks lived within a few hundred miles of each other, they had virtually no contact during the Axial Period. Their spiritual breakthroughs occurred independently, but their ideas would eventually meet and joint to form the spiritual basis of Western Civilization.

THE SIGNIFICANCE OF THE AXIAL PERIOD

Fundamental changes in human thought occurred during the Axial Period. People began to distinguish more sharply between a spiritual reality and the natural, material world in which they lived. The polytheistic worldview held that two realities existed—a divine and a material—but it assumed that the two were inextricably intertwined and explained them in similar terms. Gods were portrayed as looking and acting much like humans and they were thought to work through ordinary natural events such as rainstorms or the growing of crops. In contrast, many of the Axial Period thinkers emphasized a sharp divide between the natural world and a much deeper or higher spiritual reality. The Hebrews, for example, portrayed God as radically superior to nature, and the Buddha conceived of *nirvana* as a detachment and spiritual separation from the material world. Karl Jaspers refers to this change in thought as "spiritualization," a growing human awareness of a spiritual realm above or behind the natural realm.[7] Another historian, Benjamin Schwartz, calls it a "strain toward transcendence," a search for a reality that surpasses the material world.[8] Whatever the terminology, the Axial thinkers usually conceived of the change in one of two ways: as a supreme supernatural being (such as the Hebrew god or the Zoroastrian Ahura-Mazda) or a supernatural order (such as the Greek conception of a lawful *cosmos* or the Taoist search for the fundamental way of nature).

People also began to think in universal terms during the Axial Period, in contrast to the earlier tribalistic or regionalistic notions about gods. The Axial leaders professed teachings that were universally applicable to all people. The Buddha taught that release from the material world was possible for all, not just the Brahmin priesthood. The Confucians believed that a harmonious life was possible for all who cultivated the appropriate virtues. The Hebrews believed that God ruled the entire universe, and the Greeks contended that the laws of the *cosmos* applied everywhere. In practice, the universalistic implications of these teachings were limited. The Hebrew God was originally revealed only to the Hebrews, and the Hindu conception of rising through the caste system in successive reincarnations made sense only in a society where a caste system existed. Nevertheless, the Axial thinkers thought in more universal terms than did those of earlier religious traditions and, therefore, developed systems of belief that could be adopted by entire civilizations. This is why the Axial Period witnessed the birth of several "world" religions. World religions did not literally encompass the entire world, but they were shared throughout an entire civilization (such as Confucianism in China or Hinduism in India) and they often had at least some appeal to those living outside the civilization.

In the Axial Period, people became more self-conscious, more aware of themselves as independent beings. Previously, most people thought of themselves as parts of nature intertwined with natural processes. The Axial thinkers defined humans as somewhat spiritual creatures, distinct from the natural world. The Confucians, for example, stressed harmony within and between people and society; they said almost nothing about a person's relationship with nature. The Taoists talked about harmony with nature, but they were referring to a philosophical understanding of an underlying natural reality, not to the visible natural world. The Hebrews thought of humans as spiritual beings created in the divine image. The Greeks contended that humans were rational beings superior to nature and thus uniquely qualified to govern themselves. The effect of these teachings of the Axial Period was to proclaim a kind of human freedom and spiritual independence from nature. With this new-found freedom went responsibility. Polytheistic religions demanded of humans only that they perform the appropriate rituals at the appropriate time. The religions of the Axial Period taught that humans had to obey the moral standards imposed by whichever god or conception of the good life they followed. Confucians had to adhere to ways of behavior that produced harmony, Buddhists to the Eightfold Noble Path, Hebrews to God's commandments. Humans were in the process of becoming moral creatures governed by moral canons.

The spiritual transformation of the Axial Period destroyed a simpler world and produced spiritual uncertainty for many people. During the long millennia when animistic religions prevailed, most humans shared the same basic assumptions, the same mentality. With the Axial Period came a deep spiritual chasm between the spiritual leaders—such as the Buddha or the Hebrew prophets—and many ordinary people. The spiritual leaders taught new ways of understanding the world, ways that were so complex and profound that many ordinary people preferred to continue the traditional polytheistic practices that were familiar and more comforting. Ordinary people, after all, had a great deal to lose. The nature religions made people feel like they were a part of nature and at home in the world. This comfortable feeling of unity with nature began to disappear during the Axial Period; many people regretted the loss, and for that reason various aspects of the nature religions continued to be a part of popular beliefs for centuries to come.

CONCLUSION

Western Civilization is unique. That uniqueness originated during the Axial Period. Looking back at world history since the Axial Period, we can see first, as previously mentioned, that many peoples were unaffected by the Axial breakthroughs and continued to practice animistic religions. We can also see that the great Asian civilizations became dominated by religions that stressed harmony; for Hindus and Buddhists, it was harmony with the universe; for Confucians, it was social harmony; and for Taoists, it was harmony with nature. Thus, Asian religions encouraged people to cooperate rather than compete, to be agreeable rather than aggressive. Certainly, religious distinctions cannot account for all of the differences among civilizations, but it is significant that Western Civilization, in contrast to other societies and civilizations, developed a worldview that honored human assertiveness and aggressiveness. This worldview originated with the Hebrews and the Greeks.

From the Hebrews, Western Civilization inherited its dominant form of religion—the belief in one God who is the sole ruler of the universe but who cares about people and expects humane moral behavior from them. This religion contained distinctive attitudes toward both nature and human history. With respect to nature, the Hebrews de-spiritualized the natural world by believing that God is separate from and superior to nature. (The implications of this belief are explored in Chapter 3.) From this belief Western Civilization eventually derived the view that, since nature is inanimate, humans can dominate it and use it with impunity. Thus, Hebrew beliefs helped create the spiritual underpinning for that Western technology that sought successfully to understand and use the forces of nature. With respect to human history, the Hebrews believed that God revealed himself to humans through historical events (the Exodus, for example, which is also discussed in Chapter 3). They concluded that what happened in history was meaningful and purposive, in the sense that God was leading them forward toward some great goal. (This is the origin of the "linear" conception of history—that history advances like a line. Most ancient peoples other than the Hebrews tended to accept a cyclical view of history; that is, that historical events repeat themselves in endless cycles.) From this Hebrew conception of history, Western Civilization evolved the broad assumption that God wanted people to participate actively in the political, social, and economic affairs of this world and not retreat passively into a life of spiritual contentment. In sum, then, Hebrew religion encouraged Western people to be assertive, both in exploring and using nature and in being involved in worldly affairs.

From the Greeks, Western Civilization inherited the idea of *law*. The Greek belief that nature is governed by law is one of the philosophical foundations of Western science. Science assumes that nature can be understood because natural events occur, not randomly, but in regular patterns in accordance with natural laws. The Greek idea of law also led to the development of constitutional government (government by laws). Thus, the Greeks also encouraged Western people to be assertive; they taught that humans were intelligent, noble beings capable both of understanding the workings of nature and governing themselves.

The story of Western Civilization begins around the eastern end of the Mediterranean Sea with first the Hebrews and then the Greeks. It continues with the Romans, who brought Hebraic and Greek ideas together.

THINGS YOU SHOULD KNOW

The Axial Period
Some causes of the Axial revolution
The significance of the Phoenician alphabet
Confucianism
Taoism
The impact of religion on Chinese history
Hinduism
Caste system
Buddhism
Jainism
The impact of religion on Indian history
Zoroastrianism
Judaism
Greek thought
The significance of the Axial Period

SUGGESTED READINGS

Karl Jaspers, *The Origin and Goal of History* (New Haven: Yale Univ. Press, 1953) is the basic work on the Axial Period, but it is somewhat difficult to read. Much more accessible and an excellent introduction to some of the world's religions and philosophies is Abraham Kaplan, *The New World of Philosophy* (New York: Random House, 1961). More specific works include W. Norman Brown, *Man in the Universe: Some Continuities in Indian Thought* (Berkeley: Univ. of California Press, 1970) and R. C. Zaehner, *Hinduism* (New York: Oxford Univ. Press, 1966) on Indian thought, and Benjamin I. Schwartz, *The World of Thought in Ancient China* (Cambridge, Mass.: Harvard Univ. Press, 1985) on Chinese thought.

Particularly interesting on the relationship between Western and Asian civilizations is Joseph Needham, *Within the Four Seas: The Dialogue of East and West* (Toronto: Univ. of Toronto Press, 1969). The dynamism of Western Civilization is perceptively explored by Lynn White, Jr., *Machina ex Deo: Essays in the Dynamism of Western Culture* (Boston: MIT Press, 1968) and *Medieval Religion and Technology* (Berkeley: Univ. of California Press, 1978).

NOTES

[1] Karl Jaspers, *The Origin and Goal of History* (New Haven: Yale Univ. Press, 1953), pp. 1–6.

[2] Herbert J. Muller, *Freedom in the Ancient World* (London: Secker & Warburg, 1961), p. 107.

[3] Quoted in Abraham Kaplan, *The New World of Philosophy* (New York: Random House, 1961), p. 284.

[4] Quoted in Benjamin I. Schwartz, "Transcendence in Ancient China," *Daedalus* (Vol. 104, no. 2, Spring 1975): p. 66.

[5] Kaplan, p. 209.

[6] Ibid., p. 252.

[7] Jaspers, *The Origin and Goal of History*, p. 3.

[8] Benjamin I. Schwartz, "The Age of Transcendence," *Daedalus* (Vol. 104, no. 2, Spring 1975): pp. 2–3.

3

The Hebrews: 2000 to 100 B.C.

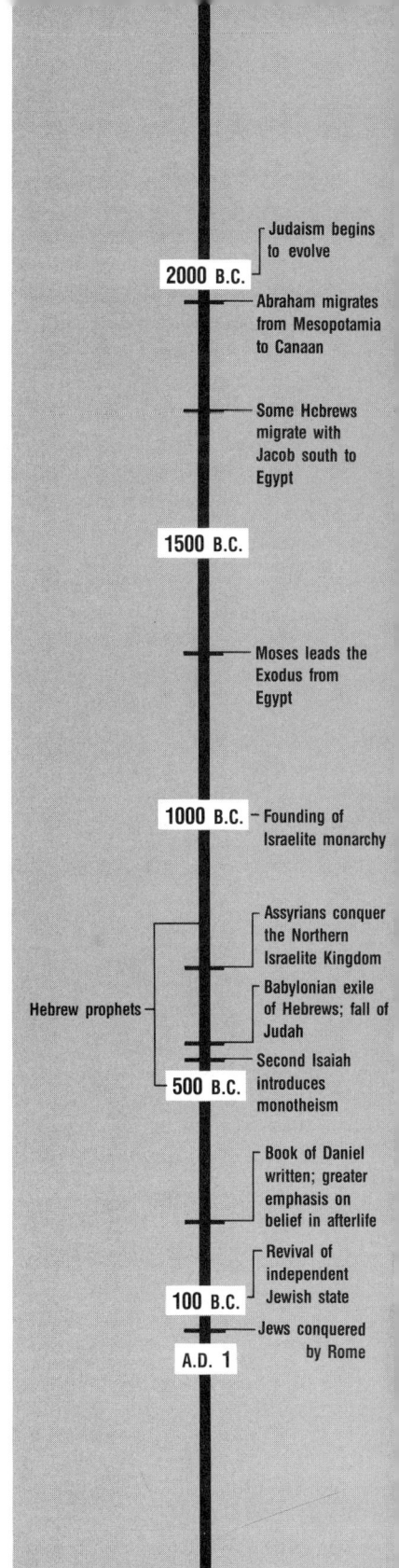

2000 B.C. — Judaism begins to evolve
— Abraham migrates from Mesopotamia to Canaan

— Some Hebrews migrate with Jacob south to Egypt

1500 B.C.

— Moses leads the Exodus from Egypt

1000 B.C. — Founding of Israelite monarchy

Hebrew prophets
— Assyrians conquer the Northern Israelite Kingdom
— Babylonian exile of Hebrews; fall of Judah
— Second Isaiah introduces monotheism

500 B.C.

— Book of Daniel written; greater emphasis on belief in afterlife

— Revival of independent Jewish state

100 B.C.
— Jews conquered by Rome

A.D. 1

Between 2000 and 100 B.C., Hebrews gradually evolved the religion that became known as Judaism. Judaism was distinct in two ways: (1) it was *monotheistic* (belief in one God) rather than polytheistic, and (2) it stipulated that God expected moral behavior from people rather than the performance of magical rituals. The evolution of Judaism proceeded in three stages. In its first stage, the Hebrew religion was a form of *monolatry*, meaning that Hebrews worshipped one God but did not deny the existence of other people's gods. In its second stage, the religion became monotheistic, as the prophets insisted that God was a universal deity who ruled all peoples. In its third stage of development, Judaism placed new emphasis on certain beliefs, such as the promise of eternal life after death and the expectation of the future coming of a Messiah.

THE BOOK OF GENESIS

According to the Hebrew Old Testament, "In the beginning God created the heavens and the earth" (Genesis 1:1).* This one sentence announced a spiritual revolution. By saying that God "created" the earth, the Hebrew writer (whose name is unknown to us) was proclaiming that only one God exists and that God is distinct from nature. The Hebrews repudiated the belief in several gods existing within nature. They also saw God as masculine, thus denying the existence of mother goddesses symbolizing fertility as well as the sexual rituals that had accompanied this belief.

The Book of Genesis also contains some striking passages about the creation of human beings. It refers to the first man as "Adam," but in Hebrew "Adam" means "the man," so the Genesis writer was referring to humankind in a general sense. From Adam, God took a rib and made it into a "woman" named Eve, a companion for man. But being a secondary creation, Eve was considered inferior to Adam. (This religious view of sexual inequality was common among most ancient peoples.) Adam and Eve were portrayed as living in the Garden of Eden, but their sense of human pride got them into trouble. God told them not to eat of the "tree of the knowledge of good and evil," but when Eve

> saw that the tree was good for food, and that it was a delight to the eyes, and that the tree was to be desired to make one wise, she took of its fruit and ate; and she also gave some to her husband, and he ate. (Genesis 3:6)

The eating of the fruit from the tree of knowledge was an act of rebellion, a grasping for total knowledge that only God can possess. Humans were

---

*Unless otherwise noted, all quotations from the Old Testament are taken from the Revised Standard Version.

thus portrayed as assertive and even arrogant, a view significantly different from conceptions of humanity in Asian religions. So God said, "Behold, the man has become like one of us, knowing good and evil; and now, lest he put forth his hand and take also of the tree of life, and eat, and live for ever," he must be banished from the Garden of Eden (Genesis 3: 22–23). People had come to know good and evil and were therefore "like" God, but God refused to let them eat of the tree of life, become immortal, and "be" God.

The first chapters of Genesis tell an entrancing story about the relationships between God and nature and between God and humans. The story reflects the ideas and beliefs held by most Hebrew people, for the Book of Genesis was compiled from a number of documents written by different authors. What is important about Genesis is not the facts, but what the facts represented to Hebrews and later to other peoples. (It makes little difference, for example, whether the Creation occurred in six twenty-four-hour days or in six eons.) The underlying message of Genesis is simple: there is one God who is the creator of all things, this God is a concrete personality who has a special relationship with humans rather than with nature, but humans are independent of God and free to choose between good and evil.

Although the underlying message of Genesis may be simple, the quest to understand that message was a complex one for Hebrews. Hebrew monotheism evolved gradually over more than a thousand years, so the story of the Hebrews is also the story of the spiritual awakening of a people.

THE ORIGINS OF HEBREW RELIGION

Abraham

Little is known of the origins of the people we call Hebrews. They were probably a seminomadic Semitic tribe who lived as sheepherders and craftspeople in and around Mesopotamia. Their story as we know it begins with Abraham, who sometime early in the second millennium B.C. had a religious experience that induced him to leave Mesopotamia. Abraham and his family migrated westward to the land then called Canaan, near the southeastern end of the Mediterranean Sea.

Abraham and his descendants (Isaac, Jacob, and so on) were the patriarchs, or fathers, of the Hebrew people. Yet, in a sense, the real father was the divine spirit that the Hebrews worshipped, for Hebrew identity came from their adherence to a unique religion, not from living in a certain area or from building a particular governmental structure. Their religion focused on the worship of one God, whose original name we do not know but who was later called the "God of Abraham." Modern scholars often use the word *Yahweh*—derived from the Hebrew sacred letters *YHWH*—to refer to the God of the early Hebrews. Yahweh insisted that Abraham and his descendants worship only him; in return, Yahweh would protect and aid the Hebrews in various ways. But Yahweh did not deny the existence of other gods for other peoples. Exodus, for example, poses the question, "Who is like unto thee, O Lord, among the gods?" (15:11). Thus, early Hebrew religion was a form of monolatry; eventually, though, it would develop monotheistic ideas.

Hebrew patriarchs believed that God was more concerned with human moral behavior than with rituals. In Genesis, God is depicted as angry about human moral blindness: "The Lord saw that the wickedness of man was great in the earth, and that every imagination of the thoughts of his heart was only evil continually" (6:5). Although the Hebrews were as bloodthirsty as any other people in their wars, they came to believe that they should behave more humanely in their dealings with each other. Thus, Hebrew religion had no sexual orgies or human sacrifices, though it did have animal sacrifices. A unique feature of the religion was a kind of questioning spirit, a willingness by the patriarchs to argue with God to ensure that justice was done. For instance, when God said that he was going to destroy Sodom because of the wickedness of its citizens, Abraham objected and God agreed to spare Sodom if there were at least ten righteous men in the city. In the end Sodom was destroyed because ten righteous men could not be found, but the important point is that Abraham was able to negotiate with God and to insist that he be fair and just.

Although some Hebrews remained in and around Canaan indefinitely, Abraham's grandson, Jacob, led others south to Egypt, probably in search of better farming possibilities. This occurred at about the same time the Hyksos from Asia invaded and conquered Egypt (sometime between 1700 and 1500 B.C.). Hebrews remained in Egypt for several centuries. However, as the Egyptians tried to reestablish national unity after driving out the Hyksos, they began to insist that Hebrews give up their religion and worship Egyptian gods instead. If the Hebrews had agreed to do so, they probably would have ceased to be a separate people and gradually would have integrated with the Egyptian people. But sometime around 1300 B.C., the Hebrews rebelled against the Egyptians under the leadership of Moses, forcing their way out of Egypt in what would become known as the Exodus. Ever since, the Exodus has been considered by Hebrews a great historical event, for it was God who led them out of Egypt in order to protect them. Also significant about the Exodus is that God was portrayed as supporting rebellion against a monarch. Thus it inspired among Hebrews a strong dislike of political despotism, especially political authority that purports to replace divine authority.

TECHNOLOGY
The Consequences of the Book of Genesis

What is the relationship between an ancient religious document such as the Book of Genesis and modern technology? Some scholars argue that the Hebrew conceptions of God, nature, and humans created a religious and philosophical orientation that encouraged Western people to develop technologies that could explore and use nature. Although all peoples have developed technologies and used nature to some extent, Western Civilization has been much more aggressive than have other civilizations in its use of technology. The question is, then, what accounts for this aggressiveness?

One important element in the Hebrew religious and philosophical orientation is its de-spiritualization of nature. By believing that God is distinct from nature, the Hebrews were implying that nature is inanimate, empty of gods and spirits. Over the centuries, this idea gradually persuaded many Western people to view nature as a reality that could be used to their advantage. Thus, people were free to develop tools and techniques for exploring nature in any way they saw fit.

The Hebrews also considered human beings to be exalted creatures, entitled to help rule and use the earth. God is quoted as saying, "Let us make man in our image, after our likeness; and let them have dominion over the fish of the sea, and over the birds of the air, and over the cattle, and over all the earth" (Genesis 1:26). The sense of human superiority is also expressed in Genesis 2:19: "So out of the ground the Lord God formed every beast of the field and every bird of the air, and brought them to the man to see what he would call them; and whatever the man called every living creature, that was its name." When Genesis says that God lets "man" name the animals, he is implying that humans are participants in the Creation as a kind of subsidiary partner of God.

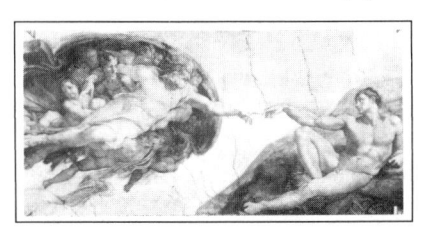

The Creation of Man *The story of the Creation was painted by the Renaissance artist and sculptor Michelangelo on the ceiling of the Sistine Chapel (see Chapter 10). Here, God reaches out to give life to humans, Michelangelo portrays God as distinct from his creation and the earthly world; humans are portrayed as creatures of great worth, created in the divine image. (The Granger Collection)*

Moses

Little is known with certainty about Moses. We know that he was a decisive figure in Hebrew history and that he lived sometime between 1350 and 1250 B.C. We also know that he was a political leader who guided the Hebrews out of Egypt into the Sinai desert, where they wandered for several decades waiting for divine guidance from Yahweh to return to the "Promised Land" (Canaan). Moses was also a religious teacher, who reinvigorated the covenant between God and the Hebrews that had originally been made with Abraham. In particular, Moses received from God the Ten Commandments, a set of moral codes that governed the behavior of Hebrews.

The religion that Moses taught was in the same tradition as that followed by Abraham. Although Yahweh did not deny the existence of other gods, he insisted that Hebrews worship only him. Yahweh was clearly different from other gods in several respects. As a spiritual deity, he could not be identified with any one place and would not tolerate "graven images" of himself. Yahweh also had a special relationship with Hebrews, one that was embodied in a covenant by which he promised to protect Hebrews if they obeyed his commandments. The covenant was unique in several ways. For one thing, it was based on free moral choice on both sides. Most other peoples of the time believed that they had no choice but to worship the gods of their particular areas. The Hebrews were not bound in this way, as they were free to choose to worship Yahweh, and Yahweh was similarly free to leave the Hebrews if they did not obey his commandments. Also unique about the covenant was its moral content, most notably the Ten Commandments (see Exodus 20:1–17). Thus obeying Yahweh meant adhering to certain moral standards. Yet another unique element of the covenant was its assumption of equality. The covenant applied equally to all Hebrew people, not just to priests, tribal leaders, or the upper classes.

THE ESTABLISHMENT OF A HEBREW STATE

Canaan was populated primarily by the polytheistic Canaanites, but during the decades before and after 1200 B.C., Hebrews gradually invaded the land. This invasion was in part a series of battles to defeat and conquer the Canaanites and in part a gradual and peaceful infiltration into Canaan. Sometime after 1200 B.C., twelve Hebrew tribes formed a sacred confederation among the people of Yahweh. This confederation was called *Israel*, and Hebrews were subsequently known as *Israelites*.

The sacred confederation lasted from around 1200 to 1020 B.C. During that time, Israel was united only by the covenant with Yahweh and had no central governnment or capital city. It was endangered,

Moses Michelangelo's statue of Moses (c. 1515–1516) portrays the ancient Hebrew leader as a powerful, majestic figure, holding the tablets containing the Ten Commandments. (The Granger Collection)

however, when the Philistines began to occupy Israelite land. The Philistines were a militarily powerful people who lived to the west of the Hebrews, on the shores of the Mediterranean. They were probably related to the Phoenicians, who lived north of the Israelites.

Unlike the historical records of most other ancient peoples, which contain few accounts of clearly defined individual personalities, the account of the Israelite resistance to the Philistines contains several memorable and distinct human personalities. Samson, for example, is a heroic figure known for his great strength, allegedly having killed a thousand Philistines with the jawbone of an ass. Samson, of course, was undone by Delilah, a beautiful Philistine woman who by enchanting him was able to cut off his hair and thus destroy the source of his strength. David, another folklore hero of the Israelite resistance, is said to have destroyed the Philistine giant, Goliath, in an epic battle. Goliath was armed with a spear while David fought with a slingshot, a highly developed weapon at that time.

To defend themselves against the Philistines, the Israelites instituted a monarchical government sometime around 1020 B.C. The first king was Saul, a man who was periodically seized by spiritual frenzies and thus presumed to have been anointed by Yahweh. After Saul came David, who eventually ended the Philistine threat and organized a central government in the capital city of Jerusalem. The Israelites thought of David as a model king; indeed, Jesus would later be identified as a descendant of David. David was succeeded by Solomon, a powerful ruler who acquired a reputation for being wise. Solomon conquered additional territory for Israel and increased its prosperity by developing extensive commercial ties with other states and rulers (including possibly the Queen of Sheba in Africa). He also used some of this wealth to build the temple at Jerusalem, which became the center of Yahweh worship.

During the reigns of David and Solomon, much of the Old Testament was written. An extraordinary body of literature, the Old Testament was inspired in various ways by Israel's religious spirit. Some of it took the form of devotional poetry:

> As the hart panteth after the water brooks,
> So panteth my soul after thee, O God.
> My soul thirsteth for God, for the living God:
> When shall I come and appear before God?
>
> Psalms 42:1–2

Some of it inquired about what constitutes a good life. The following passage declares the meaninglessness of material possessions:

> Vanity and vanities, saith the Preacher;
> Vanity of vanities, all is vanity.
> What profit hath man of all his labor,
> Wherein he laboureth under the sun?
> One generation goeth, and another generation cometh,
> And the earth abideth for ever.
> The sun also ariseth and the sun goeth down,
> And hasteth to his place where he ariseth.
>
> Ecclesiastes 1:2–5

Yet other parts of the Old Testament were written as lyrical poetry. The following passage expresses the passionate love of a young shepherd and shepherdess (or, in a more religious interpretation, the love of God for Israel):

> The voice of my beloved! behold he cometh,
> Leaping upon the mountains, skipping upon the hills. . . .
> My beloved spake, and said unto me:
> Rise up, my love, my fair one, and come away;

THE ESTABLISHMENT OF A HEBREW STATE 55

David Michelangelo's statue of the Israelite King David presents him as a heroic figure full of youthful vitality. (B. Glassman)

For lo, the winter is past,
The rain is come and gone;
The flowers appear upon the earth,
The time of the pruning is come.

Song of Songs 2:8–12

These words express well the exuberance felt by many Israelites in the days of David and Solomon. But this exuberance was soon overshadowed by political quarrels within the Israelite kingdom. Although some Israelites had always opposed the establishment of the monarchy, the voices of protest grew louder during Solomon's reign. Solomon was an enormously wealthy and sometimes despotic ruler who had seven hundred wives and three hundred concubines. To support his entourage and continue his construction projects, he imported slaves from Phoenicia (present-day Lebanon) and imposed labor requirements on lower-class Israelites. Solomon's policies resulted in a sharp division between the classes—poverty and sometimes slavery for the lower classes and wealth and power for the upper classes.

Soon after Solomon's death (c. 922 B.C.), a rebellion erupted as his empire disintegrated into two weak states—the Northern Kingdom of Israel (sometimes called Samaria) and the Southern Kingdom of Judah. The two kingdoms lived side by side for a time, until the Northern Kingdom was destroyed by the Assyrians in 721 B.C. and Judah was conquered by the Babylonians in 597 B.C. In both events, many Israelites were either killed or carried off into exile to become slaves.

In addition to these political calamities, the Israelites faced religious problems as well. These problems originated when the Israelites first settled in Canaan. Canaanite religion was polytheistic and focused on soil fertility and good crops. Like the religions of many other ancient peoples, the Canaanites believed in the analogy of human fertility and that of the soil, and they practiced the rituals common to this belief—sexual orgies, sacred prostitution, and sometimes even human sacrifice. As the Israelites settled among and often intermarried with the Canaanites, they began to absorb some of the Canaanite religious practices. Yahweh worship gradually became intermingled with Canaanite religion, and Yahweh was sometimes identified with Baal, the Canaanite god of storms and vegetation.

The Israelite tradition was thus changed in two major ways. One was political and economic in nature: the Israelites lost their equality in political and economic status when under their monarchy they became divided into the rich or the poor. The other major change in Israelite tradition was religious, propelled by the intermingling of Israelite and Canaanite beliefs and practices. These changes, in turn, led to the prophetic movement, in which the prophets protested against what they saw as religious corruption and social injustice in Israelite society. As we will see, the prophetic movement transformed Israelite religion during the eighth to sixth centuries B.C.

THE PROPHETIC MOVEMENT

The word *prophet* is broadly defined as "one who is called." More specifically, it refers to one who is called by God to transmit God's messages. Prophets had long been a part of Hebrew history, serving as advisers to Israelite kings. It wasn't until the ninth century B.C., however, that some prophets began to criticize the behavior of monarchs. The ninth-century prophets were mostly ecstatic visionaries, whereas those of the eighth century B.C. began to write and preach in more reasoned and literary terms. Indeed, their pronouncements constitute large parts of the

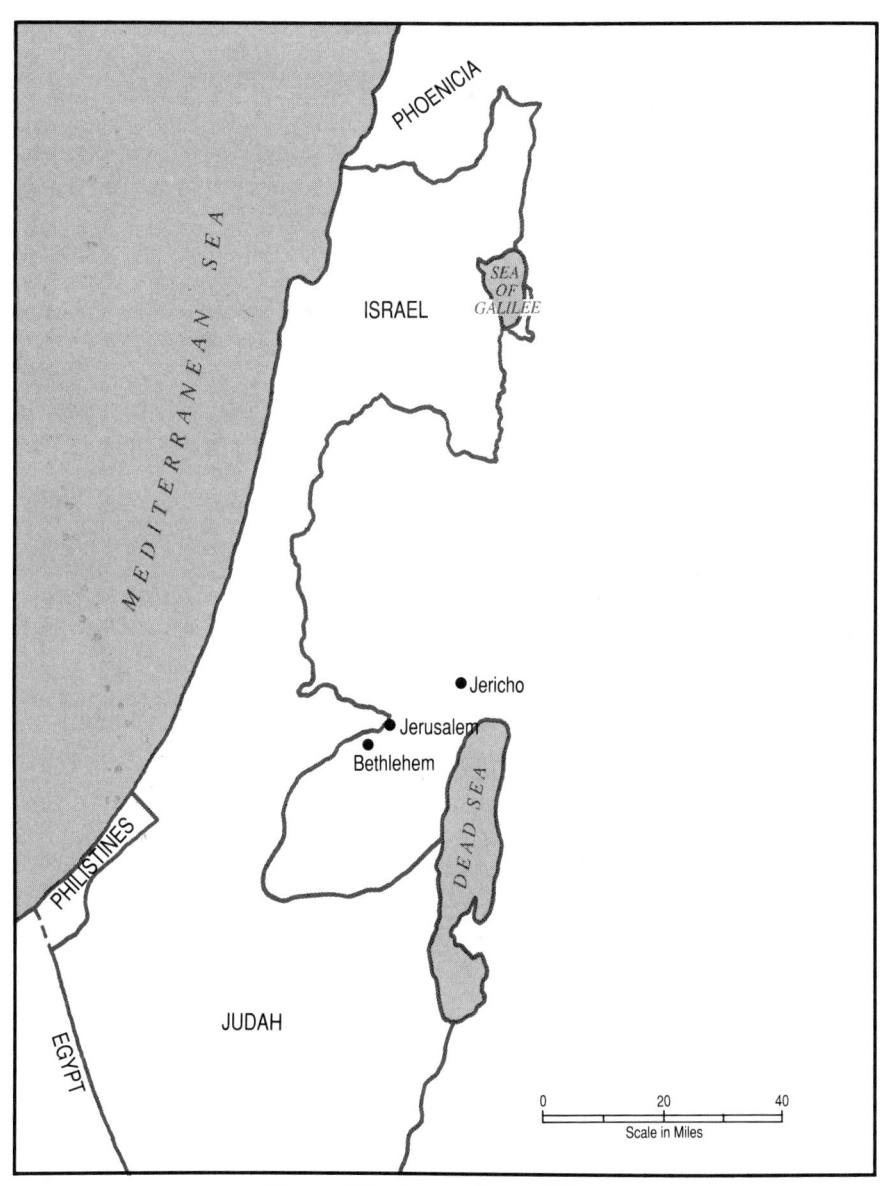

Figure 3.1 Ancient Israel, 800 B.C.

Old Testament. It is not known precisely who put the prophetic books in written form. Probably the sayings of the prophets were passed on orally for a time and then written down.

The prophets of the eighth century B.C. came from the lower classes and hence were not highly respected. They were often provocative and even insulting in their criticisms of Israelite society. As a result, they were usually disliked and sometimes punished. The prophet Jeremiah, for example, was flogged several times by order of various monarchs of Judah who were angered by his prophecies that Judah would soon be destroyed. Yet the prophets were great religious teachers who stressed above all monotheism and morality. Although monotheism and morality had long been implicit in Hebrew religion, the prophets were the first to teach explicitly that one God rules all people and demands morality, not rituals, from them.

The first of the eighth century prophets was Amos, a sheepherder who around 750 B.C. burst onto the Israelite scene by breaking up a religious service that included fertility rites. Amos quoted God as denouncing the rituals:

> Even though you offer me your burnt offerings and cereal offerings, I will not accept them.
>
> Amos 5:22

Amos told the Israelites that God wanted justice for the poor rather than rituals, and that people would be judged according to the moral quality of their lives:

> Seek good, and not evil,
>   that you may live;
> and so the Lord, the God of hosts, will be with you,
>   as you have said.
> Hate evil, and love good,
>   and establish justice in the gate.
>
> Amos 5:14–15

"Establish justice in the gate" meant helping the poor and oppressed who often congregated around city gates. Amos warned the Israelite upper classes that God would punish them if they continued to seek personal wealth and ignore the needs of the lower classes. One of Amos's successors, Hosea, described God's punishment in graphic terms:

> They shall fall by the sword,
> Their infants shall be dashed in pieces,
> And their pregnant women ripped open.
>
> Hosea 14:2

Hosea's prediction was realized as small kingdoms were crushed by larger empires and the Northern Kingdom of Israel was conquered by the Assyrians in 721 B.C. More interesting, though, was that the prophets viewed the Assyrian conquest as a carrying out of God's purposes. According to traditional religious thought, God was assumed to protect

Hebrews from all enemies; his failure to do so would reveal his inferiority to the Assyrian gods. Refusing this traditional assumption, the prophets preached that the Assyrians were instruments of God used to punish the Israelites for their sins. In effect, the prophets portrayed God as ruler of both Assyrians and Israelites, thus marking a major step in the development of monotheistic religion. The Assyrian conquest was for the Israelites a political disaster but it was also a spiritual breakthrough.

Still more political calamities ensued. The Southern Kingdom of Judah was destroyed by the Babylonians early in the sixth century B.C., and most of its surviving population was taken into exile in Babylon. At this time, Israelites were increasingly known as Jews, a name derived from Judah. Unlike their counterparts from the Northern Kingdom, the Judean exiles were able to survive as an identifiable community and were able to continue worshipping in their traditional faith.

The experience of exile raised a fundamental spiritual issue: if God is responsible for everything that happens, then why does he allow the good to suffer and the wicked to prosper? This question is confronted in the Book of Job, a long series of poems about a good man who suffers greatly and who wonders what he has done to deserve such suffering. God responds by telling Job that humans will never understand divine ways and must simply accept their fate. The broader message, of course, is that a monotheistic God is so transcendent, so far beyond human comprehension, that his ways cannot be understood.

Babylon was conquered by the Persian Empire in 539 B.C. The Persians were more benevolent than the Babylonians and allowed many Jewish exiles to return home. This good fortune was celebrated by the last of the great prophets, the Second Isaiah. His real name is unknown, but he is called the Second Isaiah because he wrote the last parts of the Book of Isaiah. Ironically, this poet is regarded as one of the greatest writers and spiritual leaders of all time. He was an explicit monotheist and the first prophet to state unequivocally that there is only one God:

> I am the first and I am the last;
> besides me there is no God.
>
> Isaiah 44:6

Although some early prophets hinted at the concept of monotheism, the Second Isaiah was the first to make its true meaning clear. Jews responded to monotheism by asking the question: If only one God exists, why do only Jews know him? The Second Isaiah explained that Jews were designated by God to suffer for the sins of others and thereby to transmit the divine message to all people. Suffering then, was a sign of the love of God and a means through which people could attain purification and redemption. This concept of the "suffering servant" is described by the Second Isaiah in the following words:

> He is despised and rejected of men;
> A man of sorrows, and acquainted with grief. . . .
> He was wounded for our transgressions,
> He was bruised for our iniquities. . . .
> With his stripes we are healed. . . .
> The Lord hath laid on him the iniquity of us all.
>
> Isaiah 53:3, 5–6

The prophetic movement ended sometime late in the sixth century B.C. Although led by a relatively small number of people, the movement had a tremendous impact on Jewish religion. The prophets universalized Jewish religion by teaching that God ruled the entire universe. They also universalized morality in the sense that they spread the idea of equality among all people in the eyes of God. The prophets were not political revolutionaries, nor did they attempt to overturn the established political order. But their demands for social justice place them among the first social reformers in Western history.

JUDAISM AFTER THE PROPHETS

The people of Judah kept the Hebrew tradition alive; thus their religion came to be known as *Judaism*. Judaism bound the Jewish people together by giving them an identity even though they no longer constituted a politically independent nation. The Jewish people were controlled by the Persians until the second half of the fourth century B.C., when they were absorbed into Alexander the Great's empire (see Chapter 4). After a brief period of Judean independence (142–63 B.C.), they were conquered by the Roman Empire in 63 B.C.

Judaism continued to evolve during the last five centuries B.C. Among the most important developments were new beliefs about the afterlife, which had previously been a minor concern of Judaism (since the Jews assumed that God would reward them in this life by protecting them from enemies). However, encouraged by the political calamities that continued to befall them as well as some Zoroastrian influence (see Chapter 2), Jews began to contend that God's rewards and punishments would be given to them after death. Thus they began to teach that in this life people had to choose between following God, the source of goodness and righteousness, or following Satan, the embodiment of evil. Further, bodily resurrection would occur in the afterlife followed by a divine judgment, at which time the pious would achieve immortality in heaven and the wicked would be damned to eternal hell.

Particularly significant to the development of these ideas about the afterlife was the Book of Daniel, written sometime during the second century B.C. Daniel is apocalyptic—that is, it makes predictions about the ultimate destiny of the world—and much of it is written in allegorical, obscure language. In particular, the Book of Daniel was highly influential in teaching about the "last things"—the resurrection of the dead and the final reign of God.

Another development in Judaism was a belief in the coming of a *Messiah*, meaning one who is "anointed" by God. Some Jews believed that God would send a political Messiah to restore their political independence; others assumed that the Messiah would be a spiritual leader unconcerned with politics. In either case, the belief in a Messiah gave Judaism a sense of expectation, a sense of waiting for some great event. This sense of expectation would later contribute to the rise of Christianity, since the followers of Jesus believed that he was the awaited Messiah.

CONCLUSION

The spiritual journey of the Jewish people had several major impacts on the history of Western Civilization:

1. From it emerged, directly or indirectly, three major religions—Judaism itself, which remained the religion of many Jews; Christianity, which developed out of Judaism in the first century A.D.; and Islam, inspired in part by Judaism in the seventh century A.D.
2. As noted earlier, the Jewish conception of a monotheistic God superior to nature had the effect of de-spiritualizing nature. Since nature was no longer regarded as having spirits, Western people eventually came to believe that they could investigate and use nature to their advantage. Over the centuries, the de-spiritualization of nature encouraged the development of Western science and technology.
3. The Jewish belief that humanity is God's greatest creation helped create a strong sense of pride among Western people. It also supported the idea of freedom, in that people were portrayed as being able to choose between good and evil. Ultimately, Western people came to believe that they could accomplish great things, and this tendency helped make Western Civilization a dynamic and aggressive force in world history.
4. The Jewish belief that God cares for all people helped create a sense of moral responsibility. According to the historian Harry Orlinsky, the prophets taught that "justice was for the weak as well as the strong, . . . that one could not serve God at the same time that he mistreated his fellow man."[1] In Leviticus is the admonition: "And you shall love your neighbor as yourself" (19:18). Jewish moral precepts were far more humane than those of other ancient peoples; indeed, they would ultimately become the source of the most noble, ethical teachings in Western Civilization.
5. The Jewish conception of history was unique. Most other ancient peoples took the fatalistic view that history repeats itself in ever-recurring cycles (see Chapter 2). This cyclical view assumes that every society proceeds through a predetermined sequence of

events—birth, maturity, and inevitable death. The Jews, however, looked forward to a future golden age—the final judgment of God and the entry of the pious into paradise. The effect was to portray history as developing in a linear fashion, as progressing toward a goal. This idea of progress became a fundamental assumption in Western history. Eventually, the Judeo-Christian belief in spiritual progress was modified to include material progress, the presumption that life on earth can be made continually better.

6. Ironically, even though the Jews are cofounders of Western Civilization, they have been persecuted by other Western peoples over the centuries. Christians, for instance, have often perceived Jews as religious and racial enemies, the result being periodic outbursts of anti-Semitism and sometimes the torturing and killing of Jews. The ultimate example of anti-Semitism is the twentieth-century Holocaust, the murdering of more than six million Jews by German Nazis and their collaborators during World War II.

THINGS YOU SHOULD KNOW

Early Hebrew religion
Abraham
Moses
Genesis and Western technology
The Israelite monarchy (1000–900 B.C.)
The prophetic movement
Amos
Job
The Second Isaiah
Judaism after the prophets
Daniel
Messiah
The significance of Judaism

SUGGESTED READINGS

The Old Testament is, of course, the fundamental source on the spiritual journey of the Jewish people. The stories contained in the Old Testament—such as the life of Moses or the liaison of Samson and Delilah—are not always historically reliable, but they have inspired the writing of many literary works and musical compositions over the centuries.

A good modern analysis of the Old Testament is Dane R. Gordon, *The Old Testament: A Beginning Survey* (Englewood Cliffs, N.J.: Prentice-Hall, 1985). Three good histories of ancient Israel are John Bright, *A History of Israel* (Philadelphia: Westminster Press, 1976); Harry M. Orlinsky, *Ancient Israel*, 2nd ed. (Ithaca, N.Y.: Cornell Univ. Press, 1960); and G. W. Anderson, *The History and Religion of Israel* (New York: Oxford Univ. Press, 1966).

NOTE

[1] Harry M. Orlinsky, *Ancient Israel*, 2nd ed. (Ithaca, N.Y.: Cornell Univ. Press, 1960), p. 144.

4

The Greeks: 1200 to 30 B.C.

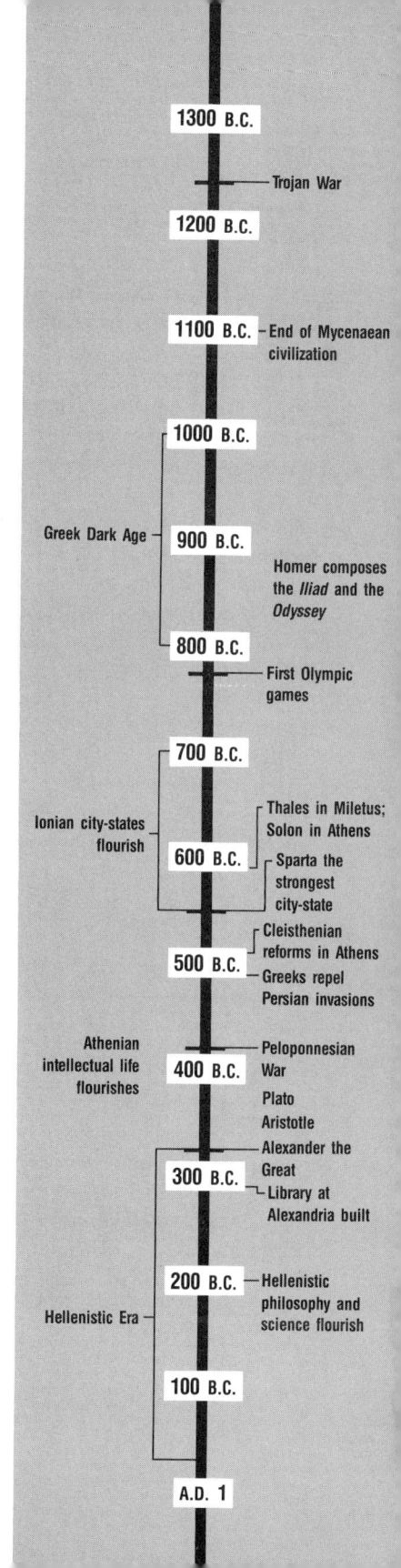

	1300 B.C.
	— Trojan War
	1200 B.C.
	1100 B.C. — End of Mycenaean civilization
	1000 B.C.
Greek Dark Age	900 B.C.
	Homer composes the *Iliad* and the *Odyssey*
	800 B.C.
	— First Olympic games
	700 B.C.
Ionian city-states flourish	Thales in Miletus; Solon in Athens
	600 B.C. — Sparta the strongest city-state
	Cleisthenian reforms in Athens
	500 B.C. — Greeks repel Persian invasions
Athenian intellectual life flourishes	— Peloponnesian War
	400 B.C.
	Plato
	Aristotle
	— Alexander the Great
	300 B.C. — Library at Alexandria built
	200 B.C. — Hellenistic philosophy and science flourish
Hellenistic Era	
	100 B.C.
	A.D. 1

We live round the sea like frogs around a pond," wrote the philosopher Plato of himself and his fellow Greeks. The heart of ancient Greece was the Aegean Sea, with its European and Asiatic coasts on either side and many islands in the middle. There, in that small world, grew an extraordinary civilization founded by one of the most fascinating peoples who ever lived. In terms of material wealth and military power, ancient Greece was not impressive, but in the realm of the human spirit the Greeks were magnificent. In many ways, they "discovered" the human "mind" through their philosophy and rational thought ("rational" meaning the intellectual power of humans to think logically and coherently). The Greeks also developed politics, in that they were the first people to create governments in which decisions are the product of public debate among free citizens. The creations of rational thought and politics were interrelated, since both philosophy and political debate drew on the reasoning powers of the mind.

We do not know with certainty when or how Greek civilization began. Even the Greeks knew little of their origins. Their legends contain only vague references to two older civilizations: the Minoan and the Mycenaean. Minoan civilization flourished on the Greek island of Crete until the middle of the second millennium B.C. (see Chapter 1). Mycenaean civilization was composed of Greek-speaking people who dominated much of mainland Greece from about 2000 to 1100 B.C. The Mycenaeans were a harsh people, predatory warriors who used their military strength to full advantage. They are most famous for their participation in the Trojan War, waged against the city of Troy on the Asiatic coast. The Trojan War of around 1200 B.C. marks the beginning of Greek history as we know it.

THE HOMERIC AGE

The Trojan War is immortalized in the *Iliad* and the *Odyssey*, two epic poems probably written by Homer in the eighth or ninth century B.C. For later Greeks these poems were virtually a "bible" that contained both a religious system and a moral code by which people lived. Homer was thus a religious and moral teacher who more than anyone else formed the Greek spirit. But we know little else about him or even if he indeed wrote both epic poems. Most scholars agree that Homer lived sometime during the so-called Dark Age (1100–800 B.C.), the time after Mycenaean civilization collapsed due to civil wars and attacks by the Dorian peoples who settled in southern Greece. According to Greek legend, Homer was a "blind poet" who wandered through the Greek part of the Asiatic coastland and earned his living by "singing" stories that had been handed down from past generations. In written form, these stories became the *Iliad* and the *Odyssey*.

The *Iliad* and the *Odyssey* portray a brutal world in which success and winning were attained at any cost. The battle scenes described in the poems tell of heads being cut off and bowels gushing out of wounded warriors. The historian Frank Frost describes Homeric warriors as "crude supermen breaking other people's heads, destroying cities, and in general crashing through life with the maximum noise and inconvenience to others."[1]

However, the epic poems are not only vivid accounts of war; for Greeks they were a form of moral and religious instruction. Achilles, the hero of the *Iliad*, is described as "godlike"; he personified for Greeks the brave, courageous warrior who sought everlasting fame through the performance of great deeds. Achilles was a symbol of the model warrior, and later Greeks would honor and imitate him. Similarly, the *Odyssey* is a story about the hero Odysseus, a middle-aged warrior who wandered into all sorts of adventures during his ten-year-long journey back to Greece after the Trojan War. Odysseus is characterized in the poem as wise and curious, traits that later Greeks would admire and seek to emulate.

The attitudes exemplified by Achilles and Odysseus in the Homeric sagas formed what historian C. M. Bowra calls the Greek "heroic outlook."[2] This outlook embodied a strong sense of human worth and thus encouraged Greeks to perform great deeds and to seek honor and fame. The Greeks called it *arete*, meaning "excellence" in the sense that a person should strive to surpass all others in the society. The Greeks' admiration for excellence and greatness was the primary source of their creativity. However, it also imparted a ruthless character to Greek life. Since the goal of life was to surpass all others, the effect was to glorify the superiority of the strong and to degrade those who were considered physically weaker, including women.

The heroic outlook was embodied in Greek religion as well. The Greeks followed a polytheistic religion taught to them by both Homer and Hesiod (the latter poet wrote the *Theogony*, or "genealogy of the gods," sometime during the eighth century B.C.). The most prominent Greek gods were the Olympians, so named because they were reputed to live on Mt. Olympus. These gods usually represented either natural forces (such as Zeus, who controlled the sky) or human forces (such as Aphrodite, who symbolized beauty and the power of attraction between people). Other Greek gods included Poseidon, god of the sea; Hades, god of the underworld; Apollo, god of light and intelligence; Dionysus, god of the vine; Ares, god of war; and Hera, wife of Zeus and goddess of motherhood. The Greeks usually portrayed their gods as constantly fighting, partying, and fornicating. Zeus, for example, the chief Greek god, was notorious for his love affairs and his violent temper. In one story, Zeus ate his first wife just before she gave birth, because he was afraid the child would eventually dethrone him. But having second

The Laocoön Group This marble statue, a good example of Hellenistic art, is a Roman copy of a work done by Agesander, Polydorus, and Athenodorus from the island of Rhodes in the second century B.C. It portrays the priest Laocoön and his two sons, who according to Greek legend were strangled by sea serpents for offending the gods. (Vatican Museum, Rome)

thoughts about the child, Zeus had his own head cleaved open with an axe so that the child—Athena—was born fully grown from Zeus's head.

Although the stories of the Greek gods may seem strange to us, for the Greeks they contained an underlying message. The gods behaved and looked like humans, although they were more powerful than humans—superhuman, higher forms of humanity—and, unlike humans, they could expect to live eternally. A Greek saying expressed this idea well: "What are men? Mortal gods. What are gods? Immortal men."[3] The Greeks were so impressed by human potential that they could not imagine anything higher.

Thus, Greek morality and religion celebrated human greatness. In the early periods of their history, the Greeks stressed the individual's pursuit of fame and glory. Beginning in the sixth and fifth century B.C., however, the Greeks began to emphasize participation in a communal greatness.

IONIA AND THE DISCOVERY OF THE "MIND"

The Greek Dark Age ended early in the eighth century B.C., and a new period of Greek history began (one that historians know much more about). The Greeks themselves dated this new period from 776 B.C., the year of the first Olympic games. Olympia was an old site used for religious festivals honoring Zeus, and the games—a celebration of human strength and power—were one way of paying homage to the humanlike gods. The competitions were all-male affairs that eventually included foot races, chariot races, javelin throws, boxing, wrestling, and many other athletic contests.

Politically, there was no unified "Greece," for the Greeks were divided into several hundred independent communities. The mountainous terrain contributed to this political disunity, since the people of each valley or plateau tended to guard their independence jealously. Each community was known as a *polis* (the origin of the English word *political*) or "city-state." Physically, a *polis* consisted of a city and the surrounding farmland, the entire area often being no more than twenty to forty miles across in any direction. Spiritually, it was a closely knit community bound together by worship of a patron god or goddess. Most of the Greek city-states were small, poor farming areas that had little impact on history. Others, however, became prosperous and powerful merchant cities with populations of three to four hundred thousand.

In the seventh and sixth centuries B.C., the most vigorous Greek city-states were in Ionia, a region on the Asiatic coast in present-day Turkey. It was here that a spiritual and intellectual revolution began— the creation of rational thought. This revolution marks the beginning of a transition in human thought as people began to use "reason"—the intellectual powers of the human mind—rather than mythology to explain natural and human events.

Why did an intellectual revolution occur in Ionian Greece? It occurred partly because the Ionians were open to new ideas and new ways. They lived in a frontier area far from the Greek mainland and, therefore, tended to disregard the old customs and to be skeptical about traditional religion. Furthermore, the Ionian cities were large commercial centers that conducted trade all over the eastern Mediterranean. As a result, the Ionians were stimulated by contacts with the older Egyptian and Persian civilizations. Most influential, though, was the Ionians' idea of *law*—that both nature and human society should be governed by regularities. We do not know with certainty how the Ionians came to develop this concept. One possibility is that it grew out of the Homeric conception of fate; that is, fate controls human destiny in much the same way as laws control nature and society.

The Ionian intellectual revolution was intimately connected with a political revolution. The Ionian cities were dominated by a merchant class that developed written law codes by which it governed. Although written laws were not new to the world, the Ionian laws were the first to express the political will of citizens. Previously, decrees expressed the will of some higher authority, such as a king or a small group of nobles. This is not to say that all Ionian citizens were permitted to express their political views, for women, slaves, and usually the lower classes were excluded. But this was the first time in Western history that people were governed by written rules that at least some ordinary citizens had helped fashion. Political decisions were increasingly made as a result of some public debate, encouraging citizens to learn how to think, reason, and persuade one another. Thus, the habit of reasoned argument developed in the political life of some Ionian cities, and the same habit was carried over into the intellectual realm.

Thales and Other Ionians

Thales of Miletus, born around 625 B.C., was the most prominent figure in the Ionian intellectual revolution. Later Greeks considered him one of the seven "wise men" and frequently recounted stories about him. One typical story about an absentminded intellectual told of Thales falling head over heels into a well because he was gazing at the stars and forgot to watch where he was going.

Thales is regarded as the first Western philosopher, primarily because of his contention that water is the basic reality in the universe. He probably was not saying that everything comes from water; rather, he was trying to account for life in the universe by portraying water as the fundamental sustaining principle of life. Thales's contention was unique in several respects. Perhaps most significant is the fact that he attempted to explain life by analogy to a natural substance—water—instead of to a god of water. Thales viewed nature as a thing not as a realm full of spirits. His view marks an important change in Western scientific thought. Another significant thesis in Thales's theory is that all living things are derived from one fundamental reality. He was assuming, therefore, that there is a fundamental order that underlies the diversity of life. This was another important change in Western thought, the beginning of the idea that nature is governed by law. Perhaps most significant, though, is the fact that Thales based his argument not on myths or some other authority, but solely on his own ability to think and reason. In effect, he was saying that "I" think all things are made of water, not the "gods" or the "ancient authorities." For the first time in Western history, a man was appealing to human reason, the rational mind, as the arbiter of truth.

Thales was not a lone original genius; he was a part, perhaps the most important part, of a long tradition of curiosity and inquisitiveness that flourished in Ionian Greece. Lyric poetry, for example, had been created long before Thales's time. Through it Ionians like Sappho and Archilochus expressed their personal feelings, even erotic desires, thereby displaying the individual human voice. Sappho, one of the few women to make a mark on Greek history, established a finishing school for young women on the island of Lesbos (hence the English word *lesbian*), and often wrote love poems to other women. An example is a poem written to

Aphrodite, the goddess of love: "Ornate-throned immortal Aphrodite,/ wile-weaving daughter of Zeus, I entreat you:/do not overpower my heart, mistress, with ache and anguish,/but come here." Archilochus was even more exuberant in proclaiming his desires. Speaking of his girlfriend, he wrote that he wanted "to fall upon her busy paunch and thrust belly against belly, thighs against thighs." After being reproached for running away from a losing military clash, he said: "One of the Saians is rejoicing in the shield/which I left reluctantly by a bush. . . ./But I saved myself. What does that shield matter to me?/It can go to hell! I'll get another one some day just as good."[4]

After Thales came a long succession of "wise men," who became known as "philosophers" (*philosophy* means "love of wisdom"). They included Anaxagoras, Anaximenes, Pythagoras, Heraclitus, and Empedocles. Some of these philosophers applied the idea of law to the entire universe and thereby created the concept of a *cosmos* ("world order"), the assumption that the universe is governed by one fundamental force and can be understood by the human mind. Other philosophers applied the powers of human reason in different ways. *History* was born in Ionia; the first known historians—Cadmus and Hecataeus—were from Miletus. Their writings did not survive, but most scholars agree that they were the first to apply the critical, rational approach to the study of human affairs and human history.

Despite their intellectual creativity, the Ionians did not endure long. During the second half of the sixth century B.C., they were threatened by the rising power of the Persian Empire. Most of the Ionian cities were soon conquered or destroyed by the Persians, marking the end of the Ionian period. The center of Greek life then shifted from Asiatic Ionia to the Greek mainland.

SPARTA

On the Greek mainland, Sparta was the most powerful and prestigious city-state during the sixth century B.C. It was also unique in one respect, for the Spartans had organized themselves into a tightly disciplined military state. The Spartans believed that the law code that defined their way of life had been established by Lycurgus, a quasi-legendary figure who may have lived in the eighth century B.C.

Located on the Peloponnesus peninsula in the southernmost part of the Greek mainland, Sparta was one of the most fertile agricultural areas in all of Greece. But the rich land was not alone sufficient to support Sparta's growing population; thus, sometime during the eighth or seventh century B.C., the Spartans conquered neighboring lands and enslaved those who lived there. These state-owned slaves, called *helots*, did all of the farm work necessary to supply the citizens with food.

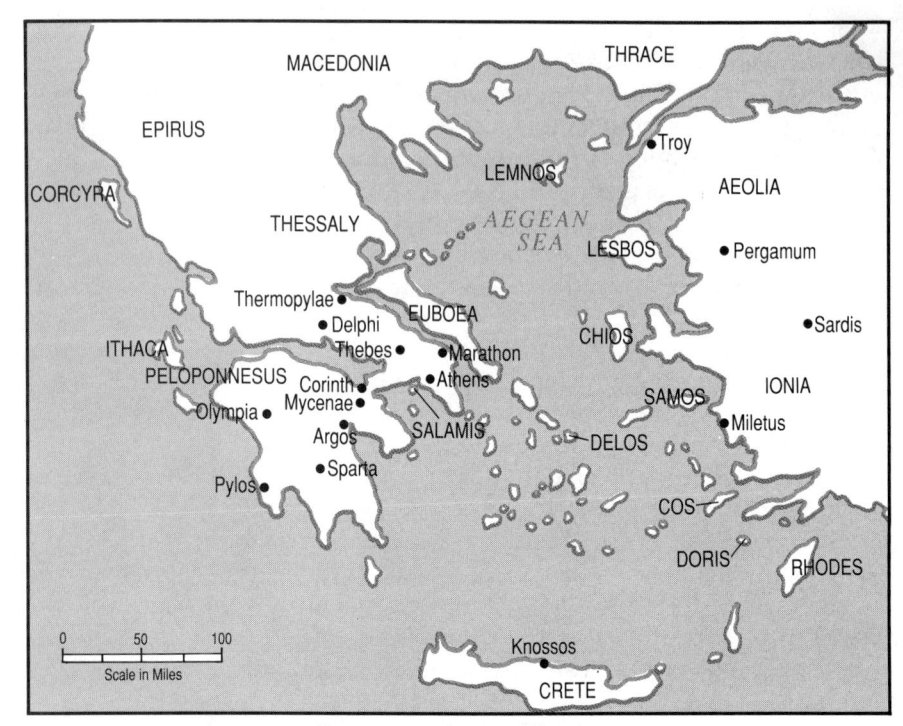

Figure 4.1 Ancient Greece

By the sixth century B.C., the helots outnumbered the Spartan citizens by approximately ten to one, and the Spartans constantly feared the possibility of slave revolt. One such revolt occurred between 650 and 620 B.C.

To protect themselves against slave revolt, the Spartans became a nation of soldiers. They left farm work to the *helots* and business and commerce to another class of noncitizens—the *perioeci.* Only male Spartans were citizens, and they spent their entire lives in the army. All male children were examined at birth by a council of elders for deformities or other signs of weakness. Those deemed weak or deformed were taken to a local mountainous area and left to die. Those who passed this first test would remain at home until the age of seven, at which time they were sent to a military barracks and trained for military service. These young boys were taught to suffer pain without complaining, to obey their elders without questioning, and to eat sparingly (the basic Spartan food was an unappetizing wheat porridge). The military training period lasted until the young men turned twenty. At this time, Spartans entered the army and continued to serve there until the age of sixty or until death.

Even though Spartan males spent most of their lives in the military, they were still expected to marry and to produce male children. Celibacy, in fact, was a crime in Spartan society. According to one Greek story, if male Spartans reached adulthood without being married, they might be pushed into a dark room containing an equal number of women and left to choose their wives in the darkness. The role of married Spartan women was crucial. Since Spartan men were nearly always in the army and away from home, the women had the primary responsibility of raising the children and supervising the household. The household work, however, was done by slaves. In general, Spartan women had greater freedom and were better educated than women in other Greek city-states.

In effect, everyone who lived in Sparta was a slave of some sort. Spartan men, although considered free citizens and the governors of the state, were actually enslaved to the military system. Spartan women had no choice but to perform their assigned roles—marrying and raising children. The helots lived under a perpetual reign of terror: a secret police watched them constantly and killed any who were even suspected of causing trouble. Once a year, the Spartans proclaimed a state of siege during which any citizen could kill any helot with impunity.

Such a way of life might seem extraordinarily unappealing. Other Greeks greatly admired the Spartans but refused to imitate them. The Athenians quipped that the Spartans were willing to die for their city because they had no reason to live. Nevertheless, most Spartans were probably content with their situation, for they were known to be enormously proud and protective of their city. During the sixth and fifth centuries B.C., Sparta had the most powerful army in Greece and was a recognized leader among the city-states.

In the end, however, the Spartan way of life produced the seeds of its own destruction. Obsessed with a military-based life-style, the Spartans became notoriously narrowminded and unable to adapt to change. In the fourth century B.C., Spartan's power as a city-state began to decline and many of the helots were freed. Sparta never flourished again.

ATHENS

Athens is the best known of the Greek city-states, both because it created a *democratic* form of government and because the new democracy helped stimulate several generations of intellectual and artistic genius. *Democracy* is here defined as government by citizens, meaning the free men of Athens. Athenian democracy was much more limited than the twentieth-century perspective, since only free males had political rights and foreign residents, women, and slaves—the bulk of the Athenian population—did not. Nevertheless, Athens defined for the first time the concept of democracy and was more open and democratic than most other societies of its time.

Political Evolution

Why did Athens, rather than some other city or nation, create the first democratic government? One reason may be its close relationship with the Ionian city of Miletus, where public debate and reasoned argument emerged during the seventh to sixth centuries B.C. Another reason may be the Phoenician alphabet, which enabled many Athenians and other Greeks to become literate. Yet another reason may be that Athens was a sufficiently wealthy commercial city to support a large citizenry. Finally, Athens produced creative political leaders at crucial times in its history.

Creative leadership was needed in Athens to respond to a social and economic crisis. Like Sparta and other parts of the Greek world, Athens became overpopulated by the seventh century B.C., and the result was a land shortage. (Unlike Sparta, though, Athens did not respond to this problem by installing a military system of government.) Many Athenian farmers were in debt and were sold into slavery to pay off their debts. This situation not only produced considerable social turmoil among the farmers but also threatened to weaken or destroy the Athenian army. Since the Athenian army included citizens who were farmers, Athens could not afford to allow too many citizens to become slaves.

The Athenian government was at this time an aristocracy, in which a few noble families dominated the life of the city. Around 594 B.C., the nobles, fearful that the economic crisis would lead to social revolution, designated a man named Solon to resolve the situation. Fortunately for Athens, Solon was a political genius who had gained the confidence of both the nobility and the indebted lower classes. He immediately established a number of social reforms, including a prohibition on selling debtors into slavery, a program for buying freedom for those already enslaved for debts, and a procedure for allowing some limited political participation by the lower classes. According to Greek legend, Solon insisted that the Athenians agree to maintain these measures for at least ten years and then set off on a tour of the world.

Solon's reforms, which guaranteed the freedom of lower-class citizens, were the first major step toward the creation of democracy. Although social turmoil continued in Athens for a while—the lower classes clamored for a redistribution of land and the noble families struggled among themselves for control of the government—it came to an end when the government appointed another reform-minded statesman, Cleisthenes, to overhaul the entire Athenian political structure. Cleisthenes came to power around 508 B.C., and with popular support he formulated a democratic constitution for Athens. The Cleisthenian reforms consisted of four major elements:

1. Athens was divided into a number of local units called *demes* (hence the word *democracy*), from which representatives were

The Parthenon (built between 447 and 432 B.C.) Towering above Athens, the Parthenon, a temple to the goddess Athena, was built on a high mountain known as the Acropolis. The great structure could be seen for miles and also symbolized the Athenians' pride in their city. (B. Glassman)

elected by the free men—the citizens—to a Council, or *Boulê*, of five hundred members. The Council carried out the daily business of the city, and many citizens participated since membership was limited to two years.
2. The public assembly, a legislative body that could debate and approve or reject all major governmental decisions, was open to all citizens. The assembly became the heart of Athenian democracy and its meetings were often boisterous affairs, with speakers being applauded, jeered, and even shouted down.
3. A board of ten generals was elected each year to lead the city in times of war. Since a general could be reelected indefinitely, the board became a center of strong leadership.
4. A unique custom known as *ostracism* was designed to prevent a powerful leader from becoming a tyrant. Each year a ballot could be held, if it was felt necessary, and whoever received the largest number of votes was banished from the city for ten years.

The Cleisthenian reforms guaranteed citizen participation in government. However, only adult males were considered citizens, and they numbered only about 42,000 out of a total Athenian population of

400,000. Excluded from political participation were women and slaves, the latter representing about half of Athenian population.

The Position of Women and Slaves

Athenian women were not permitted to vote, make contracts, conduct business involving large sums of money, or serve as witnesses in legal cases. A woman was always under the authority of a man. Before marriage, a woman's father controlled her, and after marriage, her husband assumed control. Athenian women spent most of their lives secluded at home; their roles in society were to work in the household and to produce future Athenian citizens. It is difficult to describe much more than this with great accuracy, since Athenian women were uneducated and therefore left few writings that tell of their thoughts and feelings. One interesting point, though, is that the great Athenian dramatists often portrayed strong female characters, usually of noble birth. This suggests that there may have been some assertive, independent women in Athens.

The Athenian practice of subordinating women had several side effects. One was the acceptance of homosexuality. Many Athenian men believed that love between men was natural, and some suggested that, since men were superior to women, homosexual love was superior to heterosexual love. Another manifestation of female subordination was the acceptance of widespread prostitution. So many female slaves became prostitutes that in many Greek cities the young males knew prostitutes better than women who remained at home. Athens, in particular, had a great variety of prostitutes. Most were ordinary prostitutes, known as *pornai* (hence the modern word *pornography*), who sometimes wore sandals that had nails on the soles spelling "Follow Me!" in the mud of the street. The higher-class prostitutes, called *hetairai*, were usually well-educated and attractive women who had managed to accumulate some money. In one sense, the hetairai were the most "liberated" women in Athens, since they were the only females allowed to mix freely in male company. Their freedom was limited, however, in that neither they nor their children could ever become citizens. Some of the hetairai became famous among the Athenians. Lais of Corinth, for example, was so renowned that many Greeks claimed she was the greatest conqueror they had ever known.

Athenian males considered their various sexual practices nonexclusive. Most believed that the same man could love his wife heterosexually, love a male friend homosexually, and also have sexual relations with prostitutes.

The other subjugated people in Athens were, of course, the slaves. The Greeks accepted slavery as natural. Most slaves were captured in warfare, and since war was thought to be natural, slavery was as well.

Legally, slaves were just pieces of property, but some were treated reasonably well. A housemaid or a field hand on a small farm might have become virtually one of the family. Many slaves who were skilled craftsmen worked alongside free citizens, and an enterprising slave might have saved enough money to rent his own home and even eventually buy his freedom. Other slaves, however, were treated harshly. Girl and boy slaves were often sexually abused, and many adult slaves died from hard labor in the silver mines at Athens. One of the anomalies of the Greek experience is that as the Athenians were evolving a democratic constitution they were also operating a slave market from which tax revenues were a major source of income for the democratic state. (Much the same can be said about the early history of the United States.)

The Persian Threat

Despite the fact that Athenian democracy was so limited, Athens was still closer to being a self-governing community than any other society of the time. But the new democracy soon faced a severe threat. The mainland Greeks, especially the Athenians, had helped the Ionian Greeks in their fight against the Persians. Thus, to exact revenge and also to continue their imperial expansion, the Persians invaded Greece in 490 B.C. Many Greek city-states surrendered to what appeared to be the overwhelming might of the great Persian Empire from the east, but Athens and a few others successfully defeated the Persian invasion at the battle of Marathon (490 B.C.). In the aftermath, a professional runner named Pheidippides allegedly ran the first "marathon" race by carrying the message of Athenian victory from Marathon back to Athens. According to the story, Pheidippides was so exhausted by his exertions that he ran into the city, announced the victory, and fell over dead.

The Persian threat continued, however, and in 480 B.C. the Persians invaded again. This time they won a hard-fought battle at Thermopylae, but were defeated at the naval battle of Salamis. This was the last major attempt by the Persian Empire to subjugate the Greeks.

Intellectual and Artistic Creativity

By the end of the year 480 B.C., the Athenians could look back on a remarkable thirty-year period in which they had not only created a democratic government but also had taken the lead in twice defeating the mighty Persian Empire. These achievements naturally produced great pride and self-confidence, and for the next sixty to eighty years Athens was at its peak. During that time, politicians and citizens debated momentous political issues in the assembly, dramatists debated questions of justice in their plays, philosophers argued about how humans

Woman Vase From the fifth century B.C., this vase portrays a young Greek woman in typical ancient Greek dress. The lyre, a stringed musical instrument, was often played while reciting poetry. (Metropolitan Museum of Art, NY)

could attain greater knowledge, historians told stories about the great events of the past and present, and artists and sculptors sought to capture the essence of beauty in their work. In short, for a few brief decades Athens became the center of a "prolonged conversation." This conversation focused on the questions that Athenians regarded as most important—how to live well, how to create a just society, how to create beauty in an often brutal and ugly world. The Athenians never regarded economic matters as the only important thing in life. Rather, they often preferred to devote their energies to a consideration of how to use what wealth they had to live a good life.

One of the most brilliant voices in the Athenian conversation was that of the dramatist Aeschylus (525–456 B.C.). Drama was one of the Greeks' favorite art forms. Dramatic productions attracted large audiences; they were not only a form of public entertainment but also a means of moral and religious education for the Greek community. Tragic dramas, in particular, were educational, often communicating to their audiences the Greek conception of life. The tragedians taught that humans are great and noble but not perfect; even the greatest suffer from a "flaw" that will eventually destroy them. Aeschylus presented this view in a series of plays that focused on the character Prometheus. Prometheus, though a god, was also a symbol of humanity because he stole fire from the gods and gave it to humans, who used the gift to build civilization. Thus, Prometheus represented both the greatness and weakness of humanity. Zeus, the chief god, punished Prometheus's rebellion by having him chained to a rock, where each day an eagle ate his liver, which then grew back at night so that it could be eaten again the next day. Zeus also punished humankind by sending to earth a young woman named Pandora, who brought with her a box that, when opened, released numerous evils into the world. The introduction of evil into the world was associated with female figures in both the Greek tradition—Pandora—and the Hebrew tradition—Eve. Aeschylus thus used a myth to teach the Athenians about great moral issues.

Sophocles (496–406 B.C.), the second of the great tragic dramatists, composed in *Antigone*, a long meditation on what happens when one moral good conflicts with another. Antigone was required by traditional family obligations to bury her dead brother, but the king of her city opposed a proper burial for her brother because he had perished in rebelling against the city. The king argued that obedience to the law was a moral good that outweighed Antigone's family obligations. When Antigone insisted on following the laws of her conscience as opposed to the laws of her city, she was executed.

At the same time that Sophocles was writing, Herodotus (490–425 B.C.) was reciting his histories in the Athenian marketplace (the *agora*). Often called the "father of history," Herodotus said that he wanted to ensure that the great deeds of the past would be remembered. Thus he told the story of the Persian Wars, in which he portrayed Athens as a hero defending Greek freedom against Persian tyranny. His story, in written form, is the first great historical work of Western culture.

These and other creative activities quickly turned Athens into an intellectual and artistic center. From all over Greece came a number of men called *Sophists* ("wise men"), who offered to educate young men in the art of politics. The Sophistic declaration that "man is the measure of all things" was an affirmation of human ability, particularly the ability of people to govern themselves. The education that the Sophists provided was an education in how to persuade an audience, how to speak well in the citizen's assembly. The subjects they taught—grammar (how to write), rhetoric (how to speak), dialectic (how to think)—became the core of what would later be called "liberal arts education." The Sophists' reputation eventually suffered, however, partly because they insisted on being paid for their services at a time when most teachers were independently wealthy nobles. The Sophists also lost credibility because other philosophers (principally Plato) accused them of being cynical relativists who cared only about winning arguments and not about truth.

Athenian Society

It would be inaccurate to say that Athens became a pristine paradise in which great and noble people did great and noble things, for all its creative vitality occurred in a poverty-stricken, even squalid society. In terms of such basic things as housing, dress, and food, the ordinary Athenian was quite poor. His house was small, without plumbing or heating. His dress was a woolen blanket, designed to be wrapped around his body, and a pair of shoes, both made to last a lifetime. The typical Athenian diet consisted of coarse bread, cheese, some vegetables, watered-down wine, and occasionally some meat. Garbage and sewage were thrown in the streets until washed away by the rain. The streets were narrow and dirty, and in the hot, dry summers must have given off an extraordinary stench.

Obviously, economic wealth was greatly limited in Athenian society. Many Athenians were poor farmers, eking out a living on a small plot of land. In the city, most Athenian men worked as merchants or craftsmen in small shops, while women remained at home. The result of this poverty in Athens and most other Greek city-states was that the Greeks were unable to provide for all of the children they produced. Consequently, the Greeks exposed unwanted children, particularly females. It was not uncommon in a Greek city to see an infant left alone to die on the streets or in some other place. These infants usually either died of exposure or were taken and reared by slave dealers.

To understand Athenian society, we must, in the words of historian Alfred Zimmern, "learn how to be civilized without being comfortable."[5] The Athenians, in spite of, and perhaps because of, their primitive living conditions, sought to civilize and beautify their city. On the Acropolis, the mountain in the middle of the city, they built the Parthenon between 447 and 432 B.C., a temple to the goddess Athena. The Parthenon is considered one of the most beautiful of all the Greek architectural creations. (The most lavish Greek buildings were often temples, usually in the form of rectangles with the roof supported by rows of columns.)

The Parthenon and other buildings on the Acropolis were embellished by sculptures created by numerous artists. Greek art was representational, meaning that the artist sought to copy or imitate some aspect of the natural world—the human body, for example. (Partly because of Greek influence, the representational approach to art dominated Western history for much of the next two thousand years.)

Athenians and other Greek sculptors wanted, in particular, to represent the human body. Some of the most notable examples are the statues of Zeus and Athena by Phidias, the *Discus Thrower* by Myron, and the *Aphrodite of Cnidus* by Praxiteles.

The Peloponnesian War

Athens's greatest age began to decline during the last third of the fifth century B.C. A major reason for the Athenian decline was the Peloponnesian War (431–404 B.C.); the underlying cause of the war was fear of Athens by other Greeks. After the Persian invasions of 480 B.C., Athens had organized the Delian League, a military alliance of Greek cities designed to ward off future Persian threats. Over the years that followed, the Delian League came to be more like an Athenian empire than a military alliance, as Athens dominated the other cities and collected taxes from them. The Athenians became enormously proud of their city, and their great political leader Pericles (governed 460–430 B.C.) sought to make Athens the "school of Hellas," a shining example of democracy and beauty to the other Greek cities. But the other cities, led by Sparta, saw Athenian pride as arrogance and began to resist Athens's expanding influence. Thus the war broke out in 431 B.C.

The Peloponnesian War was a full-scale Greek civil war—Athens and its allies against Sparta and its allies—that lasted twenty-seven years. In military terms, it was a relatively small affair. Fighting was sporadic and scattered; the largest battle of the first ten years involved only seven thousand Athenian soldiers against a similar number from the city-state of Boeotia. But the war gradually brutalized and undermined Greek society. A plague struck Athens and killed about a quarter of its population. Both Sparta and Athens began to execute prisoners, and in some cases entire cities were destroyed by fire or famine.

The pace of the Peloponnesian War was slow, so the Athenian political and intellectual conversation continued. In fact, the war provided much of its subject matter. Euripides (485–406 B.C.), the most radical of the great tragic dramatists, condemned warfare and slavery in *The Trojan Women*. Thucydides (460–403 B.C.), one of the greatest historians of all time, wrote his history of the Peloponnesian War while in exile from Athens. For him, the city of Athens was a tragic hero, proud and great but "flawed." In effect, Thucydides was celebrating Athenian spiritual and political greatness, even though he knew his native city was losing the war.

The man who cheered Athens through the dark hours of the Peloponnesian War was Aristophanes (450–385 B.C.), the greatest of the comic dramatists. Comedy began in bawdy revels and became an integral part of the Greek theater. The Greeks knew that humans could be obscene, ridiculous, and absurd as well as heroic and great. Aristophanes used this comic tradition to oppose and mock those who encouraged the war. In *Lysistrata,* for example, he portrays a general strike of Athenian women who refuse to sleep with their husbands until the men agree to stop the fighting. The drama is both a satire on the stupidity of men and a plea for peace. It is also a hilarious farce, in that the women are so oversexed that they can barely stay away from their husbands and the men are so sex-starved that they cannot concentrate on the peacemaking process.

The Peloponnesian War ended with the defeat of Athens in 404 B.C., though military conflicts continued to erupt for another sixty or seventy years. The war gravely weakened all of the Greek city-states. Athens, occupied by Sparta for a few years after the war, managed to rebuild and maintain its democratic government for another century and a half. Its greatest days were over, though, as the Athenian population steadily declined and its economic strength slowly dissipated. Only in the field of philosophy did Athens remain a leader in the fourth century B.C.

The Great Philosophers

Socrates Socrates (469–399 B.C.) was the greatest Athenian philosopher of the late fifth century B.C. A village "character," he was an obese and unattractive man who spent his days roaming the streets of Athens and arguing ethics and politics with young men. Forceful and argumentative, Socrates often browbeat his opponents. The nineteenth-century German philosopher G. W. F. Hegel once labeled Socrates the "patron saint of moral twaddle." At his best, though, Socrates taught people to think. His teachings were recorded (by his student Plato) in dialogue form, thereby displaying the intellectual activity of discussion and the search for truth. Socrates believed that the good life meant a continual quest for knowledge, that knowledge produced good moral conduct, and that good conduct led to happy, good citizens. He may have been right, but his questioning, irreverent attitude enabled his enemies to portray him as a subversive influence. He was brought to court on charges of corrupting the youth and being "impious" toward the gods. He was convicted and forced to drink poison. Socrates' revenge on his enemies, of course, was that his death created an enduring image of himself as a brave philosopher who died for his beliefs.

Plato The philosophical tradition was carried on by Socrates' student Plato (427–347 B.C.), considered one of the most influential philosophers in Western history. Plato traveled about the Mediterranean for a while before returning to Athens, where he founded an educational institution called the *Academy.* There he taught and wrote such works as *The Republic,* in which is examined the nature of human knowledge and the

ATHENS

ideal of a perfect society. Many of Plato's works are written in dialogue form, thus emphasizing that knowledge is the product of debate and intellectual conflict.

As a philosopher, Plato was an idealist; that is, one who believes that truth and reality are spiritual. He argued that the material world in which humans live cannot be ultimate reality because things in the material world are always changing (people grow older, for example) and ultimate, perfect reality would by definition never change. Thus Plato concluded that truth had to be sought in a spiritual realm where perfection exists. The idea of perfect justice, for example, exists in a spiritual realm, and earthly forms of justice are imperfect copies of the perfect justice. In *The Republic,* Plato uses the analogy of men chained in a cave. Because the chained men (symbolically representing humanity) faced the inside of the cave, they could only see and know whatever shadows appeared on the cave walls. Thus real knowledge is available only to those few—philosophers—who can free themselves from the chains and go outside the cave to see reality in the bright sunlight.

Plato's search for perfection led him to prescribe what an ideal society would be like. His ideal was nondemocratic, reflecting his pessimism about Athens in the aftermath of the Peloponnesian War. Plato contended that a perfect society would be one where justice dominates. Justice requires that each person do what he or she is best suited to do. Some people are more suited to farming or to carrying on business, so they should be in a producing class. Others more strong and courageous are best suited to defending the society, so they should be in a warrior class. Still others—the rational and intelligent—should rule, these being in Plato's words the "philosopher-kings."

Aristotle After Plato came Athens's last great philosopher—Aristotle (384–322 B.C.). A prolific writer who collected and organized information on such diverse subjects as biology, logic, politics, ethics, and metaphysics, Aristotle's approach to the search for knowledge was different from Plato's. Whereas Plato followed the deductive method—reasoning from general principles to the particular fact—Aristotle used the inductive method—studying and reasoning from specific facts to form a basis for defining general principles. For example, to determine the true meaning of justice, Plato would say that we would have to begin with some standard through which we could identify particular forms of justice. Aristotle, however, would say that we would have to study a variety of particular examples of justice before we could generalize or establish a universal standard.

Aristotle's writings are a massive summary of Greek knowledge. He defined the discipline of logic, and the information he collected on plants and animals provided the basis for much Western scientific thought over the next fifteen hundred years. Aristotle's political writings became a basis for political thought as well, for he and his assistants collected over 150 constitutions from Greek city-states. In so doing, he contended that there are only a few forms of government—government by an individual, government by a few, and government by the many. Each of these three types could, according to Aristotle, be good or bad. If an individual rules well, then government is a monarchy; if not, it is a tyranny. If the few rule well, government is an aristocracy (rule by the best); if not, it is an oligarchy or plutocracy (rule by the rich). If the many rule well, the result is government by laws (constitutional government); if not, the result is democracy (defined as government by the mob). Like Plato, Aristotle feared democratic rule.

THE HELLENISTIC ERA

The Greeks believed they were descended from an ancient ancestor named Hellen; thus they called themselves *Hellenes* and their country *Hellas*. Modern historians use the term *Hellenistic* to describe the last phase of ancient Greek history, spanning from the time of Alexander the Great to the final Roman conquest of the Greek-speaking world around 30 B.C. During this period of about three hundred years, Greek thought and culture spread throughout the eastern Mediterranean.

The Hellenistic Age began with Alexander the Great or slightly before with his father, Philip of Macedon. Philip built Macedonia, the mountainous area north of Greece proper, into a powerful kingdom, and in 338 B.C. his armies conquered the Greek city-states. Two years later, Philip was killed by an assassin and was succeeded by Alexander. Over the next thirteen years (336–323 B.C.), the new Macedonian ruler would become Alexander the Great, one of the most triumphant military conquerors of all time. By the end of his life, Alexander commanded a vast empire that extended southward to Egypt and eastward all the way to India. We do not know with certainty what Alexander's goals were as a ruler. Some historians believe that he was simply a great military leader who knew well how to fight and conquer. Others see Alexander as what he claimed to be, an apostle of Greek culture who used Greek language and institutions to unify a cosmopolitan empire. Once, for example, Alexander sought to encourage the mixture of peoples by presiding over a mass wedding, in which several thousand of his Greek soldiers married a similar number of Persian women.

Alexander died in 323 B.C. Almost immediately, his empire fell apart as his generals fought among themselves and eventually divided the empire into three separate kingdoms—the Antigonid kingdom on the Greek mainland, the Seleucid in the Near East, and the Ptolemaic in Egypt. These Hellenistic monarchies ruled large areas for their own profit, using Greeks and Macedonians to staff their armies and bureaucracies. Thus, Greeks became the dominant upper class throughout

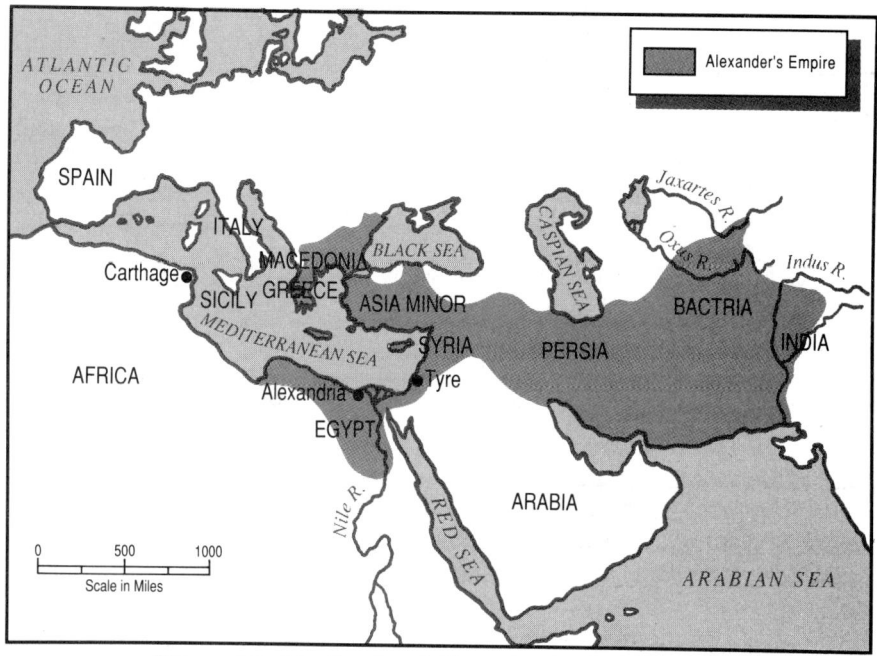

Figure 4.2 The Empire of Alexander the Great, 323 B.C.

much of the eastern Mediterranean and controlled huge masses of native farmers, many of whom were enslaved.

The Hellenistic world was in many ways a chaotic, brutal place, where powerful men competed for wealth and influence and many people lived in poverty. Hellenistic cities were often larger than the old Greek city-states and usually contained large slum areas inhabited by rootless people searching for some well-being and security in their lives. It was no accident later on that Christianity, which offered hope to the struggling masses, would grow rapidly in this harsh environment.

Hellenistic Creativity

Hellenistic intellectual life was vibrant. It gave birth to two new schools of philosophy that sought to instruct people on how to attain individual happiness in a chaotic world and that had considerable impact on the Hellenistic upper classes and later on the Roman aristocracy. One was *Epicureanism,* named after its founder Epicurus (371–270 B.C.) Believing that the gods have nothing to do with humans, Epicurus told people not to fear divine forces or punishment in an afterlife but to seek happiness on earth. For Epicurus, happiness meant withdrawing from the material world into a life of contemplation, but his philosophy was misinterpreted by many to mean "enjoy yourself" and "eat, drink, and be merry."

The other philosophy to emerge from Hellenistic culture was *Stoicism*, founded by Zeno of Citium around 300 B.C. The Stoics envisioned the universe as controlled by a divine force. Thus, people were taught to accept their role in life without questioning it. Self-control and the ability to accept one's fate were considered great virtues. Another implication of Stoicism was a general notion of equality. Since it was presumed that one god controls all people, then it followed that they are equal in some fundamental sense. The Stoics never went so far as to consider freeing the slaves or establishing political equality, but their idea of equality, or what they called "brotherhood," would be influential in later ages.

Hellenistic culture also produced a creative proliferation in science, mathematics, and technology—much of it centering in Alexandria, Egypt. The Ptolemaic rulers of Egypt (323–30 B.C.) built a large library and museum called the "House of the Muses" at Alexandria around 300 B.C. The library eventually gathered over half a million manuscripts and the museum became a scholarly research complex that included laboratories, astronomical observatories, private study areas, and lecture halls. For several hundred years—from the third century B.C. to the fourth century A.D.—Alexandria was a vibrant center of scientific research. The well-known mathematician Euclid wrote *Elements of Geometry*, and Archimedes did much research in higher mathematics. Herophilus studied anatomy, traced much of the human nervous system, and continued the medical tradition begun by Hippocrates (460–377 B.C.), the "Father of medicine." The geographer Erastosthenes calculated the circumference of the earth, while the astronomer Aristarchus theorized that the earth revolves around the sun. (His view, however, did not prevail; in the second century A.D., the astronomer Ptolemy convinced most scholars that the earth was the center of the universe. Ptolemy's view dominated until the sixteenth century A.D., when Copernicus revived Aristarchus's conception of the universe.)

Alexandria was thus the site of the greatest achievements in Western science and mathematics before modern times. Unfortunately, much of the knowledge that was accumulated in Alexandria during this time was lost when, in the fourth century A.D., Christians destroyed the museum because they thought it was a center of pagan learning. The knowledge that did survive became the foundation for further research by later scientists.

CONCLUSION

The scientific enterprise at Alexandria was the last creative surge of the ancient Greeks. Creativity had enabled the Greeks to define the concept of democracy, to develop the habit of rational thought in philosophy, and to

TECHNOLOGY
Hellenistic Inventions

The Hellenistic Era produced a number of intriguing technological developments. Pytheas of Massalia (present-day Marseilles), for example, was an enterprising navigator and one of the greatest explorers of ancient times. Late in the fourth century B.C., he refined several navigational instruments, advanced the art of mapmaking, and undertook a long voyage on the Atlantic and up around England. Few people of his time believed his account of the journey, entitled *On the Ocean*.

Alexandria was the center of technological innovations. Some homes in the city had devices that opened doors and inventions that washed clothes by delivering soap and water as needed. A few temples even had water-sprinkler systems to protect against fire. Several inventors built important labor-saving devices. Hero designed a siphon, a force pump, and even a small steam engine. The mathematician Archimedes developed a screw pump used to lift water.

By the last century B.C., Greek science and technology indeed possessed the knowledge needed to initiate an industrial revolution. Of course, such a revolution did not occur until much later in Western history, but scholars have long debated why the Greeks failed to use their knowledge to its full potential. One theory is that slave labor was less expensive than machine-powered labor, so the Greeks had no economic incentive to encourage machine construction. Whatever the reason, it would take another two thousand years before the Industrial Revolution would become a reality in the Western world.

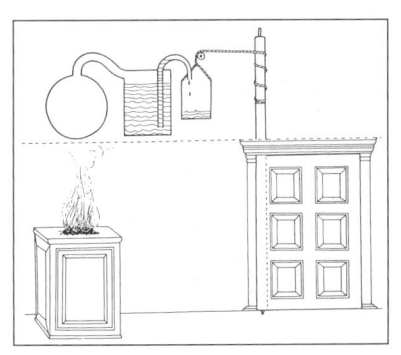

Device for Opening Temple Doors. *Hero of Alexandria, who lived in the first century A.D., understood how to produce steam power. One of his inventions opened temple doors: a sacrificial fire heated the air in a sphere; as the heated air expanded, it forced water into a receptacle that sunk under the weight of the water, which pulled cords that opened the temple doors. All but the fire was hidden so the doors appeared to open by magic. (The Granger Collection)*

do a great deal of important scientific and mathematical work. By the first century B.C., the days of political and intellectual brilliance were over, although the memories remained. The Olympic games continued until 393 A.D., and Athens retained its role as an educational center for several centuries. These and other monuments served to remind Romans and later peoples of the days when the Greeks taught humans to be proud of their physical and intellectual gifts. The words of the ancient Greek poet Pindar (518–438 B.C.) capture the essence of the Greek spirit:

> A changeable creature, such is man; a shadow in a dream.
> Yet when god-given splendour visits him
> A bright radiance plays over him, and how sweet is life![6]

THINGS YOU SHOULD KNOW

Homer
The heroic outlook
Olympic games
The Greek city-state (polis)
Why an intellectual revolution began in Ionian Greece
Thales
Sappho and Archilochus
Sparta
Solon
Cleisthenes
Women and slaves in ancient Sparta and Athens
Aeschylus
Sophocles
The Sophists
Athenian society
The Peloponnesian War
Thucydides
Aristophanes
Socrates
Plato
Aristotle
Alexander the Great
The Hellenistic Era
Epicureanism
Stoicism
Science and technology in the Hellenistic Era

SUGGESTED READINGS

Two good introductions to Greek history are Chester G. Starr, *The Ancient Greeks* (New York: Oxford Univ. Press, 1971) and Frank Frost, *Greek Society* (Lexington, Mass.: D.C. Heath, 1980). A valuable but complex study of Greek thought is C. M. Bowra, *The Greek Experience* (New York: New American Lib./Mentor, 1959). On the details of social and economic history, see John Scarborough, *Facets of Hellenic Life* (Boston: Houghton Mifflin, 1976). Sarah B. Pomeroy, *Goddesses, Whores, Wives, and Slaves* (New York: Schocken, 1976) is an excellent analysis of the position of women in Greek society. A good survey of the Hellenistic Era is Michael Grant, *From Alexander to Cleopatra: The Hellenistic World* (New York: Scribner, 1982).

For more specific subjects, see Alfred Zimmern, *The Greek Commonwealth* (New York: Modern Library, 1911), an old but still insightful history of the political evolution of Athens; and John Herman Randall, Jr., *Plato: Dramatist of the Life of Reason* (New York: Columbia Univ. Press, 1970), a lively introduction to one of the most influential philosophers in Western history. Finally, a modern historical novel that catches the flavor of ancient Greece is Mary Renault, *The Last of the Wine* (New York: Vintage, 1975).

NOTES

[1] Frank J. Frost, *Greek Society*, 2nd ed. (Lexington, Mass.: D. C. Heath, 1980), p. 14.

[2] C. M. Bowra, *The Greek Experience* (New York: New American Library/Mentor, 1957), pp. 32–33.

[3] Quoted in John Scarborough, *Facets of Hellenic Life* (Boston: Houghton Mifflin, 1976), p. 145.

[4] Quoted in Frost, *Greek Society*, p. 31.

[5] Alfred Zimmern, *The Greek Commonwealth* (New York: Modern Library, 1911), p. 217.

[6] Pindar, "Pythian Ode VIII" (ll. 95–97), quoted in Chester G. Starr, *The Ancient Greeks* (New York: Oxford Univ. Press, 1971), p. 211.

5

Rome and the Birth of Christianity, 800 B.C. to A.D. 400

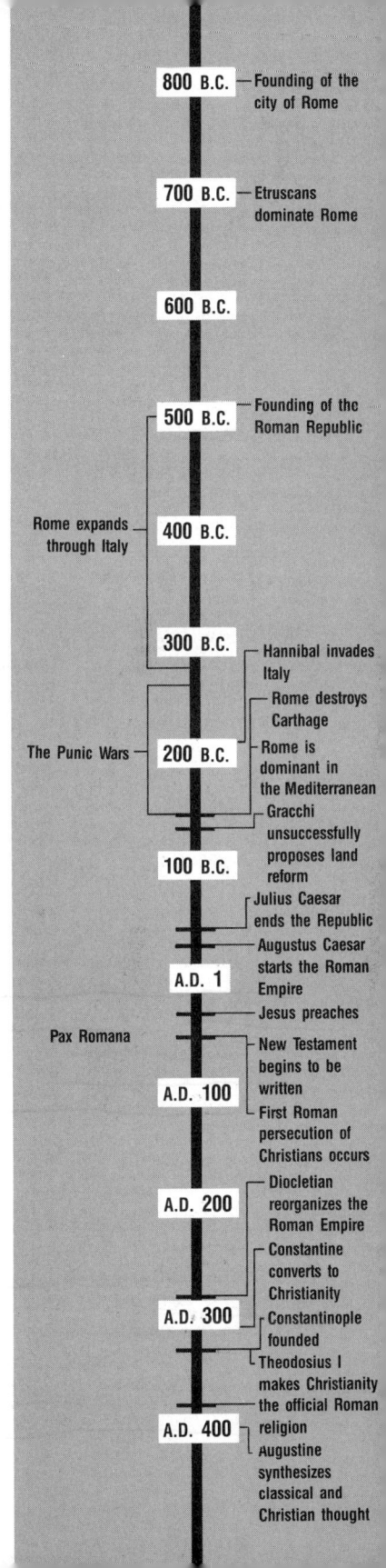

800 B.C.	Founding of the city of Rome
700 B.C.	Etruscans dominate Rome
600 B.C.	
500 B.C.	Founding of the Roman Republic
400 B.C.	Rome expands through Italy
300 B.C.	Hannibal invades Italy
200 B.C.	The Punic Wars — Rome destroys Carthage; Rome is dominant in the Mediterranean; Gracchi unsuccessfully proposes land reform
100 B.C.	Julius Caesar ends the Republic
A.D. 1	Augustus Caesar starts the Roman Empire; Jesus preaches
	Pax Romana
A.D. 100	New Testament begins to be written; First Roman persecution of Christians occurs
A.D. 200	Diocletian reorganizes the Roman Empire
	Constantine converts to Christianity
A.D. 300	Constantinople founded; Theodosius I makes Christianity the official Roman religion
A.D. 400	Augustine synthesizes classical and Christian thought

The phrase "Eternal Rome" was sometimes inscribed on ancient Roman coins. Rome, of course, was not forever lasting, but it endured so long that it seemed immortal to many people of the ancient world. Roman history extended well over a thousand years, and during that time the Mediterranean world was slowly united by two forces. The first was the Romans themselves, who conquered a vast empire and ruled the entire Mediterranean basin for several centuries. The Roman Empire eventually began to disintegrate, however, and as it did, a second unifying force emerged. This was Christianity, a new religion that by the end of Roman history won the adherence of most Mediterranean peoples and thus created a spiritual unity that replaced the disappearing political unity of Rome.

EARLY ROMAN HISTORY

We know few real facts about early Roman history. The Romans were descendants of a people known as the Latins, who settled alongside the Tiber River in central Italy sometime around 800 B.C. The agricultural village established by the Latins marks the founding of the city of Rome. For two or three centuries, the Latins remained simple farmers living between two more civilized neighbors—the Greeks, who had colonized southern Italy, and the Etruscans to the north. The Etruscans, who probably came to Italy from Asia Minor (present-day Turkey) around 850 B.C., were a wealthy and powerful people who at some uncertain point gained control of Rome. In 509 B.C., however, the Romans launched a war of independence, driving the Etruscans out and establishing a republican form of government. Nevertheless, Etruscan influence had a significant impact on several aspects of Roman life, including religion, politics, literature, architecture, military techniques, and the tradition of staging gladiatorial combats. In particular, the Roman Senate was based on Etruscan precedent, and the Romans received the alphabet from the Etruscans, who had received it from the Greeks.

These facts explain in general terms some of the events of early Roman history, but they do not convey the thoughts and beliefs of the Roman people. When the Romans talked about the early days of their city, they recited legends that told of how they were descended from heroes and how their city was destined for greatness. One such legend was told by the Roman poet Virgil (70–19 B.C.) in his great epic poem *The Aeneid*. It tells the story of Aeneas, a Trojan warrior who escaped from Troy at the end of the war with the Greeks (see Chapter 4) and migrated to Italy to father a new line of warrior heroes. Among his descendants were twin brothers, Romulus and Remus, and it was Romulus whom the Romans believed founded their city in 753 B.C. Another Roman legend tells the story of Horatius. As an invading army was approaching a bridge that led to Rome, Horatius held off the invaders single-handedly while his comrades destroyed the bridge behind him. One version of this story says that Horatius then swam across the river, whereas another version says he died heroically.[1]

The Roman belief in a heroic past was reflected in Roman religion, which was a religion of patriotism. Unlike the Greeks, the early Romans did not believe in personalized deities or gods; rather, they believed that events in this world were controlled by divine spirits or forces that could be only vaguely understood by humans. These forces had to be placated by sacrifices and offerings of various kinds, so that they would bring good fortune to Rome. Thus, the essence of early Roman religion lay not in an emotional religious experience with a personal god or in a search for eternal salvation, but in the dutiful performance of rituals designed to gain divine favor for Rome.

Early Roman history thus stressed political developments far more than intellectual or spiritual ideas; indeed, Roman creativity was often manifested in politics and government. The Romans gradually built a massive international empire held together by the rule of international law and an expanded concept of citizenship. But Roman creativity was also expressed in architecture and engineering: the Romans built roads, aqueducts, baths, and theaters in many places.

THE ROMAN REPUBLIC

The Roman Republic was established in 509 B.C. It had a republican form of government in which all governing officials were elected by the upper classes. This was inspired in large part by the recently overthrown Etruscan tyranny, causing Romans to distrust strong, centralized governments. The republican system of government prevented any one individual from dominating Rome, so for several centuries the city was governed by many upper-class Romans who held power for short periods of time. (A unique feature of Roman history was that Rome was built by an entire people and not by a great individual conqueror like Alexander the Great.)

At first, the government was controlled solely by the upper classes, called the *patricians*. Three hundred or so patricians were members of a *Senate* that held legislative powers and was the ultimate source of authority. In addition, the patricians elected each year two *consuls* to share the executive power, with the stipulation that no one consul could be reelected.

As time passed, the lower classes—called the *plebeians*—began to demand political rights for themselves. The plebeians wanted to end the practice of debt slavery, the custom of people selling themselves into slavery in order to pay off their debts. (As noted in Chapter 4, this same

A Roman Aqueduct The Romans were great builders, and some of their most impressive constructions were the aqueducts that brought water to cities. The water was pumped from mountain lakes or streams to an aqueduct, high enough to allow for a gradual drop in elevation so the water could flow downhill and be sent several miles to nearby cities. The aqueduct shown here was built about two thousand years ago and still exists today. (Italian Tourist Office)

issue led to political change in sixth-century B.C. Athens.) The plebeians also demanded political rights because they supplied most of the manpower for the army and felt they should have some voice in political decisions.

From the fifth to the third centuries B.C., the patricians and plebeians gradually compromised their political differences and a series of measures allowed broader political rights to the plebeians. A *Tribal Assembly* was created as a forum for plebeians to debate political issues. The office of *tribune* was established to protect plebeian rights, and eventually it won the power to *veto* ("forbid") legislation considered harmful to plebeians. Plebeians also gradually became eligible for election to the consulship, and finally, in 287 B.C., the Hortensian Law stipulated that decrees of the Tribal Assembly were the basic laws of government. In theory, the Hortensian Law made Rome a democratic state in which the will of the people was supreme, but in practice the patricians continued to dominate the consulship and Senate and thereby control Roman politics. Still, Rome had broadened the political participation of plebeians without undergoing a civil war or revolution, an accomplishment that few other cities in the ancient world could match. (The Roman political system was so impressive that many later peoples imitated Roman practices. The United States Constitution, for example, includes Roman conceptions of the Senate, the veto, and the principle of separation of powers.)

Internal political transformation in Rome was accompanied by external expansion. Like most other ancient peoples, the Romans had to fight small wars every summer to protect their lands from aggressors. Among the first Roman enemies were the Etruscans and the Gauls, the latter a tribe of Celtic peoples who lived in northern Italy and raided farming areas in central Italy. The Romans particularly disliked the Gauls, who sometimes stormed into battle stark naked while screaming curses and swinging large slashing swords.

The Conquest of Italy

The Romans slowly gained a reputation as defenders of Italy against the Gauls and so began to offer protection to those local cities that would give allegiance to Rome. Between 509 and 275 B.C., Rome continued to dominate more and more cities until it finally controlled most of central and southern Italy. In the process, Romans began to believe that they were natural leaders destined to conquer other peoples and other lands, and eventually they became some of the most successful imperialists of all time. Why were the Romans able to build and maintain such a large republic for centuries?

One reason for the longevity of Rome was its military strength. Roman armies were not invincible, but they rarely conceded defeat and usually maintained an offensive until victory was attained. (One example of strict Roman military discipline was the practice of *decimation*, whereby a unit that displayed cowardice in battle was condemned to have every tenth man executed.) Furthermore, Roman armies received great rewards from military success: for the common soldier, fame and prestige; for the generals, a celebratory parade or "triumph," through Rome.

Another reason for Rome's preeminence was its ability to gain and retain the loyalty of conquered subjects who appreciated relatively benevolent Roman rule. The Romans, like most other ancient peoples, were often brutal in war, but after the battle they were more tolerant and relatively good-natured people. From the Italian cities that they conquered, the Romans expected an annual contribution of soldiers to their armies but no taxes. In return, the Italians received protection as well as the freedom to govern their own local affairs. Some upper-class Italians were even granted Roman citizenship rights. Overall, it was a good bargain for the Italians, and the result was a growing allegiance to Rome.

The Punic Wars

By 275 B.C., Rome governed a population of more than one million Italians, a large number for that day. Also by this time, the Romans were coming into contact with another rising imperial power, the city of Carthage on the North African coast. The Romans and the Carthaginians soon came to regard each other as enemies, largely because both were expanding into southern Italy. The eventual result of this territorial conflict was the Punic Wars (so-named because the Romans called the Carthaginians the *Poeni*, meaning descendants of the Phoenicians).

The Punic Wars were a succession of three wars separated by two periods of truce. Together they lasted from 264 to 146 B.C. The First Punic War (264–241 B.C.) led to the Roman conquest of Sicily and Sardinia. In the Second Punic War (218–201 B.C.), the great Carthaginian general Hannibal invaded and ravaged Italy but eventually conceded victory to Rome. In 201 B.C., Rome gained control of Spain from Carthage. The Third Punic War (149–146 B.C.) was deliberately provoked by Rome and ended with the destruction of Carthage. The Romans killed all Carthaginian men and sold the women and children into slavery.

While defeating Carthage, the Romans were also expanding into the lands that the successors of Alexander the Great ruled. Between 200 and 146 B.C., Rome assumed control of Greece, Macedonia, and other eastern countries, largely to prevent other possible conquerors from taking them. By 146 B.C., Rome was the dominant military power in the Mediterranean.

HOW THE ROMAN CONQUESTS CHANGED ROME

The Roman conquests and the expansion of Rome brought about several changes and problems. Growing contact with other peoples made Rome more cosmopolitan, more open to new ideas and customs. Greek culture, in particular, strongly influenced Roman thought and art. The Romans began to identify the Greek gods with the impersonal divine forces that they had traditionally worshipped (the Greek Zeus, for example, became the Roman Jupiter), and so Roman religion was conceived of in more personal terms. The Romans also learned the philosophy of Stoicism from the Greeks, which would become highly influential by the time of the Roman Empire.

Although the Roman Republic had expanded considerably, the Romans were unwilling or unable to build an effective administrative system to govern the areas they had conquered. Usually, influential

The Colosseum at Rome The Colosseum is the most famous Roman amphitheater. Constructed in the first century A.D. for gladiatorial shows, it was a marvel of design and engineering and could seat about 45,000 people. (B. Glassman)

patricians were sent to govern a province for a year or so, but many of them used their power to enrich themselves by raising taxes and accepting bribes. One result was the gradual corruption of traditional Roman honesty and integrity; another was an increasing resentment of Romans by the peoples they conquered. In the fifth and fourth centuries B.C., the Romans governed their conquered subjects with fairness and decency. As Rome continued to expand during the third to the first centuries B.C., however, the Romans governed their colonies with less honesty and they became more despotic. The earlier tradition of good imperial government was restored only after Augustus Caesar became the first Roman emperor late in the first century B.C.

Social divisions also deepened within Rome during this time. In the early days of the Roman Republic, patricians and plebeians had similar standards of living. By the second century B.C., however, many plebeians were losing their farmland because they were spending so much time fighting in wars and could not maintain their farms. These plebeians gradually migrated to the city of Rome in search of work. However, employment was often unavailable, so the government had to provide free food and entertainment to pacify this new urban proletariat. Many patricians, on the other hand, were becoming rich from the spoils of Roman expansion and began living luxuriously. They often bought the land lost by the plebeians, combined a number of small farms into one large plantation, and imported slaves to work their new estates. This, of course, created the threat of slave revolt.

The Roman army gradually became an independent force in the society. By the late second century B.C., army commanders began to offer long-term enlistments to unemployed plebeians and to promise recruits a share in the booty captured in war. Thus, what had originally been a citizen-based army motivated primarily by patriotism slowly became a professional army (somewhat separate from the body of citizens) motivated by desires for personal wealth.

A CENTURY OF TURMOIL AND THE END OF THE REPUBLIC

By the middle of the second century B.C., a power struggle began to disrupt Roman politics. On one side were the *Optimates*, the conservative patricians who wanted the Senate to govern Rome in the traditional manner. On the other side were the *Populares*, political leaders (many of them also patricians) who sought to mobilize popular support to break the power of the Senate and institute political and social reforms.

The first great *Popularis* was Tiberius Gracchus, a tribune who in 133 B.C. tried to launch a reform program that would give land to unemployed plebeians, but he was murdered by assassins financed by patricians. Ten years later, Gaius Gracchus, brother of Tiberius, was also murdered after he too proposed land reform. The fundamental problem was that behind the issue of land reform lay the basic issue of who should control Rome: the Senate representing the traditionalists, or a popular tribune with public support? The murders of the Gracchi meant that the Senate would retain power for a time, but they inaugurated a century of political violence in Rome.

The *Optimates* soon confronted other problems. By the end of the second century B.C., Gaius Marius, a general and a popular hero, became the most powerful man in Rome. Angered by patrician arrogance, Marius had many of his opponents murdered. A Greek historian named Appian described how Marius's men "killed remorselessly and severed the necks of men already dead, and they paraded these horrors before the public eye, either to inspire fear and terror, or for a godless spectacle."[2] Another difficulty faced by the *Optimates* was the revolt of many Italian towns against Rome in 90–88 B.C. The rebels were angered by Rome's unwillingness to allow them to share in the economic benefits of the expansion, and Rome had to pacify the rebels by granting citizenship rights to all free males in Italy.

By the middle of the first century B.C., Rome was engulfed by political factions. Speaking for the *Optimates* was Cicero, a famous lawyer and

A CENTURY OF TURMOIL AND THE END OF THE REPUBLIC   97

Figure 5.1 The Expansion of Rome, 264 B.C.–A.D. 120

orator. Cicero was one of Rome's greatest prose writers, producing essays and speeches that defended liberty and republicanism. He knew that the *Optimates* were often greedy and selfish, but he argued that only the Senate could protect Rome from the dangers of military rule.

Cicero's greatest enemy was Julius Caesar, an able general who was popular with the *Populares*. In 60 B.C., Caesar, together with another general named Pompey and a financier named Crassus, formed a political alliance known as the *First Triumvirate*. But Crassus died soon thereafter, and Pompey for a variety of reasons began to support Cicero and the Senate. Civil war broke out in Rome in 49 B.C. Caesar led his armies from Gaul into Italy, eventually defeated Pompey, who was later killed, and became dictator of Rome from 49 to 44 B.C. Thus, Caesar destroyed the republican government that had been decaying for a century or more. Although the Senate still existed, its power was taken away.

Caesar ruled Rome for only five years. In 44 B.C., he was assassinated by senators claiming to be defenders of liberty. Once again, a power struggle erupted in Rome. The senators were incapable of governing

Rome and many of them, including Cicero, were soon killed. In 43 B.C., the Second Triumvirate was formed. It included Mark Antony (one of Caesar's lieutenants), an obscure general named Lepidus, and Octavian, Caesar's grandnephew and heir. Lepidus was soon forced out of the Triumvirate, so Mark Antony governed the eastern provinces and Octavian took control of the western provinces. Antony, however, soon became the lover and political ally of Cleopatra (69–30 B.C.), the queen of Egypt. (Cleopatra was the last of the Ptolemaic rulers of Egypt and was determined to become a powerful political figure in the Mediterranean world. Toward that end, she used her mind and body to entrance Julius Caesar and then Mark Antony.) Octavian gradually came to distrust Antony and Cleopatra, and the distrust grew into open conflict. In 31 B.C., Octavian's navy defeated Antony and Cleopatra's ships off the Greek coast at Actium, and soon thereafter Antony and Cleopatra committed suicide.

THE ROMAN EMPIRE

Augustus, the First Emperor

Following a century of political chaos and civil war, Octavian assumed full control of the Roman state. He quickly modified the governmental structure, transforming Rome from a republic governed by the upper classes into an empire in which one man—an emperor—directed an authoritarian regime. Although republican institutions survived and the Senate continued to meet, Octavian held absolute power. He was *imperator* (origin of the word *emperor*), meaning "commander of the armies," as well as *princeps* (origin of the word *prince*), meaning "first citizen." To signify his new exalted status, Octavian changed his name to Augustus (meaning "revered") Caesar.

Augustus ruled Rome from 31 B.C. to A.D. 14 and was in many ways an excellent emperor. He brought stability to the Roman Empire and began the process of building an administrative system that would govern the provinces fairly and honestly. He inaugurated the *Pax Romana* ("Roman Peace"), the period from 31 B.C. to A.D. 180, when most of the Mediterranean world enjoyed prolonged peace and prosperity. He also helped sponsor a literary renaissance in Rome. In *The Aeneid*, Virgil proclaimed that Rome was destined to rule the world; he defined the Roman ideal in the following words:

> Remember Roman,
> To rule the people under law, to establish
> The way of peace, to battle down the haughty,
> To spare the meek.[3]

Bust of Julius Caesar (c. 100–44 B.C.) Among Rome's greatest political and military leaders, Julius Caesar conquered Gaul (present-day France) and then destroyed the republican government in Rome. The name "Caesar" came to mean "emperor" (for example, the modern German word for emperor, *kaiser,* is derived from the word *caesar*). (New York Public Library)

Another poet, Horace (65–8 B.C.), wrote lyric poems, some of which were patriotic odes to Roman splendor. Ovid (43 B.C.–A.D. 17), however, wrote erotic poems in his *The Art of Love* that so offended Augustus, who wanted to strengthen the family as an institution, that the poet was banished from Rome.

Ovid's fate illustrates another side of the new political system in Rome, for Augustus sometimes used secret police to stifle intellectual dissent and to punish anyone who opposed him. Eventually, the authoritarian system established by Augustus would sow the seeds of its own destruction, particularly because it eliminated political and intellectual debate and thereby undermined the creativity that helps any society to thrive.

The Grandeur and Degradation of Roman Society

Before continuing a chronological account of Roman politics, we need to know something about Roman society. As we will see, life in the Roman Empire was both grand and brutal.

By the time of Augustus Caesar, the Roman Empire covered the entire Mediterranean basin and contained nearly one hundred million people from diverse cultural and linguistic backgrounds. Many of these people lived in a relatively cosmopolitan environment, in coastal towns where sea transport encouraged travel and commerce. Aristocrats usually traveled frequently, many going to Greece to study philosophy or to visit the tourist attractions at Athens and Olympia. Yet other people lived in inland areas in a more isolated, provincial atmosphere. Land transport was very difficult and expensive for these people, so they rarely traveled. They obtained most of the material goods they needed from the surrounding countryside.

Why were the Romans able to govern such a diverse mixture of peoples and societies so successfully for several centuries? One obvious reason was their military power, but less obvious was the Roman tradition of tolerance and open-mindedness. Compared to other peoples of the ancient world, the Romans were more willing to allow people to live their lives as they saw fit (provided, of course, that they remained loyal to Rome). One example of this tolerance is the Roman attitude toward women. Upper-class women, for example, attended banquets and actively helped their husbands conduct business and political affairs. Although they had no political rights, in daily affairs they could come and go largely as they pleased.

The Roman tradition of tolerance extended to imperial governance, as the Romans tended to allow conquered peoples to live in accordance with their own customs and religion. At their best, the Romans developed *humanitas*, an attitude of respect for others regardless of their race or nationality. In practice, this concept was implemented to form a body of international law to govern all peoples equitably.

The development of Roman law began around 450 B.C., when in its first phase the Twelve Tables—a listing of the then-existing laws—were written. By around 200 B.C., Roman jurists began to modify these laws to reflect the need to govern a growing empire. In this regard, the Romans did two significant things: (1) they universalized their laws so they could be applied to a variety of peoples; and (2) they conceived of law as something made by people, not god-given, and thus were able to understand law as something that can be analyzed, used, and interpreted by people. In the second phase of Roman law, from 200 B.C. to A.D. 250—the classical period—the laws were internationalized and came to be based on principles of fairness and equity. These principles would be handed down to later ages. A third phase of Roman law occurred as the

TECHNOLOGY
Roman Roads

Romans governed successfully in part because they provided many material advantages for the peoples of the empire. Roman engineers constructed large baths, theaters, aqueducts, and roads. The baths and theaters were centers of entertainment, and the aqueducts brought water from rivers to cities. The water was used for drinking, for irrigating crops, for the baths, and for ornamental fountains.

Perhaps most impressive, though, was the Roman road system. Over the centuries, the Romans built about fifty thousand miles of road to connect the various parts of their empire. The roads were adapted to local climates and weather conditions. In marshy areas, for example, the roads were made of staked-down timbers on which layers of gravel and stone were placed. In areas with solid ground, the road foundations consisted of layers of gravel and clay, with stones placed on top. In addition, milestones were placed at the appropriate points along the roads to assist the traveler, and in some areas small roadside hotels were provided.

The Roman road system was far more advanced than that of other ancient peoples. In some areas, Roman roads were better constructed than anything else that would be built until the nineteenth and twentieth centuries A.D. Some Roman roads are still in use today.

Via Appia ("The Appian Way") *The Appian Way was one of the first major roads built by the Romans, stretching over three hundred miles from Rome to southeastern Italy. In this nineteenth-century depiction, a section of the Appian Way near Rome has tombs and monuments on both sides. (The Granger Collection)*

laws were codified in large legal collections. This phase lasted until the sixth century A.D., when Justinian—discussed in Chapter 6—directed the codification of all Roman laws.

Despite Rome's great achievements, life for many in the Roman Empire was brutal. The poor always lived precariously. The rural poor survived by constant toil on the land, and they had little access to the attractions in the cities. The urban poor often lived in large, wooden tenement buildings that were vulnerable to fire, had no toilet facilities, and provided little heating. And the poor in Rome were always threatened by the possibility of unemployment, since slaves did most of the unskilled work. Wealthy Romans used slaves to perform household chores, to run errands, and to work on their farms. Some Romans owned slaves as an investment, hiring them out to others for a fee. Although some slaves were treated reasonably well, at times being accepted as virtual members of the family and eventually being granted their freedom, most slaves were treated brutally and were forced to work in mines or on farms until their death.

The brutality of Roman society was most strikingly manifested in the gladiatorial contests. The Roman government often provided so-called circuses, a form of entertainment for urban crowds, particularly the unemployed. These games were held in Rome at a huge arena called the *Colosseum*. At first, they involved trained gladiators who fought each other to the death while the large audience cheered. But as time went on, the spectators demanded novel events. Thus the gladiatorial contests came to feature such things as dwarfs fighting women, animals (crocodiles, giraffes, and elephants) fighting each other or men (often Christians), and even dramas in which the leading actor was murdered. That the crowds enjoyed and even exulted in such violence is in stark contrast to the civilized attitudes of tolerance and respect for law that the Romans exhibited in other areas of life.

First-Century Emperors

When Augustus transformed the Roman Republic into the Roman Empire, enormous tension erupted among the Roman aristocracy and continued for nearly a century. With all power concentrated in the hands of one man—the emperor—many aristocrats related to the ruling family sought to influence or even assassinate the emperor in order to attain power for themselves. The emperors, in turn, felt forced to imprison or murder suspected rivals. So, Roman imperial government in the century after Augustus was conducted in an atmosphere of suspicion and murderous intrigue.

The Julio–Claudian emperors—Tiberius, Caligula, Claudius, and Nero—ruled Rome from A.D. 14 to A.D. 68. They were all in some indirect way related to the family of Augustus Caesar (Augustus had no direct heirs). Several of them ruled effectively for a time, but fear of assassination led Tiberius, Caligula, and Nero to execute entire aristocratic families. The historian Tacitus tells of a frightened young woman being led to her execution, saying: "What have I done? Where are you taking me? I won't do it again."[4] The emperors had reason to be just as afraid as the young woman; Caligula and Nero were killed by their own guards, and Claudius was poisoned by his wife.

After Nero died in A.D. 68, a brief power struggle ensued until Vespasian became the first of three emperors of the Flavian dynasty, which ruled from A.D. 69 to A.D. 96. Vespasian's two sons—Titus and Domitian—were the other two. Vespasian was a strong ruler, in part because he was an Italian provincial and the first emperor to come from outside the city of Rome. The Roman Empire was beginning to use the talents of people outside the traditional aristocracy.

The Five Good Emperors

When the Flavian dynasty ended in A.D. 96, the Senate appointed Nerva to the throne. Nerva immediately established what would become an important reform in the method of choosing an emperor. During the first century A.D., Rome had no established way of selecting a successor to a dead emperor, and the result was often political instability. To correct this problem, Nerva instituted a reform by which an emperor could adopt his successor (someone he thought would be a good emperor). This practice of adoption led to a series of able rulers often referred to as the *Five Good Emperors*—Nerva, Trajan, Hadrian, Antoninus Pius, and Marcus Aurelius.

The period of the Five Good Emperors (A.D. 96–180) was a time of prosperity and improved standards of living for many Romans. The emperors were honest, hardworking men who provided peace, law and order, and capable government for their subjects. The Mediterranean prospered like never before in Roman history. The city of Rome had a population of nearly one million, and in the provinces were dozens of other cities, most of them dotted with baths, gymnasiums, and theaters. Even the life-style of the poor had improved as a result of welfare programs instituted by the imperial government, providing such things as food for children. The government also issued decrees that to some degree protected slaves against harsh treatment by their owners.

However, the prosperity of the Roman Empire in the second century A.D. was based on a weak foundation. The emperors, though effective rulers, held such absolute power that few others had the opportunity to make decisions. Imperial government slowly sapped the life out of the empire. Local governments gradually declined into insignificance, and political and intellectual discussion largely disappeared. Many individuals became fatalistic, as is attested to by a popular tombstone epitaph of those days: "I was not, I was, I am no more, I care not."[5]

Chaos in the Third Century

By the third century A.D., the Roman Empire was facing economic and political problems as well. Its economic production stagnated and its population declined, perhaps due to a plague. Furthermore, the empire was threatened by external foes, a revived Persian Empire in the east and Germanic barbarians from the north. The need for national defense meant that the Roman army became more powerful, intervening in politics and appointing and deposing emperors. Between 235 and 285 A.D., there were twenty-six emperors, many of them assassinated by rival army factions. Nevertheless, the empire endured through the chaos of the third century. That most Romans believed that their empire would survive indefinitely was not unreasonable, for in A.D.. 248 they celebrated the one-thousand-year anniversary of the founding of the city of Rome.

THE ORIGINS AND GROWTH OF CHRISTIANITY

During the first centuries of the Roman Empire, a new religion—Christianity—was gaining acceptance in an obscure Roman province. The Romans conquered an area inhabited by the Jewish people in the first century B.C. and renamed it *Palestine*. Palestine was a land where spiritual and religious questions preoccupied many people. Prophets and preachers wandered about the area, spreading their messages to those who would listen. Most Jews still adhered to the old Hebrew faith, the belief in one God who expects moral behavior from humans.

The Teachings of Jesus

Jesus of Nazareth was born in Palestine sometime between 6 and 4 B.C. (Logically, the birth date of Jesus should be the year 1. However, when the sixth-century A.D. monk Dionysius Exiguus invented the B.C.–A.D. system of dating, he miscalculated the years, leaving the Western calendar with some anomalies.)

Little is known about Jesus' early days, but he is said to be descended from the house of David, the great Israelite king. Furthermore, Jesus was taught the main tenets of the Jewish religious heritage. Sometime around A.D. 28 or 29, he was baptized by the preacher, John the Baptist. (Baptism—the immersion in or sprinkling of the body with water—symbolizes purification.) Jesus then began his own ministry.

According to the four Gospels of the New Testament—Matthew,

Mark, Luke, and John—Jesus healed people, exorcised demons, and preached the imminent coming of the Kingdom of God. The healings and exorcisms were, according to Jesus, signs that the rule of God had begun. The blessings of this reign of God were available to everyone, for Jesus taught an egalitarian message in which the poor were just as blessed (if not more so) as the rich and powerful. In Luke, Jesus is quoted as saying: "Blessed are you poor, for yours is the kingdom of God. Blessed are you that hunger now, for you shall be satisfied. Blessed are you that weep now, for you shall laugh" (6:20–21).* Significantly, many of Jesus' first followers were simple people—fishermen, peasants, and even prostitutes. And the morality he taught these people was one of love and gentleness toward all: "You shall love the Lord your God with all your heart, and with all your soul, and with all your mind. . . . You shall love your neighbor as yourself" (Matthew 22:37–39).

Jesus clearly believed that he had a special relationship with God, though modern scholars disagree on the precise nature of that relationship. Some scholars contend that Jesus regarded himself as the Son of God, while others point out that he usually referred to himself as the "Son of Man," a somewhat vaguer phrase. More important, though, is that the established authorities—Jewish leaders and the local Roman rulers—believed that Jesus was claiming to be the Messiah who would lead the Jews against their enemies. Consequently, when Jesus went to Jerusalem sometime in the early 30s A.D., he was condemned by the Romans as a revolutionary and crucified. (Crucifixion—the nailing of a person on a cross—was a fairly common Roman form of execution.)

Jesus' Followers

When the leaders of earlier movements were killed, the followers of those movements usually disappeared. Jesus' followers, however, came to believe that Jesus had in some sense been resurrected—raised from the dead—and that fellowship with him was still possible. The belief in the Resurrection thus had the effect of resurrecting the Christian movement.

Jesus' followers were originally known as the *Galileans* because of their association with the area around the Sea of Galilee. At first, the Galileans believed that their movement was a part of the broader Jewish religion and recognized the Jerusalem church—headed by James, supposedly the brother of Jesus—as the center of the movement. Gradually, however, the Galileans began to preach to non-Jews, or so-called *Gentiles,* and to travel to distant areas to spread their message. The Apostle Peter, for example, went as far as Rome; others traveled to Greece, Mesopotamia, and possibly Arabia. In the city of Antioch, just up the coast from Palestine, the Apostle Paul began to preach that Jesus'

---

*All quotations from the New Testament are taken from the Revised Standard Version.

Jesus Christ Holding the Orb The orb is a symbol of the earth surmounted by a cross. Here the artist, whose name is unknown, uses the orb to portray Jesus as the spiritual ruler of the earth. (Pierpont Morgan Library)

teachings were for all people, not just Jews. Paul was of Jewish heritage and at one time had been a persecutor of the Galileans, but he was converted and had a major impact on shaping the new religion. Under his influence, Jesus' followers began to call themselves *Christians,* since they believed that Jesus was the Christ, the Savior, and to think of themselves as adherents of a new religion, *Christianity*. The belief that the Galileans were a part of Judaism died with the destruction of the Jerusalem church in A.D. 70. A Jewish revolt against Rome had erupted in A.D. 67, and the Romans destroyed the city of Jerusalem and most of the Jewish Galileans in A.D. 70.

The Christian Message

As Christianity slowly grew, it developed its sacred writings and teachings. The four Gospels of the New Testament were written down sometime during the second half of the first century A.D. These accounts of Jesus' teachings and life were not written down at first, because his followers expected the end of the world to come soon. When that expectation proved false, the Gospels were transmitted from memory and oral recitation to parchment. Many other parts of the New Testament are letters written by Paul to early Christian churches around the middle of the first century A.D.

From the sacred writings of the New Testament, Christian preachers and missionaries gradually evolved the message that they wanted to transmit to nonbelievers. This message was simple: a Christian had to have faith in God and in Jesus as the Son of God. Even though all people sinned, in the sense of being separate from God, God loved them and expected them to love him and their fellow humans. Because God loved people, he allowed his Son to become human and die a horrible death. The death of Christ was a divine sacrifice that made amends for human sin. Thus, it was possible for all who believed to be forgiven for their sins, to be saved, and to attain eternal life. Soon, the early Christians taught, the Second Coming of Christ would take place, at which time the righteous would ascend into heaven and the wicked would be condemned to hell. As the years passed and it became apparent that the Second Coming would not occur immediately, this last teaching was modified to say that Christ would return at some unspecified time in the future.

The Christian message appealed to many people in the Roman Empire for a number of reasons. One reason was the promise of salvation to those who believed. Another was the message of a loving God, which was particularly appealing in a brutal age. A third reason was the growing belief that Christian exorcists could cast demons out of people, a clear sign that they were recipients of divine power.

Christian Institutions

Another aspect of the growth of Christianity was the evolution of a permanent institutional structure primarily during the first and second centuries A.D. Local Christian communities developed a sacramental system to give spiritual support to members. The two most important sacraments were *baptism,* presumed to purify and admit the recipient into the Christian community, and a celebration of the *Lord's Supper* (later known as the *Eucharist*), Jesus' last meal with his disciples.

In addition, a hierarchical church organization began to develop. The first Christian communities were informal groups directed by elders, later known as *priests.* When several communities emerged in one city or area, an official known as a *bishop* ("overseer") was appointed or elected to guide all Christians in that area. Then, as Christians sought to unify over a still larger area, the large cities—Alexandria, Antioch, and Rome—began to appoint *archbishops* to supervise the Christian communities of an entire province. Thus, over the course of two or three centuries, a church organization emerged: priests guided the local congregations, bishops directed the priests and congregations in certain areas, and archbishops supervised hundreds of bishops and priests.

The final part of the church hierarchy appeared when the bishops of Rome began to argue that they should have precedence over all other bishops, because Peter—Jesus' leading disciple—was the founder of the church at Rome. By the fifth century A.D., the bishop of Rome was increasingly called the *Pope,* meaning "father of the church."

Christianity In the Early Roman Empire

The growth of Christianity gained the attention of the Roman government. Although the Romans were usually tolerant of different religions, they feared Christians in particular for several reasons. One reason was the Christian insistence on meeting in secret, which appeared subversive to the Romans. Another reason was the Christian refusal to worship the Roman emperor, an act that to the Christians was idolatry but to the Romans was simply a sign of allegiance to Rome. Further, the Romans accused the Christians of being atheists because they questioned the existence of the traditional pagan gods.

As a result of the Romans' fear of Christians, some emperors tried to destroy Christianity through intimidation. The first imperial persecution of Christians took place in A.D. 64; others occurred sporadically over the next two and half centuries. Christians were sometimes crucified, sometimes torn to death by wild animals in the gladiatorial games, and sometimes simply murdered. Ironically, the Roman persecution of Christians increased the popularity of Christianity. Most Christians believed that dying for their faith would guarantee them salvation, so many perished willingly. Further, the spiritual strength and conviction of these Christian martyrs impressed many non-Christians as well.

By the end of the third century A.D., however, Christians were still a small minority within the Roman Empire. Many people continued to worship the traditional pagan deities, with the sun god being particularly popular (*Sunday* was a "divine" day for many). Others turned to religions that, like Christianity, promised human salvation. Mithraism, for example, told of the god Mithras, who ascended to heaven from where he offered redemption to the faithful. Thus, Christianity was at this point only one of several competing religions.

THE POLITICAL TRANSFORMATION OF THE ROMAN EMPIRE

The political structure of the Roman Empire changed fundamentally in the late third and early fourth centuries A.D. One change was the growing militarization of the empire, accompanied by an increase in the power of the emperor. Another fundamental change was the Christianization of the Roman Empire, as Christianity won a political victory over other religions of the time and became the official religion of Rome.

Militarization

Beginning around A.D. 260, a succession of Roman emperors implemented a military revolution designed to make the army more effective in fighting the Persians in the east and the Germanic tribes in the north. Military commands were no longer given to senatorial aristocrats but to professional soldiers. The new commanders instituted tighter discipline and new military tactics, which enabled the Roman armies to defeat the foreign foes. The long-range effects of the military revolution were to turn the military into a major source of political talent and to allow army leaders to replace aristocrats in the governing councils of the empire.

Centralization of Power

Additional changes occurred when Diocletian became emperor in A.D. 285. He launched a thorough reorganization of the imperial administration, designed to restabilize the empire after the political instability and economic stagnation it faced in the third century. Politically, he turned the Roman Empire into an autocracy, in which the central government was in complete control. Diocletian was known as "Lord and God" and held absolute power. He used his power in particular to persecute Christians throughout the empire. Diocletian's economic reforms included making occupations hereditary; for example, the sons of peasants had to remain peasants. His purpose here was to stabilize economic production by forcing people to remain at their assigned tasks.

Through his reforms, Diocletian transformed the Roman Empire into an armed camp governed by an absolute monarch. The reforms worked throughout much of the fourth century A.D., a time of stability and prosperity in Rome. At the same time, though, basic Roman institutions were being undermined. In the western half of the Roman Empire, Diocletian's economic reforms hindered commerce and thereby weakened the economic foundation of the cities—the heart of Roman society. Also in the west, Germans from northern Europe (see Chapter 6) were being recruited into the Roman army to fight other Germans, who were pushing against the Roman frontiers in the north.

Christianization

The Christianization of the Roman Empire advanced rapidly after the emperor Constantine was converted in A.D. 312. In A.D. 313 the new convert issued the Edict of Milan that decreed governmental toleration of Christianity. Thereafter, the number of converts grew steadily—many hoped that conversion would gain them favor with the government and others were impressed by the popular belief that Christians could perform miracles. One story of the time told of a pagan prophet who challenged a bishop to a debate, but was struck dumb and died before she could utter what Christians called her "blasphemies."

Constantine also built a new capital for the empire. In A.D. 330, Constantinople was founded on the site of the ancient Greek village of Byzantium. Its location—on a peninsula commanding the sea route between the Black Sea and the Mediterranean—enabled Constantinople to become the principal city and capital of the eastern half of the Roman Empire. More important to Constantine was the fact that the new city was a Christian capital, distinct from the old pagan capital of Rome.

By the late fourth century A.D., Christianity was becoming the dominant religion within the Roman Empire and Christians were actively trying to destroy paganism. Those who had once been the persecuted now became the persecutors, as Christian mobs ransacked pagan temples and intimidated pagans into converting to Christianity. Religious feelings were so strong that at times they caused riots in which people had their eyes torn out or tongues cut off.

The final political victory of Christianity over paganism came in A.D. 380, when the emperor Theodosius I decreed Christianity to be the official state religion and thereby transformed Rome from a pagan empire into a Christian one. Theodosius I was also significant in that he was the last emperor to govern the entire empire effectively. At his death, his two sons divided control of the empire and the two halves were never again united. Thus, the reign of Theodosius I (A.D. 379–395) marked both the end of the old pagan Rome that ruled the entire Mediterranean basin and the beginning of a new Christian world still being born (discussed in Chapters 6 and 7).

THE SPIRITUAL TRANSFORMATION OF THE ROMAN EMPIRE

Christianity became the state religion of Rome in large part because of a spiritual transformation that was occurring among the people of the Roman Empire. Pagan, classical thought was slowly giving way to Christianity, and the transition produced the most profound intellectual debate since the great days of Athens in the fifth century B.C.

On one side of the debate were the Hellenes, those who still adhered to the ancient ways of learning that had originated in Greece a thousand years earlier. The Hellenes defended human reason as the primary vehicle for discovering truth, and in the universities they studied the ancient Greek philosophers. They argued that the best life for humans lay in the *polis,* a city where intelligent, free people could debate political issues and try to create the good life on this earth. The Hellenes were at this time recopying the texts of the Greek philosophers for use by later generations.

On the other side of the debate were the Christians, who were defining an alternative way of life. One aspect of this new way of life was the movement known as *monasticism,* which began with an extraordinary man named Anthony of Egypt. Anthony took literally Jesus' admonition to "sell all you have and give to the poor and follow me." In A.D. 269, Anthony moved into the Egyptian desert to live as a hermit, believing that solitude would enable him to pray and worship God without distraction. His example stirred others to do the same, and within a century the monastic movement spread to Syria. There Simeon the Stylite allegedly squatted on top of a fifty-foot column for forty years, so that, like Anthony, he could concentrate on meditating and worshiping God. Anthony and Simeon had many imitators, some of whom embarrassed other Christians by engaging in such extreme actions as starving themselves to death to demonstrate contempt for their bodies. So, church leaders gradually began to organize these people into monasteries, communities where monks lived by an iron discipline that focused on constant prayer and meditation. Gradually, a number of monastic orders for women were established as well. By the late fourth century A.D., dozens of monasteries existed in Egypt, and the monastic movement was growing rapidly. Over the next several centuries, monasticism would be one of the most vital institutions within Christianity.

Another aspect of the new Christian way of life was the attempt by Christian theologians to define precisely what Christianity meant. The greatest of these theologians was Augustine (A.D. 354–430), who for over three decades was bishop of Hippo in northern Africa (present-day Algeria). Northern Africa had long been one of the more prosperous areas of the Roman Empire. Africa produced large quantities of grain, and some cities, such as Alexandria in Egypt, were centers of intellectual life. By the third and fourth centuries A.D., Africa was the home of many important Christian theologians and teachers.

Augustine wrote two books that had a decisive impact on Christian thought. *Confessions* is an autobiographical examination of his own search for spiritual truth. In it Augustine focuses on himself as an individual personality, marking a new kind of thinking that stressed the importance of the individual. According to the traditional classical thought, a person was part of a community and the community was more important than any one individual. In contrast, Christianity argued that every person has an individual soul, and so each individual is valuable in the eyes of God. This belief was manifested in Christian condemnations of ancient practices that were cruel and harsh to individuals—such as fatal exposure for deformed infants and the practice of gladiatorial contests.

Augustine's other great work is the *City of God*, an assault on classical philosophical thought. In it Augustine argues that all humans live in one of two spiritual worlds, the City of Man or the City of God. According to Augustine, Romans who lived in the spiritual City of Man saw the good life as something that could be defined in terms of political and economic well-being, and believed that human reason alone could discover truth. In short, the City of Man placed its ultimate confidence in people. Those who lived in the spiritual City of God saw reason and faith as essential to the attainment of truth, and professed to put the service of God before the service of people. Only in this way could people overcome the pride and greed for material possessions that characterized the City of Man. Augustine contrasts the two cities in the following words:

> That which animates secular society is the love of self to the point of contempt for God; that which animates divine society is the love of God to the point of contempt for self. The one prides itself on itself; the pride of the other is in the Lord; the one seeks for glory from men, the other counts its consciousness of God as its greatest glory.[6]

Augustine, educated in ancient classical thought, did not repudiate it entirely. He only insisted that classical thought was incomplete and that faith in God had to be added to confidence in human reason. Thus, Augustine defined a new synthesis of human experience, a Christian synthesis that combined the Greek faith in reason with the Jewish and Christian faith in God. This new synthesis and its resulting tensions would dominate the Western world in the succeeding centuries.

CONCLUSION

Roman history spans over a thousand years. During those years, the Romans conquered and ruled one of the largest empires ever assembled, and made enduring achievements in the areas of law and government. Furthermore, the Roman Empire was the site of a major spiritual transformation in Western Civilization, as Christianity gradually became the dominant religion of Western peoples.

The decline of Roman power from the third to the sixth centuries A.D. marked the end of a major phase of Western history. The events of ancient history centered around the Mediterranean Sea, but as we will see in Chapters 6 and 7, the center of Western Civilization after Rome shifted to Western Europe.

THINGS YOU SHOULD KNOW

Virgil and *The Aeneid*
The governmental structure of the early Roman Republic
The Punic Wars
How the Roman conquests changed Rome
The Gracchi
Cicero
Julius Caesar
The Roman Empire
Octavian (Augustus Caesar)
Roman law
Roman roads and other technologies
Gladiatorial contests
The Julio-Claudian Emperors
The Flavian Dynasty
The Five Good Emperors
Jesus of Nazareth
The Galileans
The Apostle Paul
Early Christian teachings
The organization of the early Christian church
Roman persecution of the Christians
The growth of Christianity
The political and spiritual transformation of the Roman Empire
Diocletian
Constantine
Theodosius I
monasticism
Augustine

SUGGESTED READINGS

Two good introductions to the history of Rome are Finley Hooper, *Roman Realities* (Detroit: Wayne State Univ. Press, 1979), and L. P. Wilkinson, *The Roman Experience* (New York: Knopf, 1974). Geza Alfoldy, *The Social History of Rome* (Baltimore: Johns Hopkins Univ. Press, 1988) is a good account of the details of social history. For the Roman Empire, see Chester G. Starr, *Civilization and the Caesars: The Intellectual Revolution in the Roman Empire* (New York: Norton, 1965). Robert Graves, *I, Claudius* (New York: Random 1989) is an historical novel that captures the atmosphere of intrigue and fear that surrounded the first Roman emperors.

On the early history of Christianity, see Martin Marty, *A Short History of Christianity* (New York: New American Library, 1959), and Ramsay MacMullen, *Christianizing the Roman Empire* (New Haven: Yale Univ. Press, 1984). Edward Gibbon, *The Decline and Fall of the Roman Empire* (New York: Penguin, 1983) was written in the late eighteenth century but remains a masterpiece of historical literature. An excellent modern analysis of the decline of Rome and the rise of Christianity is Peter Brown, *The World of Late Antiquity*, A.D. *150–750* (New York: Harcourt Brace Jovanovich, 1971). Finally, a high-level but rewarding work on the intellectual struggle between Christian and classical thought is Charles Norris Cochrane, *Christianity and Classical Culture* 2nd ed. (New York: Oxford Univ. Press, 1957).

NOTES

[1] Quoted in Finley Hooper, *Roman Realities* (Detroit: Wayne State Univ. Press, 1979), p. 37.

[2] Ibid., p. 204.

[3] Quoted in Chester G. Starr, *Civilization and the Caesars: The Intellectual Revolution in the Roman Empire* (New York: Norton, 1965), p. 181.

[4] Quoted in Hooper, *Roman Realities*, p. 368.

[5] Quoted in L. P. Wilkinson, *The Roman Experience* (New York: Knopf, 1974), p. 193.

[6] Quoted in Charles Norris Cochrane, *Christianity and Classical Culture*, 2nd ed. (New York: Oxford Univ. Press, 1957), p. 489.

6

The Great Migrations, Byzantine Civilization, and Islamic Civilization, A.D. 400 to 700

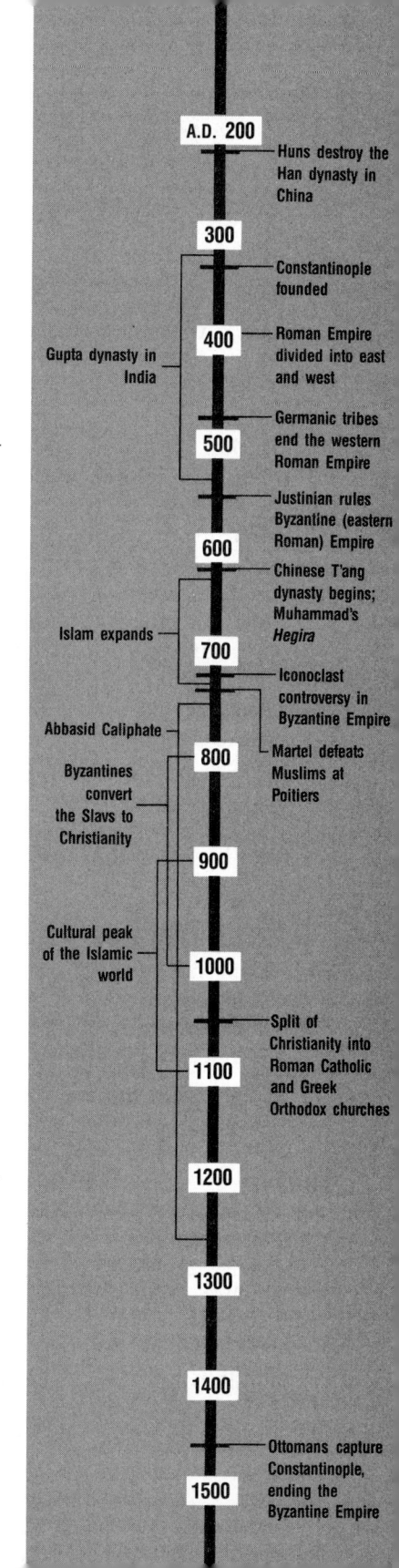

A.D. 200	Huns destroy the Han dynasty in China
300	Constantinople founded
400	Roman Empire divided into east and west
	Germanic tribes end the western Roman Empire
500	
	Justinian rules Byzantine (eastern Roman) Empire
600	Chinese T'ang dynasty begins; Muhammad's *Hegira*
700	Iconoclast controversy in Byzantine Empire
	Martel defeats Muslims at Poitiers
800	
900	
1000	
1100	Split of Christianity into Roman Catholic and Greek Orthodox churches
1200	
1300	
1400	
1500	Ottomans capture Constantinople, ending the Byzantine Empire

Gupta dynasty in India

Islam expands

Abbasid Caliphate

Byzantines convert the Slavs to Christianity

Cultural peak of the Islamic world

In *The Decline and Fall of the Roman Empire,* the eighteenth-century historian Edward Gibbon created an enduring image of the Roman Empire declining, falling, and disappearing. The image is somewhat exaggerated, for Rome neither fell suddenly nor disappeared completely. Rather, it slowly disintegrated and in its place emerged three new cultural realms that inherited much from the Greco-Roman-Christian past. In the western parts of the empire, the imperial government was gradually overwhelmed by Germanic peoples and replaced by a Western Christian society that eventually became the basis for Western European Civilization. In the east, centered in Constantinople, an eastern Roman Empire (later known as the Byzantine Empire) endured for another thousand years after the western half of Rome disappeared. In the seventh century A.D., the Arabic peoples created a new religion—Islam— and surged out of the Arabian peninsula to expand over much of what had been the southern part of the Roman Empire and to seize some territory from the Byzantine Empire.

The transformation of the Mediterranean world from one united Roman Empire into three distinct cultural realms occurred roughly between A.D. 400 and 700 and involved a vast movement of peoples. Various Germanic tribes—for example, the Goths, Franks, Vandals, Lombards, Angles, and Saxons—migrated from northern Europe into Italy, France, Spain, and North Africa. The Slavs, who first appeared in northeastern Europe (or present-day Poland), spread over much of eastern Europe. The Huns, an Asiatic people from somewhere near Mongolia, invaded parts of Europe but eventually left and soon disappeared from Western history. The Avars, another Asiatic people, moved into southern Russia and part of eastern Europe, but they too eventually disappeared. Finally, the Arabs, a Semitic people from southern Arabia, spread into some eastern Mediterranean lands and across North Africa. These various migrations were a part of a vast movement of peoples across much of the Eurasian landmass that affected not only Rome but other civilized areas as well.

CIVILIZATION AND NOMAD INVADERS ACROSS EURASIA

Four civilized areas stretched across central Eurasia: Rome, Persia, India, and China. In the third to fourth centuries A.D., each of these civilizations was internally weak. One source of their weakness was political fragmentation, as central governments were increasingly unable to maintain control of their vast realms. Another source of weakness was technological stagnation, particularly in agriculture where continued use of inefficient tools and techniques restricted productivity. Internal weakness left the civilized areas of central Eurasia vulnerable to external attack by nomad invaders. Thus, between A.D. 200 and 600, several waves of nomads swept across Eurasia. Many of the nomads came from Mongolia, peoples known in China as the *Juan-juan* and in Europe as the Huns. The origin of the Huns is somewhat obscure, as are the reasons they invaded Eurasia at this time. Historians know with certainty only that the Huns were nomads and skilled horsemen who probably moved through Eurasia in search of food and pasture for their animals.

The first encounter between the Huns and the civilized world occurred in China. The Han dynasty (202 B.C.–A.D. 222) ruled a stable and prosperous China for several centuries, but its power declined after A.D. 100 and the ensuing disorder bore many similarities to events of the same period in the Roman Empire (as we will see later in this chapter). The central government in China slowly lost power to local warlords, who used their new strength to assert greater control over the peasantry. Although the long-suffering peasants sometimes rebelled against the warlords, many of them lost their farms and some were forced to sell their children into slavery to survive. The Han dynasty collapsed in A.D. 222, and over the next two or three centuries China was plagued by civil wars among the warlords and invasions by the Huns. China was more resilient than Rome, however, for late in the sixth century the Sui dynasty drove most of the nomads out and restored a central government. The Sui were soon succeeded by the T'ang dynasty (A.D. 618–907), which sustained a long period of stable government in China.

While China was suffering social disorder and war, India was thriving both politically and culturally. In the fourth century A.D., the Gupta dynasty (A.D. 320–535) imposed political unity in northern India. The Gupta period quickly became one of the greatest cultural eras in Indian history. During this time, the Indians developed one of the greatest human creations—a new and improved numerical system (see the Technology box on page 119). Indian creativity was also expressed in literature, as writers produced dramas and romantic poetry and transcribed the epic poems that had earlier been transmitted orally. Two new forms of entertainment—chess and animal fables—were also developed in India at this time. Indian art and culture began to expand throughout eastern Asia, primarily through the efforts of Buddhist missionaries who were seeking converts. As a result, Buddhism and Indian culture became a cultural bond not only for Indians but for many Chinese, Koreans, Japanese, and Indonesians as well. This great age of Indian culture began to decline, however, when the Gupta dynasty was undermined by Hun invaders in the mid-sixth century A.D. The Huns were unable to establish a centralized government, so India became politically fragmented. It remained culturally united, however, through Hinduism and adherence to the caste system.

Nomads also attacked but were unable to defeat a revived Persian Empire. After A.D. 226, the Sassanian (from *sasan*, the Persian word for commander) monarchs formed what was known as Sassanian Persia, a deliberate imitation of the ancient Persian Empire of the sixth to fourth centuries B.C. Although Sassanian Persia was strong enough to repel Hunnish and other invaders, it was finally defeated by the Muslims in the seventh century A.D.

Consequences of the Nomad Invasions

The Huns eventually moved into Europe and helped precipitate the fall of Rome, a sequence of events that is examined later in the chapter. We first need to examine the nomad invasions in terms of their religious and political effects and their role in the destruction of three empires—the Han in China, the Gupta in India, and the western half of the Roman Empire. We also need to consider why only two civilized areas—Sassanian Persia and the eastern Roman Empire—were able to resist the nomad invasions.

One important effect of the invasions was the expansion of world religions. Many people sought spiritual consolation in this age of war and chaos. Christianity spread throughout most of the Mediterranean and into Ethiopia as well. Zoroastrianism was revived by the Sassanian monarchs in Persia. Islam emerged in the Arabian peninsula during the seventh century A.D., and eventually supplanted Zoroastrianism in Persia and Christianity in most of North Africa. (Since Zoroastrianism had few adherents outside of Persia, it ceased to be a significant religion after Islam gained wide acceptance in the Sassanian Empire.) In addition, Buddhism was carried throughout Asia by Indian missionaries and became a major influence in Korea, Japan, Southeast Asia, and parts of China. Interestingly, though, Buddhism gradually lost influence within India as a revived Hinduism became the religious tie among most Indians. Buddhism also lost influence in China. Although it had spread into China after the collapse of the Han dynasty in A.D. 222, the Sui and T'ang dynasties sponsored a revival of Confucianism during the late sixth and seventh centuries A.D. Confucianism again became the dominant religion in China, with Buddhism having only marginal influence.

Three major developments thus occurred across much of Eurasia between A.D. 400 and 700. First, the old centers of civilization—Rome, Persia, India, and China—were either destroyed or fundamentally transformed because of internal weakness and external attacks. China and India were able to recover and rebuild fairly quickly, but the collapse of the western half of the Roman Empire meant that a new civilization would be formed in Western Europe. Second, religious revival gradually brought new spiritual values and attitudes to civilized peoples. The religious influence of the Axial Period (see Chapter 2) spread rapidly during this time, as an increasing number of people were turning away from polytheistic and nature religions and developing loyalties to more

TECHNOLOGY
A Better System of Numbers

A modern numeral—6,789
The Roman numeral for 6,789—VMDCCLXXXIX
Performing addition of roman numerals and arabic numerals:

Roman Numerals	Arabic Numerals
CCLXVI	266
MDCCCVII	1807
DCL	650
MLXXX	1080
MMMDCCCIII	3803

Using Roman numerals, the problem is difficult if not impossible to solve.

Over history, different peoples have used different systems for writing and calculating numerals. Prior to the Gupta dynasty in India, most peoples used cumbersome numeral systems that were difficult to manipulate. The Romans, for example, used letters to designate numerals.

The Indians developed a new numerical system that used only nine digits (1 to 9) and a special sign—the zero—that enabled the nine digits to be continually reused. The zero was the key to the development of a positional system of numeration. By putting a numeral in a position to the left of where it had been, it then designated a higher power, ten or a hundred (or more) times as great as the original. Thus the number 1 with a zero added to it became the number 10, with two zeroes it became 100, and so on. The zero was first used in ancient Babylon and passed from there into India. Between the third and eighth centuries A.D., the Indians gradually adopted the zero and made it a part of their new numerical system. The system was eventually passed on to the Arabs and then to the Europeans late in the tenth century A.D. The Europeans referred to the nine digits as arabic numerals, as we still do today. However, it is more accurate to call it the Hindu-Arabic numeral system since the Indians developed it.

The Hindu-Arabic system of numbers is much less complex than the old roman numeral system. The Europeans slowly adopted the Hindu-Arabic system, and it eventually became the mathematical system used in modern science and technology.

universal and transcendental religions. Third, civilized institutions and skills were spreading into uncivilized areas. Japan, Korea, and Southeast Asia came under the influence of both China and India. The Arabs came into contact with more civilized peoples when Islam expanded, and the Germanic peoples were civilized in part through their conversion to Christianity. (It is interesting to note that civilization was also spreading in the Americas at this time with the development of the Mayan and the Incan civilizations.)

THE GERMANIC PEOPLES AND THE END OF ROME IN THE WEST

The Germanic peoples lived in a number of independent tribes, but they were interrelated and spoke variants of a common Germanic language. They were simple agricultural people who had not developed city life, had little written language, and no "civilized" political, educational, or legal systems. Their politics consisted of allegiance to a king or chieftain; their laws were simply customs and traditions handed down from past generations.

The Germanic tribes originated somewhere around present-day western Russia or Scandinavia. In about 500 B.C., they began to move south in search of better land and a warmer climate. By the second and first centuries B.C., many Germanic tribes were in central Europe where further movement was naturally blocked by the Rhine and Danube rivers—the northern frontiers of the Roman Empire. For the next several centuries, Romans and Germans coexisted peacefully, with some commerce being conducted across the rivers and some Germans moving into the empire as slaves or soldiers in the Roman army. But by the late fourth century A.D., two factors persuaded the Germanic tribes to push their way into the Roman Empire. One was the division and weakening of the imperial government after the death of the Emperor Theodosius in A.D. 395 (see Chapter 5), which encouraged the Germanic peoples to take over Roman farmland. The other was a fear of the Huns, whose movement toward Europe caused the Germanic tribes to seek protection within the Roman Empire.

The Visigoths were the first Germanic tribe to move into the boundaries of the Roman Empire. They were admitted peacefully in A.D. 376. However, various quarrels over where the Visigoths should live led to the battle of Adrianople in 378, in which the Visigoths defeated a large Roman army. That Roman defeat left the Danube frontier unprotected, causing many peoples, including the Huns, to drive into the empire. In A.D. 406, the Roman government brought in troops from the Rhine in an attempt to control the situation, but this left the Rhine frontier unprotected. Thus, during much of the fifth century, Germans and Huns moved back and forth through the empire. Some of the movements were violent: the Visigoths sacked Rome in A.D. 410; the Huns attacked Italy before eventually being driven off; and the Vandals terrorized Spain and North Africa (thereby inspiring the word *vandalize*). Other movements were relatively peaceful, for most of the Germanic tribes wanted only to settle on good farmland and enjoy the benefits of Roman government.

The Germanic invasions were primarily a result of the migration of immigrants seeking a better life. They did not intend to destroy the Roman government. But their migrations weakened Rome's political and military institutions, severed its communication and transportation ties, and undermined its educational and legal structures. Controlling and civilizing the immigrants was more than the weakened Roman Empire could manage. A symbolic event occurred in A.D. 476, when a Germanic general deposed the last official Roman emperor in the west, a young boy ironically named Romulus Augustulus.

Western Europe after the Fall of Rome

Even after A.D. 476, the Roman emperor in Constantinople still claimed to govern the entire empire, but that claim had no substance. The west was now controlled by the Germanic tribes, and some of their chieftains tried to build kingdoms and rule the mixed populations of Romans and Germans. In Britain, the Angles, Saxons, and Jutes each formed small kingdoms; later the name "Angleland" would be transformed into "England." In Gaul, the Franks built "Frankland," later shortened into "France." The Visigoths organized a kingdom in Spain, the Ostrogoths in Italy, and the Vandals in North Africa. But most of these kingdoms survived only briefly, since the Germanic tribes did not possess the governing and administrative skills necessary to sustain large political structures. What had been the western half of the Roman Empire slowly collapsed into chaos and confusion.

We do not know with certainty what happened to ordinary people in these chaotic times. Some wealthy landowners were probably able to withdraw to their estates and build fortress-like villas for protection. Others probably joined monasteries to seek spiritual consolation. The poor either worked on the estates or took to the mountains and survived by robbery. The situation varied in different areas; in some places absolute confusion reigned while in others a semblance of Roman civilization remained. Historian Peter Brown describes the atmosphere of this time as follows:

> A Roman senator could write as if he still lived in the days of Augustus, and wake up, as many did at the end of the fifth century A.D., to realize that there was no longer a Roman emperor in Italy. Again, a Christian bishop might welcome the disasters of the

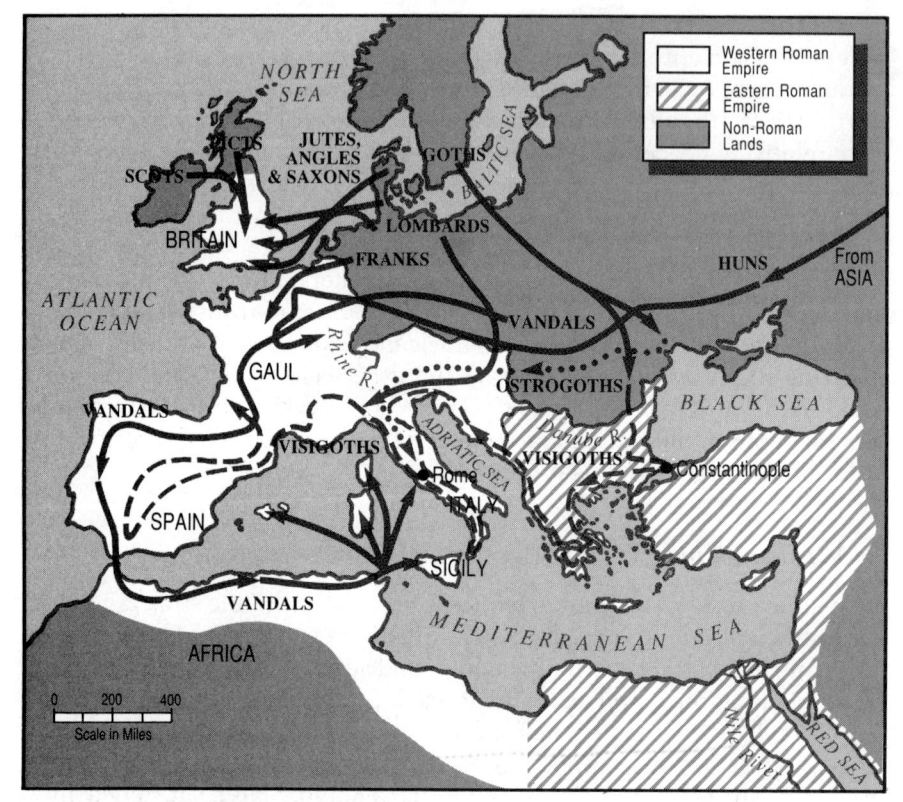

Figure 6.1 Barbarian Invasions and the Division of the Roman Empire

barbarian invasions, as if they had turned men irrevocably from earthly civilization to the Heavenly Jerusalem, yet he will do this in a Latin or a Greek unselfconsciously modelled on the ancient classics: and he will betray attitudes to the universe, prejudices and patterns of behavior that mark him out as a man still firmly rooted in eight hundred years of Mediterranean life.[1]

Roman attitudes toward the Germanic invaders varied. Some Romans spoke well of their attempts to maintain effective government, as in this description of Theodoric, an Ostrogothic king of Italy:

> He so governed two races at the same time, Romans and Goths, . . . that by the Romans he was called a Trajan or a Valentinian, whose times he took as a model; and by the Goths . . . he was judged to be in all respects their best king.[2]

Other Romans described the barbarians as dirty, violent, and drunken: "Happy the nose that cannot smell a barbarian." Gregory of Tours described the cruelty of one Germanic tribe—the Thuringians—as follows:

> The Thuringians murdered the hostages in all sorts of different ways. . . . They hung our young men up to die in the trees by the muscles of their thighs. They put more than two hundred of our young women to death in the most barbarous way: they tied their arms round the necks of their horses, stampeded these animals in all directions by prodding them with goads, and so tore the girls to pieces; or else they stretched them out over the ruts of the roads, attached their arms and legs to the ground with stakes, and then drove heavily-laden carts over them again and again, until their bones were all broken and their bodies could be thrown out for the dogs and birds to feed on.[3]

Underlying the cruelty and chaos was the fact that the period from A.D. 400 to 700 was, more than most, an age of transition. The historian C. Warren Hollister calls it a "twilight" age—in the sense that there is twilight at sundown when something old is disappearing and twilight at dawn when something new is being born.[4] The old was the crumbling western half of the Roman Empire. The city of Rome ultimately declined to the point where its population numbered only seventeen thousand and its Forum—the old political center of Rome—was a cow pasture. The new was the Germanic and increasingly Christian West (as we will see more clearly in the next chapter).

The transition from Roman to Germanic Europe was a significant event in the history of Western Civilization. The Roman Empire had grown stagnant and despotic, and the arrival of the Germanic tribes brought a surge of fresh energy to Western Europe. Some Germanic traditions, however, were harsh by modern standards. One such tradition was trial by ordeal: a person was considered innocent if he held a red-hot bar and the burn wound healed; he was guilty if the wound did not heal. Other Germanic customs were more positive, such as the belief that royal power could never be absolute since laws were derived from the customs of the people that could not be abridged by anyone. This belief was one source of the eventual development of the principle of government by law later on. Whether harsh or positive, Germanic ideas and traditions reinvigorated Western Europe and over several centuries helped create a new civilization there.

The Germanic invasions caused the western half of Rome to fall, but the eastern half of the Roman Empire lasted for another thousand years.

THE EASTERN ROMAN, OR BYZANTINE, EMPIRE

The history of the eastern Roman Empire began when Constantine founded Constantinople in A.D. 330. The new city quickly became the center of an empire that was both Roman and Christian and that continued to thrive while western Rome was collapsing.

The eastern empire endured for several reasons. One reason was that the strategic location of Constantinople helped to block the barbarian invasions and turn the invaders westward. A second reason for its success was that the east had a stronger economic base than the west, with more productive agriculture, particularly in Egypt, and more commercial activity in the cities. A third factor in survival was that the east had deeper cultural roots than the west; the easterners often thought of themselves as "Greeks" and heirs to a civilization over a thousand years old.

During the fifth century A.D., the emperors in Constantinople did not fully comprehend the extent of the troubles in the west, for their economy was thriving and their cities were full of merchants working and philosophers teaching. When they realized that the west was disintegrating, they began to hope of reconquering the west from the Germanic tribes and restoring the Roman Empire.

Justinian

The foremost advocate of this plan was Justinian, eastern Roman emperor from A.D. 527 to 565. Aided by the advice and encouragement of his wife, the Empress Theodora, Justinian hoped to rebuild a unified Roman Empire. Much of his reign was taken up by wars, in which his armies briefly reconquered Italy, parts of North Africa, and parts of Spain. These reconquests did not endure, however, and those areas soon fell back into Germanic hands.

More successful was Justinian's effort to restore the spiritual and intellectual foundations of imperial rule. Constantinople was at this time one of the most prosperous and productive cities in the world. There, among others, was Procopius of Caesarea, who saw himself as the spiritual heir of Herodotus and Thucydides and wrote a history of the wars fought to reconquer western Rome. Also at this time a number of jurists acting on the emperor's direction, compiled and codified all existing Roman law. The *Codex Justinianus* preserved the Roman legal tradition for later ages. Justinian personally contributed to the lively atmosphere of Constantinople by directing a massive public building program. The most famous construction project in his program was the Church of Sancta Sophia ("Holy Wisdom"). The church was among the largest buildings of the time—250 feet by 220 feet—and was dominated by a dome of 107 feet in diameter. When Justinian saw the church completed, he exclaimed; "Glory to God who has judged me worthy of accomplishing such a work as this! O Solomon, I have outdone thee!"[5]

Justinian's failure to reconquer the west marks the end of the old Roman Empire and the beginning of a new Christian empire. The people of the east continued to call themselves Romans and the intellectuals continued to study the Greek classics. But the spiritual essence of the east was no longer Roman or Greek but Christian. As a result, historians refer to the eastern Roman Empire after Justinian as the Byzantine Empire, because Constantinople was built on the site of the ancient village of Byzantium.

Byzantine Christianity

Byzantine Christianity, somewhat different from the Christianity that developed in Western Europe, affected every aspect of life in the eastern empire. In politics, the Byzantine emperors were regarded as being chosen by God, and so their powers were thought to be divine. A ruler was called the "equal to the Apostles," the "God-resembling Emperor," and a "god on earth." In practice, this meant that the Byzantines adhered to a political doctrine adapted from the Persians. This doctrine was called *caesaropapism* (*caesar* means "emperor" or "head of state"; *papism* means "pope" or "head of church"), and it held that the emperor was an autocrat who controlled both state and church. Although they exercised absolute power, Byzantine emperors were still often overthrown. The common belief was that God could withdraw divine favor from an emperor at any time. Thus an emperor who was assassinated or succumbed to a rebellion was assumed to have lost divine protection. The effect of this theory was to create a murderous competition for control of the imperial throne. During the thousand-year history of the Byzantine Empire, sixty-five emperors were forced out of power and over forty of them died as a result. Only thirty-nine Byzantine emperors died peacefully of natural causes.

Byzantine Christianity stressed the transcendence and omnipotence of God, an attitude that assumed a deep chasm separated the world of God from the world of humanity. Byzantine Christians tended to be mystics, relatively uninterested in the earthly world and whose major goal was to bridge the chasm and attain spiritual reunion with God. One device thought to help in achieving spiritual reunion was the *icon*, a statue (of Jesus or one of the apostles, for example) or some other physical representation of the divine. An icon was believed to be a point of contact between the human and divine worlds.

One effect of the Byzantine religious attitude was to de-emphasize the rational powers of the human mind, for the Byzantines believed that reason and logic were incapable of penetrating the divine mysteries and so were relatively unimportant. Another effect was to encourage Byzan-

Byzantine Empress Theodora Wife of the emperor Justinian, Theodora was one of the most powerful women of ancient times. In this mosaic from the sixth century A.D., the artist portrays her in lavish robes and jewelry and with several attendants. Mosaics were a popular Byzantine art form. (Metropolitan Museum of Art, NY)

tine monks to be almost exclusively concerned with the care of their own souls. Compared to their counterparts in Western Europe, Byzantine monks were relatively unconcerned with the spiritual welfare of the larger community and uninterested in reasoning and thinking about religious doctrine. A third effect of Byzantine religion was to encourage development of a new kind of art. Most classical Greek and Roman art had been naturalistic. In the sixth century, however, the Byzantines began to develop an abstract art in which human figures were portrayed with large, piercing eyes and in a flattened form without any sense of three-dimensional space. The purpose of this art form was to lead people to the transcendent by picturing humans as seekers after spiritual peace rather than as participants in a realistic, physical world.

External and Internal Conflict

The Byzantines' obsession with spiritual peace and reunion with God may have been influenced by the conflict and chaos that characterized their world. The Byzantine Empire was constantly threatened by invaders from two directions. From the north, a succession of nomadic invaders attacked the empire regularly; first the Huns, then the Avars, and finally the Slavs. From the southeast, the original threat was from Sassanian Persia, but the Byzantine Emperor Heraclius (A.D. 610–641) managed to subdue the Persians after a long series of wars. In the process, however, both the Byzantines and the Persians were gravely weakened and left vulnerable to the rising power of Islam. The Arabs burst out of the desert in the mid-seventh century A.D., destroying the Persian Empire and taking Palestine, Syria, and Egypt from the Byzantine Empire. The Byzantine losses seriously undermined the empire, since Egypt was a major source of grain, Syria the culmination point of trade routes across Asia, and Palestine the location of major religious shrines. Arab attacks continued for years and included several sieges of Constantinople. It was not until A.D. 863 that the Byzantines were able to defeat the Arabs decisively and diminish the Arab threat for a time.

During the late seventh and eighth centuries A.D., the territorial possessions of the Byzantine Empire were reduced to Asia Minor, some parts of the Balkan peninsula, and a few areas in Italy captured during Justinian's rule. Most of Spain and Italy was lost to Germanic invaders, much of the Balkans to the Slavs, and much of the eastern Mediterranean to the Arabs. As a result, the Byzantine Empire became increasingly militarized, since the main concern of the imperial government was national defense. Large numbers of peasants were conscripted into armies and stationed permanently along the frontiers. Also during this time arose a religious controversy known as *iconoclasm* ("breaking of icons"). Many Byzantines believed that the long succession of military defeats was a punishment from God brought on by some kind of theological error. In the A.D. 720s, the Emperor Leo proclaimed that the error had to do with icons, for in his view they were an attempt to represent the spiritual in physical form and thus constituted idolatry. Over the next several decades, the government forced the destruction of numerous statues, paintings, and other forms of religious art. But many monks were icon worshippers, so the controversy became a power struggle between emperors—who sought the destruction of icons—and monks—who demanded continuation of the iconic tradition. The struggle was often violent and many monks were exiled or even killed.

Eventually, the emperors asserted their control over the monks and the church. In the mid-ninth century A.D., however, some forms of icon worship were allowed.

The End of the Byzantine Empire

For a time during the ninth century Byzantine power was revived. In A.D. 867, Basil I came to the throne and founded the Macedonian dynasty that ruled for nearly two centuries. Under the Macedonians, the Byzantine Empire recaptured some land in Asia and the Balkans. (The fighting in the Balkans was often brutal. In A.D. 1014, the Byzantines captured a Bulgarian army of fifteen thousand and blinded their prisoners, allowing each hundredth man to keep one eye so to guide the rest back to Bulgaria.) Byzantine influence also expanded to the Russian state of Kiev, which was converted to Christianity in A.D. 989.

Contacts between the Byzantines and the Slavic peoples were increasing. The Slavs—the ancestors of the Russians, the Poles, the Czechs, the Slovaks, and the Bulgars—originated in northeastern Europe and moved into eastern Europe and the Balkan peninsula at about the same time the Germanic tribes were invading Western Europe. During the ninth to eleventh centuries A.D., various Slavic peoples established states in Bulgaria, Moravia, and Poland. Many of the Slavs were gradually Christianized by the Byzantines, although the Poles and many Czechs adopted Roman Catholic Christianity. But expansion in the east was counterbalanced by loss of Byzantine influence in the west. In the eleventh century, the empire lost its last possessions in Italy. Moreover, in 1054, a split occurred between western and eastern Christianity, caused largely by the Byzantine refusal to recognize the Roman pope as the supreme leader of all Christians.

Christianity was thus divided, with the Roman Catholic Church dominating Western Europe and the Greek Orthodox Church centered in Constantinople claiming the loyalty of Greeks and most of the Slavic world. The religious split was the most prominent aspect of a larger cultural split, for Byzantines and western Europeans were increasingly perceiving each other as religious, political, and military rivals. This rivalry intensified during the Crusades of the eleventh to thirteenth centuries (discussed in greater detail in Chapter 8). The Crusades were a response to the capture of Palestine late in the eleventh century by the Seljuk Turks (central Asian nomads who converted to Islam). Both Byzantine and western European Christians agreed that the Holy Land (Palestine) had to be restored to Christian control, and for two hundred years Crusader armies fought, unsuccessfully, to retake the area. At first, the Byzantines and the Europeans cooperated against the common enemy, but the Europeans soon turned on their allies largely because the church split of 1054 made them regard the Byzantines as heretics. In 1204, a European Crusader army attacked and captured Constantinople, an event that marks the beginning of the end of the Byzantine Empire. The Byzantines later managed to retake their capital, but the empire was gravely weakened. Then, in the fourteenth century, there appeared a new enemy: the Ottoman Turks. Over several decades, the Ottomans conquered Byzantine territory and, in 1453, took Constantinople, thereby bringing the Byzantine Empire to an end.

The Byzantine Empire was destroyed because it was caught between two rising powers—the Muslim Turks from the east and the European Christians from the west. With its destruction, the last remnant of the old Roman Empire disappeared. But during its thousand-year history, the Byzantine Empire made a number of significant contributions to human history. Among the most important contributions in terms of the history of Western Civilization was the Byzantines' preservation of much of the Greco-Roman cultural heritage, passing it on to both the Arabs and the western Europeans. The Byzantines also brought much of the Slavic world within the realm of Christian culture and civilization. And, by continually fighting off Asian and Arabic invaders, they unintentionally helped to protect Western Europe and thereby made it easier for Europeans to build the foundations of a new civilization.

ISLAM

The rise of the religion of Islam was significant in several respects. It marked the creation of a new world religion during a time when major religious changes were taking place, especially the change from the old animistic religions in the Mediterranean to monotheism (Judaism, Christianity, and Islam). It also marked the emergence of the Arabic peoples as an influential force in world history. And, the rise of Islam was the last phase in the transformation of the Roman unification of the Mediterranean into three new cultural and religious realms.

Islam originated in Arabia. For centuries Arabia played only a peripheral role in the great events occurring throughout Eurasia, since it lacked both the population base and the political unity necessary to be influential. It was primarily important as a transit area, through which passed caravans carrying goods between Asia and the Mediterranean. Agriculture was common only in the Yemen, the southern part of the Arabian peninsula. Most of Arabia consisted of waterless deserts and steppes, punctuated only by an occasional oasis. Small communities existed around each oasis, but much of the population were members of Bedouin tribes that wandered the deserts. Most Arabs practiced some form of polytheistic nature religion.

Muhammad

The traditional Arabic world was transformed largely by one man—Muhammad. Born sometime after A.D. 570, Muhammad became a trader and merchant in the small caravan town of Mecca. Mecca was one of the few Arabic areas that had much contact with the non-Arabic world, and as a result Muhammad became familiar with the Jewish and Christian religious traditions. At about the age of forty, Muhammad experienced a religious conversion and felt called by Allah (the Arabic word for "God") to preach to the Meccans. Many Meccan businesspeople disliked Muhammad's preaching, both because he opposed traditional Arabic religion and because his preaching disrupted their business. As a result, in A.D. 622, he was forced to flee from Mecca to Yathrib (later named Medina), where he had a few supporters. This flight, known to Muslims as the *Hegira* ("flight" or "exodus"), was a turning point in Muhammad's career, and eventually the year 622 was designated as the first year of the Muslim calendar. From then on Muhammad's powerful personality and his appeal of monotheism, which was more coherent than traditional polytheism, induced many Arabs to convert to Islam. When Muhammad died in A.D. 632, Islam was the dominant Arabic religion.

According to Muhammad, Islam was the last and greatest revelation from God, the culmination of an ancient religious tradition that began with the Hebrew patriarch, Abraham. (Thus Islam was the latest manifestation of an Axial Period religion.) God called Abraham to follow him, and Judaism eventually evolved from that call. Christianity developed later, after God called Jesus, who Muhammad regarded as a prophet but not the Son of God. Since neither Jews nor Christians had properly followed God's commands, God called his last and greatest prophet—Muhammad—to found Islam, the supreme embodiment of the divine revelation.

The Islamic Faith

Like Judaism and Christianity, Islam is a faith in one God who judges people, eventually sending the righteous to paradise and the wicked to hell. But there are differences in the attitude toward humans. Judaism and Christianity often portray humans as relatively strong-willed creatures prone to rebel (sin) against God. Islam, however, regards humans as weak and ignorant, needing guidance from God on how to live and what to believe. The word *Islam* means "submission to God," and a *Muslim* is "one who submits." Through submission the believer is directed to worship God through performance of the Five Pillars of Islam: (1) accepting the confession of faith that states "there is no God but Allah, and Muhammad is his prophet"; (2) praying five times a day at appointed times; (3) giving alms to the poor; (4) fasting from daybreak to sunset

Muhammad A line engraving showing an artist's conception of Muhammad, Arab prophet and founder of Islam. (The Granger Collection)

during the holy month of Ramadan; and (5) making a pilgrimage to Mecca at least once in a lifetime.

Further guidance for the believer is contained in the *Koran,* the Islamic holy book compiled by Muhammad's followers. The Koran is a collection of the revelations that God made to Muhammad and is regarded by most Muslims as the literal words of God. Every Muslim is expected as an act of worship to memorize and recite some of the Koran. Here is one example of a commonly memorized passage:

> In the name of God, the Merciful, the Compassionate: Praise belongs to God, Lord of all Being; the Merciful, the Compassionate; Master of Judgment Day. Thee we serve, on Thee we call for help. Guide us in the straight path, the path of those whom Thou art bounteous to, not those whom anger falls on, nor those who go astray.[6]

Another source of authority for Islamic followers is the *hadith,* a collection of the teachings of Muhammad compiled after his death.

No official priesthood exists in Islam, so any Muslim can perform the rituals. However, those known as *imans* or *ayatollahs* are recognized as spiritual leaders. Also, there is an informal group of religious scholars or

Suleymaneye Mosque, Istanbul (16th century A.D.) Muslims built numerous mosques as sites for public religious worship. The mosques are characterized by domed roofs and minarets, high slender towers from which the call to prayer was chanted at the appointed times of the day. (Turkish Tourist Office)

clergy called the *ulema*, whose role is to explain the teachings contained in the Koran and hadith. The ulema are expected to explain and transmit Muhammad's teachings, not to think or give their own opinions. (An ulema said once, "Piss on my opinion.")[7] The teachings in the Koran and hadith guide all aspects of Muslim life, including what Muslims can eat, how they can dress, punishments for crimes, relations between the sexes, and so on. Some of the teachings encourage toleration and love toward others. Muhammad taught, for example, that "the Arab is not superior to the non-Arab; the non-Arab is not superior to the Arab. You are all sons of Adam, and Adam was made of earth."[8] Other teachings, however, express an attitude of intolerance. Women are regarded as inferior to men in Muslim societies. They have no identity outside the family and are always under the control of a male. (In the twentieth century, some Muslim women began to assert their independence from male control.) The subjugation of women eventually led to the required practice of wearing a veil over their faces when in public, the idea being that no male outside the family should see the face of a mature woman. Another example of intolerance is the Muslim belief (here similar to Christian belief) that only they know the truth of God and that this truth applies to everyone. This belief justified the practice of holy war (*jihad*), by which Muslims sought to conquer non-Muslim societies.

Islam Expands

Holy wars dominated Arab history in the decades after Muhammad's death. *Caliphs* (or "successors") were selected to act as both political and religious leaders, and they led a series of conquests. In A.D. 636, the Arabs took Syria and Palestine from the Byzantine Empire. In 637, they conquered the Sassanian Persian Empire, and in 640–641 seized Egypt from the Byzantines. Thus, within five years the Arabs overran much of what had been the eastern half of the Roman Empire and in the process destroyed most of the influence of Greco-Roman culture in the east (much like the Germanic tribes destroyed it in the west). The Arabs were successful in part because the Byzantine and Persian empires had weakened in fighting each other and in part because religious zeal and overpopulation in Arabia impelled the Arabs to expand.

To govern the new acquisitions, the Caliph Muawiya founded the Umayyad dynasty in A.D. 661. Under the Umayyads, the Arab capital was Damascus and the government was a monarchy supported by a military aristocracy who dominated the conquered peoples. Military expansion continued, as Arab armies pushed eastward all the way to India. In the west they drove across North Africa; in A.D. 711 they launched an invasion of Spain and were quickly victorious. The growth of Arab power was soon halted, however. In A.D. 717–718, the Byzantines defeated the Arab siege of Constantinople, thereby ensuring the survival of their empire. In 733, the Frankish warlord Charles Martel defeated an Arab army at Poitiers (known today as Tours) in southern France, so further Arab expansion into Western Europe was blocked. Most of Europe remained independent of the Muslim world. But by the early eighth century A.D., the Muslim world included Spain, all of North Africa, Syria and Palestine, Arabia, Persia, Afghanistan, and parts of India.

Despite this expansion, the power of the Umayyad Caliphate was gradually undermined by two forces. One was feuds among the Arabs. The vast majority of Arabs were *Sunni, or orthodox*, Muslims, but they were opposed by a minority that became known as *Shiite* Muslims. The Shiites were originally a political faction that claimed the Umayyads had usurped power from Muhammad's cousin, Ali, and his descendants. However, they soon became a source of both political and religious opposition to the Sunni majority. The other force that undermined the power of the Umayyads was Islam itself, for all Muslims—Arab and non-Arab—were considered equal. Consequently, the Arab population was quickly outnumbered by non-Arab converts to Islam. These converts,

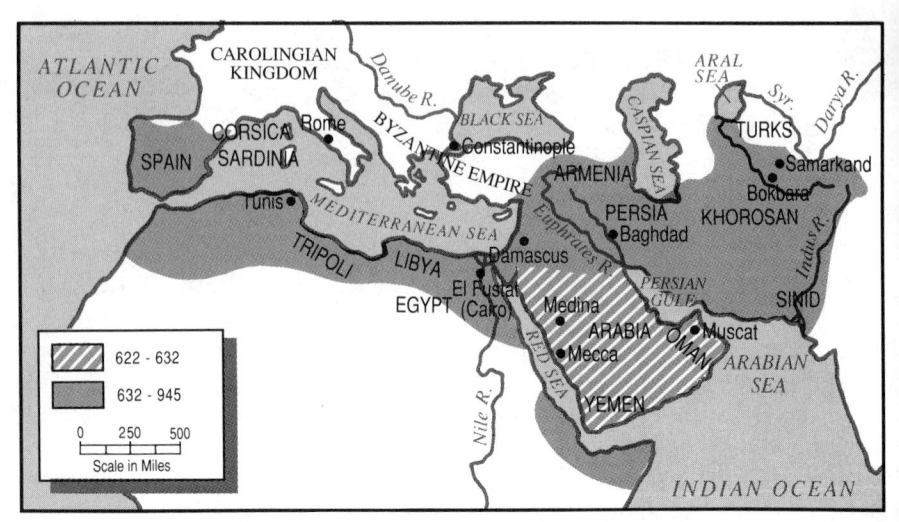

Figure 6.2 The Spread of Islam, A.D. 622–945

many of whom were urban merchants and artisans, disliked the militarism of the Arab aristocracy and wanted a new, more stable social order in which trade and agriculture would be more important than war. The tensions created by these two forces led to the Abbasid revolution of A.D. 747–750, which replaced the Umayyad dynasty with a new Abbasid Caliphate.

With the Abbasid revolution, the nature of the Muslim world changed. It was no longer controlled only by Arabs, for the Abbasids treated all Muslims equally and used Islam rather than Arab ethnic unity as the binding force of their empire. The capital was moved to Baghdad, where the caliphs became autocrats who called themselves the "Shadow of God upon Earth" and claimed that God gave them the power to rule. The caliphs governed through a bureaucracy, chosen by merit from both Arabs and non-Arabs.

Islamic Society and Culture

The Abbasid Caliphate lasted from A.D. 750 to 1258. During most of that period the Islamic Empire was both powerful and prosperous, since it was at the center of both north–south and east–west trade routes. Furs from Scandinavia came to Baghdad, as did gold and slaves from Africa. Silks and spices came from India and China, some of which were transported on to north Africa and Spain. Also from India came the new nine-digit numerical system that later became known in Europe as arabic numerals. In addition, scientific knowledge was exchanged with China. The following account tells of an Arab physician who passed his knowledge of an ancient Greek scientist named Galen to a Chinese scholar:

> A Chinese scholar came to my house and remained in the town about a year. In five months he learnt to speak and write Arabic. When he decided to return to his country, he said to me a month or so beforehand, "I am about to leave. I would be glad if someone would dictate to me the sixteen books of Galen before I go." . . . So together with one of my students we read Galen to him as fast as we could, but he wrote still faster.[9]

The cultural and intellectual life of the Islamic world reached its height during the tenth to twelfth centuries A.D. Contact with China and India as well as knowledge of the Greek philosophical and scientific heritage stimulated an explosion of Islamic talent and creativity. Avicenna, an eleventh-century philosopher and physician, wrote *The Canon of Medicine*, which became a basic source of medical knowledge both in the Islamic world and later in Europe. Averroes, a twelfth-century philosopher, composed commentaries on Plato and Aristotle, which helped revive interest in Greek philosophy in Europe. And, in the eleventh century, the astronomer Al-Biruni postulated the revolutionary theory that the earth revolves around the sun, an idea that nobody at the time accepted. Many other innovations were also developed. Eye surgery was performed in several of the larger cities, and glass-making became a major industry. Windmills were common in some rural areas, and in some places, a sweet, cool drink known as sherbet was available.

Islamic art also flourished, emphasizing the depiction of natural forms because Islam prohibited the display of human forms in art. The most notable Islamic style was known as *arabesque*. Arabesque is a highly ornamental art form that stresses elaborate designs, infinite patterns, and graceful flourishes. The style is so intricate and complex as to suggest a source of inspiration beyond the natural world. One example is the Topkapi Palace at Constantinople, the interior of which is decorated with so many representations of flowers and trees that it resembles a flower garden. Another is the Alhambra Palace in Granada, Spain, in which virtually all interior surface areas are covered with vivid colors and geometric designs.

The political unity of the Islamic world began to weaken in the ninth and tenth centuries A.D. Local governments in Egypt, North Africa, and Spain asserted independence from the central government in Baghdad. Then, in the late eleventh century, a growing spirit of religious conservatism began to stifle the creative impulses of Islamic learning and scholarship. In 1258, the Mongols, a nomadic people from Mongolia in northern China, captured Baghdad and ended the Abbasid Caliphate. After that, the Islamic world remained important in many ways, and

Islam continued to expand in Asia. The great days of political power and intellectual creativity, however, were over.

CONCLUSION

The centuries between A.D. 400 and 700 were a chaotic time around the Mediterranean Sea, but by shortly after 700 three cultural areas were clearly demarcated: the Germanic in Western Europe, the Byzantine, and the Muslim. The Muslims dominated the southern and eastern Mediterranean, but their defeat at Constantinople in A.D. 717–718 ensured the independence of the Byzantine Empire, and their loss at Poitiers (Tours) in A.D. 733 guaranteed the autonomy of Western Europe. One of the ironies of the time was that these three cultures were very much alike but continually hostile to one another. They shared a monotheistic religion inherited from the Hebrews and together cultivated the Greco-Roman cultural heritage. Yet, despite—or perhaps because of—their similarities, the three fought one another during the seventh to eighth centuries and would fight again later in the Crusades (see Chapter 8).

Finally, it is significant that after A.D. 700 the Mediterranean Sea was no longer a major center of civilization. The Byzantine Empire was in the northeastern Mediterranean, the center of the Islamic world shifted eastward toward Persia, and the center of Western Christian culture shifted northward into the heart of Europe. It was there in Europe that a dynamic new civilization would develop—our focus in the following chapters.

THINGS YOU SHOULD KNOW

Constantinople
The Huns
The Han dynasty in China
Hindu-Arabic numeral system
Gupta Age in India
The Germanic tribes
Justinian
Byzantine Christianity
Iconoclasm

The Slavs
Muhammad
Basic teachings of Islam
Expansion of Islam
Umayyad dynasty
Abbasid Caliphate
Islamic philosophy, art, and medicine

SUGGESTED READINGS

Edward Gibbon, *The Decline and Fall of the Roman Empire* (Baltimore: Penguin, 1983) is the classic work on the decline of Rome. C. Warren Hollister, *Medieval Europe: A Short History* (New York: McGraw, 1982) and William R. Cook and

Ronald B. Herzman, *The Medieval World View: An Introduction* (New York: Oxford Univ. Press, 1983) contain good discussions of the Germanic migrations into the Roman Empire. Two good introductions to the Byzantine Empire are Robert Browning, *The Byzantine Empire* (New York: Scribner's, 1980) and D. A. Miller, *The Byzantine Tradition* (New York: Harper & Row, 1966). A more detailed work, on the wife of the Emperor Justinian, is Antony Bridge, *Theodora: Portrait in a Byzantine Landscape* (Chicago: Academy Chi. Pubs., 1984). On Islam, Marshall G. S. Hodgson, *The Venture of Islam*, vol. 1: *The Classical Age of Islam* (Chicago: Univ. of Chicago Press, 1974) is excellent. A good biography of Muhammad is W. Montgomery Watt, *Muhammad: Prophet and Statesman* (New York: Oxford Univ. Press, 1974). Also important are Bernard Lewis, *The Arabs in History* (New York: Harper & Row, 1966) and R. M. Savory (ed.), *Introduction to Islamic Civilization* (Cambridge, Engl.: Cambridge Univ. Press, 1976).

NOTES

[1] Peter Brown, *The World of Late Antiquity*, A.D. *150–750* (New York: Harcourt, 1971), p. 8.

[2] Quoted in William R. Cook and Ronald B. Herzman, *The Medieval World View: An Introduction* (New York: Oxford Univ. Press, 1983), pp. 128–29.

[3] *Ibid.*, pp. 127–28.

[4] C. Warren Hollister, "Twilight in the West," Lynn White, Jr.(ed.), *The Transformation of the Roman World: Gibbon's Problem After Two Centuries* (Berkeley: Univ. of California Press, 1966), p. 179.

[5] Quoted in Robert Browning, *The Byzantine Empire* (New York: Scribner's, 1980), pp. 39–40.

[6] Quoted in Marshall G. S. Hodgson, *The Venture of Islam*, vol. 1, *The Classical Age of Islam* (Chicago: Univ. of Chicago Press, 1974), p. 185.

[7] Quoted in Michael Cook, "The Emergence of Islamic Civilization," in *The Origins and Diversity of Axial Age Civilizations*, ed. S. N. Eisenstadt (Albany: State Univ. of New York Press, 1986), p. 482.

[8] Quoted in Joseph Needham, *Within the Four Seas: The Dialogue of East and West* (Toronto: Univ. of Toronto Press, 1969), p. 208.

[9] Quoted in L. S. Stavrianos, *A Global History: The Human Heritage*, 3rd ed. (Englewood Cliffs, N.J.: Prentice-Hall, 1983), pp. 124, 126.

7

The Early Middle Ages: A Dynamic Frontier, 500 to 1000

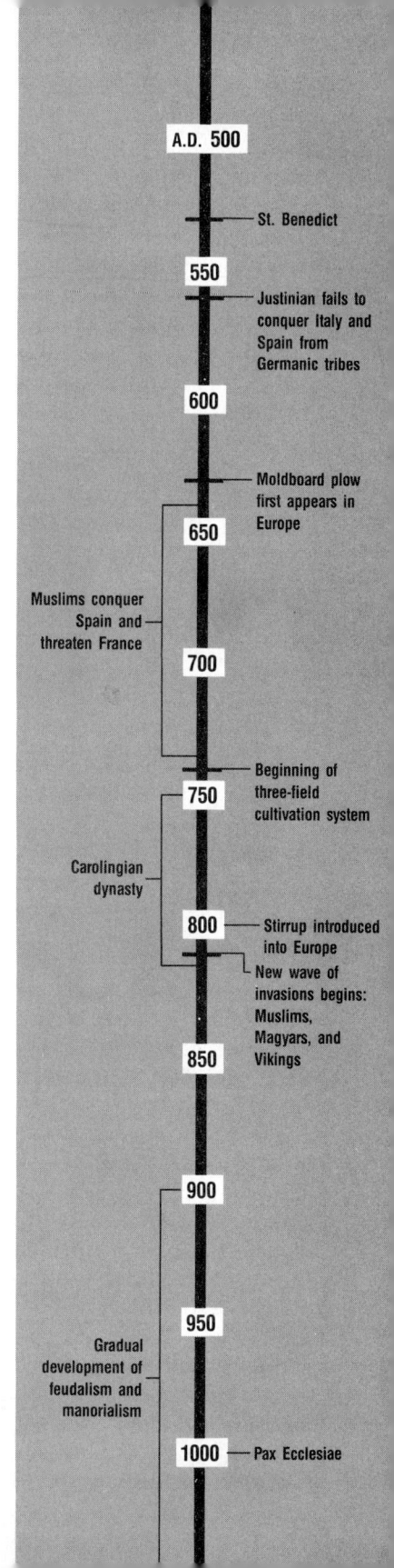

A.D. 500	
	St. Benedict
550	
	Justinian fails to conquer Italy and Spain from Germanic tribes
600	
	Moldboard plow first appears in Europe
650	
	Muslims conquer Spain and threaten France
700	
	Beginning of three-field cultivation system
750	
	Carolingian dynasty
800	Stirrup introduced into Europe
	New wave of invasions begins: Muslims, Magyars, and Vikings
850	
900	
950	
	Gradual development of feudalism and manorialism
1000	Pax Ecclesiae

European history from roughly A.D. 500 to 1400–1500 is traditionally designated as the *Middle Ages,* or the *medieval* period, because it came between ancient history and modern history. The traditional term for the early Middle Ages is the *Dark Ages,* since it was a time of decline in comparison with the highly developed civilizations of the ancient world. In many respects, the so-called Dark Ages were a bad time; most governmental structures disappeared, educational and social institutions collapsed, and economic conditions were harsh. Historian Georges Duby describes early medieval Europe this way:

> A mere handful of men—unending emptiness stretching so far west, north, and east that it covers everything . . . clearings here and there, wrested from the forest but still only half-tamed; within this food-producing area . . . huts of stone, mud, or branches, clustered in hamlets surrounded by thorn hedges and a belt of gardens; . . . sparsely scattered towns, the mere whitened skeletons of Roman cities invaded by rural nature, streets in ruins . . . , fortifications haphazardly repaired, stone structures dating back to the Roman Empire that have been turned into churches or strongholds.[1]

Despite the harsh living conditions of the early Middle Ages, it is somewhat of a misnomer to refer to this period as the Dark Ages. Western Europe at this time was more like a dynamic frontier in two senses: (1) it was a relatively underpopulated area, much of it untamed by human settlement; and (2) this was a time of great creativity, when a new civilization—Western European Civilization—was being born. As the historian L. S. Stavrianos remarks, "It was an age of birth as well as of death, and to concentrate on the latter is to miss the dynamism and significance of a seminal phase of human history."[2]

THE SIXTH TO EIGHTH CENTURIES

Western Europe was buffeted by successive waves of migrations and invasions between the sixth and eighth centuries. The various Germanic tribes fought one another sporadically for control of land. The Byzantine Empire under the rule of Justinian tried to reconquer Italy and Spain in the sixth century. Arab armies subdued Spain and threatened France in the eighth century. Constant violence and warfare changed the way people lived. Travel and communications were difficult, so political and economic life became concentrated on the local level. Long-distance commerce all but vanished. Architecture was modified, as the wealthy sought protection by building their homes like fortresses with thick walls and small windows. The poor sought help from the wealthy, but, as usual, they suffered the most. Archaeological finds from this time commonly include skeletons and bones deformed by malnutrition.

A few educated people realized the significance of the disappearance of Roman civilization. Pope Gregory the Great wrote in the late sixth century, "For where is the Senate? Where is the People? The bones are all dissolved, the flesh is consumed, all the pomp of the dignities of this world is gone. The whole mass is boiled away."[3] A few scholars tried to preserve the Greco-Roman cultural heritage. Cassiodorus (480–575), for example, helped Christianize the Ostrogoths in Italy and transcribed several ancient manuscripts to ensure their survival. Boethius (c. 480–524) wrote the *Consolation of Philosophy*, one of the last ancient works to look to pre-Christian philosophy for spiritual truth and comfort.

Preserving the Greco-Roman heritage was important, for it became one of the elements from which Western European Civilization would be formed. The other two elements important to Western European Civilization were the spiritual and moral tradition of Christianity and the political and cultural tradition of the Germanic peoples who now populated most of Europe. These three elements were first brought together by monks and nuns—people who withdrew from ordinary society to devote their lives to God—who more than anyone else converted the Germans to Christianity and also preserved the Greco-Roman heritage for later ages.

CONTRIBUTIONS OF MONKS AND NUNS

In 597, Pope Gregory the Great sent a mission of monks to England to convert the Angles and Saxons, who practiced animistic religions, to Christianity. His mission found that a movement of Irish monks had already developed in western Scotland, Ireland, and Wales. According to legend, many Irish had been converted to Christianity by St. Patrick in the mid-fifth century. The Irish monks were unique in that they followed a tradition of pilgrimage and voluntary exile from their native land, going wherever God called them to go. One story, for example, tells of three monks ". . . who stole away from Ireland in a boat without any oars because they would live in a state of pilgrimage for the love of God, they recked not where."[4]

During the seventh and eighth centuries, Irish monks migrated throughout much of Western Europe, establishing dozens of monasteries and converting large numbers of German peasants to Christianity. The monks were joined by thousands of nuns, many of whom built large convents that controlled great amounts of land. Hilda of Whitby, for example, founded and governed several large monasteries in England in the seventh century, and Herlinda of Eika (Belgium) became known in the eighth century as a skillful copier of manuscripts. For both women and men in the early Middle Ages, the monastic life offered a sanctuary for those who were especially devout and provided a center of activity for those who were especially ambitious.

The Benedictine Rule

As monasticism spread, it gradually became organized according to the *Rule* of St. Benedict of Nursia (480–543). Benedict was an extraordinary individual who, like many others of his time, felt an intense antagonism between the temptations of the flesh and the pious, spiritual life he wanted to live. The following medieval account tells of how he overcame a temptation:

> For the evil spirit brought back before the mind's eye a certain woman whom he had once seen. So intensely did the Tempter inflame his mind by the sight of that woman that he could hardly control his passion. . . . Then suddenly God graciously looked upon him and he returned to himself . . . he stripped off his garments and flung himself naked upon stinging thorns and burning nettles. He rolled about there for a long time, and came out with his whole body wounded by them. So through the wound of his skin he drew out from his body the wound of the mind by changing the lust to pain.[5]

Benedict's spiritual struggles led him to found a monastery at Monte Cassino, Italy. There he developed a set of regulations to govern himself and his fellow monks. This *Rule* quickly came to dominate the lives of most monks and nuns in Western Europe.

Although the Benedictine *Rule* may seem overly demanding to us, to early medieval people it was considered moderate and reasonable. Benedict stipulated that the monk or nun had to take vows of poverty and chastity, giving up all private property and sexual gratification. Those who took the vows were expected to devote their lives to the service of God and to achieve salvation. Their daily schedule was strictly regulated—the first prayer service was held around 2:30 A.M. and followed by seven more scattered throughout the day until the last one at 7 P.M. In addition to the prayer services, there were periods set aside for reading and study and for agricultural labor to produce the food needed. This routine was followed daily, except in extraordinary circumstances.

Benedictine monasticism was different from that in other parts of the world. Buddhist monasticism, for example, denied the value of manual labor, and Buddhist monks lived by charity rather than by their own work. Byzantine monasticism stressed mysticism, and the monks lived in isolation from the rest of the world and denigrated human reason. Both were unlike the Benedictines, who read books, farmed, and performed charitable and educational activities for local peasants. In comparison with the Buddhists and the Byzantines, Benedictine monks were more practical and more interested in worldly affairs. This worldly orientation had a significant impact on at least three aspects of Western Civilization: (1) Western conceptions of time, (2) Western attitudes toward education and learning, and (3) Western beliefs about the value of manual labor.

St. Benedict A fifteenth-century drawing of St. Benedict giving instructions to two monks. St. Benedict, who established many of the rules that now govern monks around the world, founded twelve monasteries in Italy that eventually became the centers of European monasticism. (Pierpont Morgan Library)

In the ancient world, time was a vague concept. People lived by the rhythms of nature, rising at sunrise and going to sleep at sundown. They were not concerned with the "time of day" as we are today. Although medieval peasants also lived by the rhythms of nature, the Benedictines and some other Christians were interested in time measurement. According to Benedict, "Idleness is the enemy of the soul," and so he established an elaborate schedule to absorb the energies of monks and nuns. Punctuality was important in this schedule, for lateness might make it necessary to shorten a prayer service. The importance of being on time was expressed by the English monk, Bede: "I know that the angels are present at the canonical hours, and what if they do not find me among the brethren when they assemble? Will they not say, where is Bede? Why does he not attend the appointed devotions with his brethren?"[6] This Benedictine concern with punctuality and schedules would slowly help to develop a growing Western consciousness of time. The late Middle Ages would see the invention of the mechanical clock (the importance of which is discussed in Chapter 8).

The Benedictines also exhibited a new attitude toward education, for they believed that reading and copying books was a form of worship. Cassiodorus said once:

> Oh, blessed the perseverance, laudable the industry which preaches to men with the hand, starts tongues with the fingers, gives an unspoken salvation to mortals and against the iniquitous deceits of the Devil fights with pen and ink. For Satan receives as many wounds as the scribe copies words of the Lord.[7]

Monks and nuns respected books and in many cases organized monastic schools for the local population. Their interest in education was a decisive departure in Western history, for the Benedictines were the first organized group to do both intellectual and manual labor. In the ancient world, the two forms of labor were divided socially, with intellectual labor reserved for the educated upper classes and manual labor assigned to slaves and the lower classes. The monks helped to weaken the social barrier between the intellectual and the manual and thus helped create in Western history a respect for learning that was both theoretical and practical. This new attitude would eventually lead to modern science, in that it encouraged early scientists' interest in pure scientific thought and in practical experimentation.

The ancient world generally associated manual labor with slaves and viewed it as degrading. That monks and nuns gardened and did other work with their hands began to impart a new dignity to the performance of manual labor. Christianity developed more of a mixed attitude. In Genesis, for example, labor is portrayed as a punishment for sin—"by the sweat of thy face shalt thou eat bread" (Genesis 3:19). But the Apostle Paul supported the value of work—"if any would not work, neither should he eat" (2 Thessalonians 3:10). Benedict stated that "to labor is to pray" and stipulated that monks should work regularly. The Benedictines did not regard manual labor as good in itself; rather, it was a form of penitence for sin and a remedy for the idleness that could invite temptations from the devil. Nevertheless, since monks and nuns were the most admired people in the early Middle Ages, their work had the effect of slowly raising the social and spiritual prestige of labor, even though the upper classes continued to shun manual labor. Other factors also contributed, most notably the reality that in a frontier society manual labor was necessary for survival.

The Benedictines were the first in Western history to place a spiritual value on work. This attitude later helped to produce the Western belief that work (in the sense of practical, productive activity) is both socially useful and spiritually important.

THE PEASANTS CREATE AN AGRICULTURAL REVOLUTION

At the same time that the Benedictines were dignifying manual labor, the peasants—who still did most of that work—were creating the first of several European agricultural revolutions. This revolution would eventually enable Europe to be more productive than ancient Rome or Greece had ever been. The ancient Roman and Greek economies were based on slave labor, which did not foster technological creativity and thus caused economic production to remain at a low level, leaving most people to live in poverty. Medieval society, however, encouraged creativity and thus developed several technological innovations that increased agricultural productivity and provided a foundation for a better economy.

The medieval agricultural revolution was carried out by large numbers of ordinary peasants whose names we do not know; it was, in a sense, a democratic revolution. The peasants adapted farming techniques to local conditions all over Europe and, in the process, slowly learned better ways of doing things. The first agricultural breakthrough was a new moldboard plow (see the Technology box).

The moldboard plow changed the lives of peasants in several ways. Since the plow required several oxen for its operation and few peasants had more than one or two oxen, they had to pool their animals and work together. This led to a communal farming system, in which the peasants of a community worked in one large field with each being entitled to a certain share of the produce. In addition, cattle were allowed to graze on another large field that was left fallow for the next year's planting, so their droppings fertilized the soil. In some places, manure piles became recognized as a sign of wealth.

Another agricultural breakthrough was the substitution of a three-field system for the earlier two-field one. In the sixth and seventh centuries, most peasant villages divided their land in half, with one field being cultivated each year and the other lying fallow so that soil nutrients could be naturally replenished. But increased manure from animals so enriched the soil that in the eighth century some peasants north of the Alps moved to a three-field system. By dividing land into thirds and cultivating one field in autumn and another in spring, these peasants increased the amount of land farmed each year from one-half to two-thirds. The result, of course, was increased productivity.

The horse was the focus of other agricultural innovations in the ninth century. The Romans had been unable to use the horse with their scratch plow, since the harness was simply a lasso placed around the neck that choked the animal when it pulled anything heavy. They used either oxen or slaves to pull the plows, both of which were slow and inefficient. Two inventions in early medieval times—the shoulder harness and the horseshoe—enabled peasants to use the horse, faster and cheaper than the ox, to operate the moldboard plow in Europe. The shoulder harness was probably developed in central Asia and brought to Europe in the ninth century. It allowed animals to pull greater weights. The horseshoe, which appeared in Europe by the ninth century, protected the horse's hooves from breaking or wearing down.

The life-style of the peasant gradually improved as a result of this agricultural revolution. The most basic improvement was an increase in the amount of food grown. Another was the opportunity for peasants to live in larger communities. A horse could move faster than an ox, so peasants could live further from their fields and congregate in villages of several hundred people rather than in small hamlets. The village offered greater safety, access to a church, and in some cases the availability of water-powered grain mills (the mills are discussed in the Chapter 8 Technology box).

Why were European peasants more willing and able than their ancient counterparts to invent or develop so many new agricultural technologies? There are at least five interrelated answers to this question.

1. Medieval peasants were more free than ancient peasants. While most ancient peasants were actually slaves under the control of their owners, medieval peasants were either free citizens or serfs (farm workers controlled by an upper-class authority) and were often able to make their own decisions about how to farm.
2. Medieval peasants lived on a frontier and had to be creative in order to survive. They thus had to develop new tools to meet new conditions, such as the moldboard plow discussed in the Technology box.
3. The peasants, most of whom were of Germanic descent, inherited a tradition of developing innovations to cope with the cold climate of northern Europe. Over the centuries, the Germans either invented or adopted from other peoples the chimney and the easily heated compact house, trousers and sleeves, and the ski.
4. The successive waves of invasions of Europe—by the Germans, Byzantines, Arabs, Slavs, and so on—destroyed most of the old customs and habits derived from Roman civilization. Thus, Europeans had to begin anew.
5. Christianity's conception of nature gradually encouraged Europeans to exploit the natural world more aggressively. As discussed in Chapter 3, the Judaeo-Christian perception of God as transcendent and separate from nature encouraged the idea that nature is spiritless or inanimate. The early Germans did not share this conception, since they perceived nature as full of divinity and spirit. As they became Christianized, however, the Germans slowly modified their conceptions of religion and nature. Peasants, for example, began to pray to Christian saints rather than to spirits in

TECHNOLOGY
The Moldboard Plow

The Romans and other ancient peoples had used a scratch plow that simply had a blade to split the soil. The scratch plow barely broke the surface of the soil, although it was adequate for the thin soil of Mediterranean lands. The wet, thick soil of the northern parts of Europe required a heavier, more efficient tool—the moldboard plow. We do not know with certainty the precise origin of the moldboard plow, but it was probably developed sometime in the sixth century A.D. by the Slavic peoples of eastern Europe. The moldboard plow appeared in parts of France and northern Italy in the seventh century, in Germany by the eighth century, and in England by the ninth century.

The real innovation was in the way the plow cut the soil. A knife, at the front of the frame, cut the soil vertically to make it easier for the "share" behind it to split the soil horizontally down to the grass-roots. Behind the share was the moldboard, a curved board diagonal to the frame, which lifted the cut sod and threw it to the side. Wheels on the front allowed the relatively large plow to be moved more easily.

The two most important advantages of the moldboard plow were (1) its effectiveness in the wet soils of northern and Western Europe and (2) its ability to cut deeply into more nutrient-rich soil. The result was an increase in agricultural production for many medieval peasants.

The Moldboard Plow *In this drawing (c. 1340), English peasants are using the moldboard plow. The knife in the front of the plow cut the soil, the share behind it and parallel to the ground split the soil, and the long moldboard turned over the soil. (The Granger Collection)*

nature. Over several centuries, peasants gradually came to perceive nature as spiritless and to believe that they could use nature without fear of retribution from any gods or spirits. This change in perspective occurred slowly and haltingly. Furthermore, it was not a complete break with the past, for peasants had always used nature to some extent. Nevertheless, European peasants were evolving a more aggressive attitude toward nature, and one reason for that was their different conception of the natural world. The question of why Byzantine Christianity did not also create a more aggressive attitude toward nature is an interesting one. One possible reason may be that Byzantine Christianity was more contemplative and less action oriented than Western Christianity. The Byzantine Christians taught, for example, that sin largely results from theological error, whereas Western Christians tended to think of sin as wrong action. Our example reveals a fundamental difference: Byzantine Christianity evolved a relatively passive attitude toward many earthly things including nature, whereas Western Christianity was more aggressive in its attitude toward nature and other earthly things.

Taken as a whole, the medieval agricultural revolution was one of the most significant developments in the history of Western Civilization. Its short-term effects were to expand the food supply and allow populations to grow and cities to develop, thereby providing the foundation for the creativity of the High Middle Ages (discussed in Chapter 8). It also helped to eliminate slavery in Western Europe, since the growing use of animal-powered plows reduced the need for human labor. The long-term effect of the agricultural revolution stands out even more clearly, for it displayed the technological creativity that is a fundamental characteristic of Western history.

It is important to remember that this very significant revolution was carried out by people who by twentieth-century standards were ignorant and superstitious. Medieval peasants were capable both of thinking clearly enough to develop new technologies and of believing things that later ages would regard as wildly improbable. For example, a popular story of early medieval times tells of a bishop who drove away a serpent dragon that was terrorizing the population of Paris. Another story tells of a young man who married a beautiful stranger that turned out to be a dragon. To drive off the evil spirit, the young man sprinkled holy water on his wife, who promptly jumped over their house, screamed, and vanished into thin air. The peasants were regarded with contempt by their economic and social superiors. In medieval literature, they are portrayed at best as nameless creatures who did the manual labor, at worst as barely human monsters who lived in dark forests and frightened those who traveled. The peasants were innovators unrecognized in their own time.

THE CAROLINGIAN EMPIRE

The emergence of the Carolingian dynasty brought a brief period of political stability to the early Middle Ages. It is named after its greatest ruler, Charlemagne, or Charles the Great (from the Latin *Carolus* meaning "Charles"). The greatest years of the Carolingian dynasty extended from 751 to 814, and at its height it governed much of Western Europe, including today's France, Belgium, the Netherlands, the western half of Germany, and northern Italy.

The Carolingian empire was largely agrarian—there were a few towns such as Aachen and Lyons—an empire without cities and held together by rulers who were regularly on the move and fighting to maintain their power. Its origins can be traced to the late fifth century, when the Franks conquered Roman Gaul, which then became known as Frankland and later as France. But the empire developed only in the eighth century when a series of Frankish warlords asserted control. First was Charles Martel, whose armies defeated the Arabs at Poitiers (Tours) in 733, and thus helped prevent a Muslim conquest of Europe. Then came his son, Pepin the Short (751–768), who strengthened his power by forging an alliance with the pope. It was Pepin's son, Charles (768–814), who became Charlemagne, the greatest of the Carolingian rulers.

Charlemagne was in many ways a barbarian warrior. He was a tall, potbellied man who enjoyed the pleasures of the flesh and spent much of his life on military campaigns. But Charlemagne was also a Christian who built churches and provided financial support to monasteries. Indeed, he believed that his struggles were done in the name of Christianity:

> For it is our task, with the aid of divine goodness, to defend the holy church of Christ everywhere from the attacks of pagans without and to strengthen it within through the knowledge of the Catholic faith. . . . With God, our leader and benefactor, the Christian people may always and everywhere be victorious over the enemies of his Holy Name, and the name of Our Lord Jesus Christ be proclaimed throughout the world.[8]

Charlemagne was also interested in scholarly and artistic activities. These interests resulted in what modern scholars call the Carolingian Renaissance. Even though his own writing skills were poor, the emperor established a palace school at his capital, Aachen, to which several dozen scholars from all over Europe came to settle. Under the guidance of the school's leader, Alcuin of York, many ancient manuscripts were copied and some artistic works were created. The Carolingian Renaissance ended soon after Charlemagne died in 814, but it was influential in later cultural developments in Europe.

Crowning of Charlemagne In A.D. 800 on Christmas Day, Pope Leo III crowned Charlemagne emperor of Rome. (Pierpont Morgan Library)

A significant event occurred on Christmas day in the year 800: Charlemagne was crowned emperor by the pope in Rome. His coronation designated Charlemagne as both a successor to the Roman emperors and as the political leader of Catholic Christendom. It also signified a growing sense of European independence from the Byzantine Empire. Byzantium had long claimed to be the only Christian and Roman empire, but now there was a rival claimant.

The Carolingian dynasty was the first political manifestation of a new civilization that some were already calling "European." (The word *Europe* comes from the Greek *Eurōpē*, meaning "land of the setting sun.") A surge of energy was sweeping through Europe. Peasants were clearing land to expand the area available for agriculture. A change in thought was developing, as demonstrated by the illustrations used on calendars: instead of passive, allegorical characters who represented a saint or something similar, by the year 800 calendars began to show a concrete person actively engaged in some kind of labor. These new "labors of the months," as they were called, indicated a more realistic concern with work and the practical problems of the everyday world.

The Carolingian period also saw a change in the position of women. The Germanic tribes had usually treated women as property always under the control of men. But by the ninth century, some married women were acquiring a degree of economic independence. A new custom required that just before marriage a groom give his bride a gift, usually land, which was hers to control. Furthermore, some women were able to share in the inheritance of land and other property.

The Carolingian surge of energy lasted only briefly, for the dynasty disintegrated soon after Charlemagne's death. In 843, his grandsons concluded the Treaty of Verdun that divided the empire into three parts: Louis the German received what is today known as western Germany, Charles the Bald got most of what is present-day France, and Lothair got a "middle kingdom" between the other two, which is today northern Italy and the French and German lands that center on the Rhine River. Charlemagne's grandsons thus helped initiate the process by which Europe became divided into national states, since the Treaty of Verdun marked the beginning of France and Germany and of a middle area over which the two nations would fight for the next one thousand years.

ANOTHER WAVE OF INVASIONS

One reason for the collapse of the Carolingian dynasty was a wave of invasions that afflicted Europe in the ninth and tenth centuries. In the south, Muslim pirates known as Saracens raided Mediterranean villages and drove up rivers in southern France. In the east, Magyars (Hungarians) invaded Germany and northern Italy. In the north and west, Vikings (Norsemen, or Northmen from Scandinavia) attacked the British Isles, the lands around the Baltic and North Seas, and France. The result was a breakdown of political and social order in Europe and the devastation of many towns, churches, and monasteries. It was not unusual for peasants to flee their homes and wander the countryside in search of food and shelter. Also common was the sight of monks leaving monasteries about to be attacked and carrying only some food and a few precious possessions.

The Vikings

Of all the invaders, the Vikings had the greatest impact on Western Civilization. A maritime people with the best ships and navigational skills of their time, the Vikings became raiders and conquerors in part because overpopulation in Scandinavia pushed them out of their homeland and in part because they lived in a war-oriented society that honored military

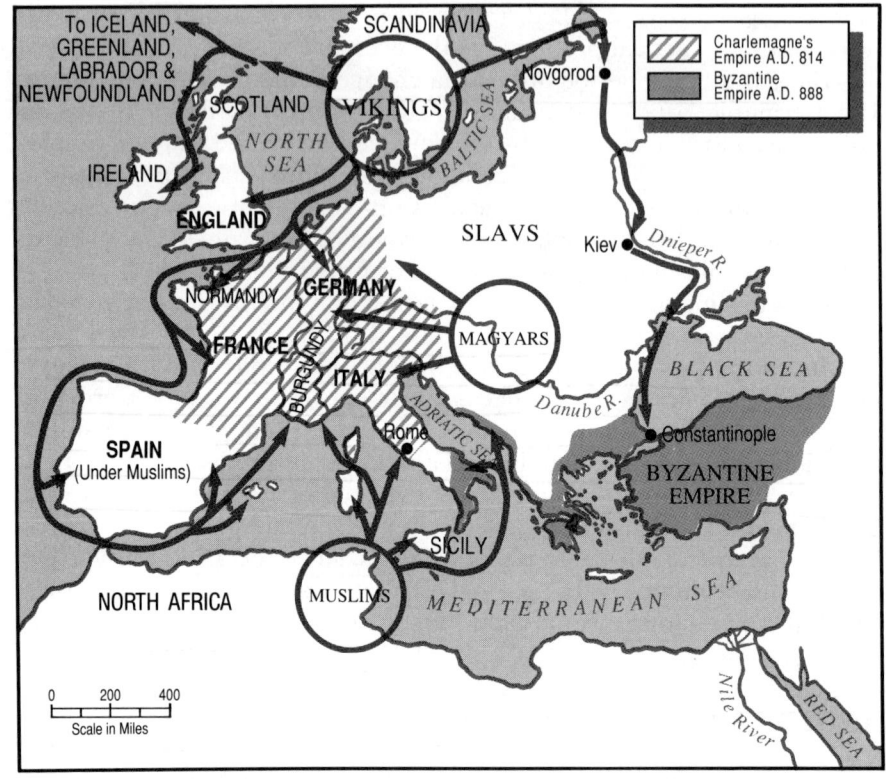

Figure 7.1 Charlemagne's Empire and Invasions by the Vikings, Magyars, and Muslims, A.D. 800–950

virtues and lived by attacking others. Their attacks were usually vicious and highly destructive.

The first recorded Viking attack occurred in 793, at the monastery of Lindisfarne in England. Over the next century, the Vikings conquered much of England, raided and settled in large parts of the French coast, sent an occasional expedition into the Mediterranean, and invaded Russia. Their most spectacular achievement was a drive across the North Atlantic. The Vikings established small colonies in Iceland and Greenland and eventually reached North America. In 986, a Viking named Bjarni Herjolfsson was blown off course in the North Atlantic and ended up in Labrador. He stayed only briefly, but a few years later Leif Eriksson led a small Viking band that tried unsuccessfully to settle on the Canadian coast.

The Viking explorations in the North Atlantic were unsuccessful. They lacked the organizational skills necessary to sustain large colonizing ventures and were operating in a harsh Arctic environment that was becoming harsher due to climatic change. One account of the survivors of

A Viking Invasion This illustration depicts an invasion of England by Danish Vikings in the ninth century A.D. As shown, typical Viking sea vessels were curved both front and back and were powered by many people with long wooden oars. (Pierpont Morgan Library)

a Viking shipwreck tells of how they saved themselves by hiking over miles of ice floes and glaciers. The Vikings were more successful in Europe. By the eleventh century, they dominated trade in Norway, Denmark, and England, and they populated much of Ireland, the French area of Normandy (named for the Northmen), and parts of northern Russia.

The Viking destructiveness was slowly tamed as they were gradually Christianized and absorbed into European populations. In the process, the Vikings imparted a new vigor to Europe. They opened up new trade routes and taught Europeans the arts of navigation that would be used later to explore the world. The age of the Vikings was the beginning of a long history of European expansion, as we will see in later chapters.

FEUDALISM AND MANORIALISM

When the Viking, Muslim, and Magyar invasions subsided in the tenth century, the Europeans began to restore some measure of social order and economic prosperity. The legal and governmental system known today as *feudalism* was a major part of that restoration of order. (The word *feudalism*, invented by modern historians, was derived from the Latin *foedum*, meaning "fief.") Feudalism originated in part as a Germanic tradition of free fighting men who swore to fight for their chieftain. In addition, feudalism characterized the old Roman patron–client relationship in which clients gave their land to more powerful patrons in exchange for protection from marauders and the right to continue using the land.

Feudalism was based on an economic system called *manorialism*, which will be discussed shortly. In the manorial system, unfree laborers known as serfs farmed under the direction of a lord.

The Feudal Relationships

The roots of feudalism lay in the chaos of the seventh and eighth centuries, when powerful nobles offered protection to less powerful nobles who, in exchange, agreed to join the military retinue of their protectors. Then, in the late eighth century, a military innovation—the stirrup—led to the practice of powerful nobles granting landed estates to the members of their retinues. Traditionally, European warriors (and the Greek and Roman warriors before them) fought on foot because a mounted warrior without a stirrup could be easily dislodged and destroyed. The stirrup, developed by central Asian nomads, came into Europe in the eighth century. It enabled the rider to bind himself to the horse. Consequently, the nobility became mounted, armored knights rather than foot soldiers, and they also needed landed estates to finance their horses, armor, and weapons.

By the tenth century, these traditional practices began to coalesce into an elaborate feudal structure. The powerful noble was a *lord* who occupied a position of authority on earth similar to that of the Lord in heaven. Those in his retinue were his *vassals*. Vassals usually owed their lords at least three things: (1) *homage*, or loyalty; (2) *aid*, which meant certain specified financial support as well as military service in the lord's army for a certain number of days each year; and (3) *advice*, or consultation with the lord about whatever public matters needed to be discussed. In return, the vassal received from the lord's army protection against bandits or foreign invaders. He also received a *fief*, a means of financial support, usually in the form of an estate with peasants to cultivate the land.

Feudalism was initially a localized arrangement by which the nobles in an area organized small armies to protect their land. As time passed, the feudal structure expanded and became more complex. Through a process known as *subinfeudation*, many vassals gave parts of their fiefs to other people, who then became their vassals. Thus, it was possible for a given person to be both a lord and a vassal, a lord to the vassal below him and a vassal to the more powerful lord above him. In some places, subinfeudation created an elaborate feudal hierarchy covering a large area, with several levels of lords and vassals owing various forms of allegiance to one another. Another complicating factor developed when some land-hungry vassals began to acquire fiefs from two or more lords (see the accompanying diagram). Since a vassal with two lords could not be loyal to both if his two lords competed or fought with each other, it became necessary for the vassal to declare that one lord was his *liege*, or first lord.

THE FEUDAL STRUCTURE

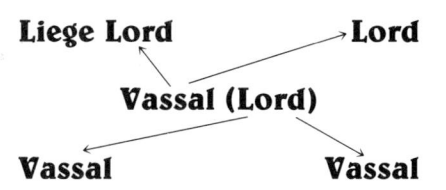

Liege Lord → **Lord**

Vassal (Lord)

Vassal   **Vassal**

Feudalism dominated much of Europe from the tenth to the thirteenth centuries. It was most prevalent in France, western Germany, and northern Italy (the heart of the old Carolingian empire), but feudal institutions also spread in varying degrees to England, parts of Spain, the Slavic lands of eastern Europe, and even to the kingdom of Jerusalem established for a time by the Crusaders. In all cases, feudalism affected legal and governmental practices. European monarchs trying to consolidate their power often forced the greatest nobles in their kingdom to swear feudal loyalty to their king. Thus, feudal oaths were a means of enforcing royal power and thereby building the national kingdoms of Europe (see Chapter 8). But feudalism did more to limit than to expand monarchical power. Under the feudal system, a monarch was always subject to feudal law (the conditions of the feudal contract) and so could not do just as he pleased. For example, the great nobles of a kingdom were often able to insist that their king could not increase taxes without their consent (an early form of "no taxation without representation"), since feudal contracts stipulated that vassals had to agree to any increase in financial payments to their lord. Another example was the feudal stipulation that vassals give advice to their lord. In some places, the obligation of the vassal to give advice was gradually transformed into the right of the vassal to advise and the obligation of the king to listen. In England, this vassal right was one of the factors leading to the emergence of the English parliament (see Chapter 8).

Vassals also had a recognized right of resistance to monarchs who broke feudal laws and customs. This right of resistance, which limited the power of monarchs, eventually helped create constitutionalism (government by laws) and representative government in Western Civilization. Other civilizations (the Islamic and Chinese, for example) that did not develop a principle of rightful resistance to governmental authority also did not evolve any significant forms of representative government.

Feudalism was not often a matter of high legal principle, however. The feudal structure applied only to the nobility—the wealthier 10 to 15 percent of the population. These nobles were a rough, rowdy group accustomed to fighting, carousing, and intimidating those less powerful. Historian C. Warren Hollister describes a typical knight of this period as "a rough-hewn warrior; his armor was simple, his horse was tough, his castle was a crude wooden tower atop an earthen mound, and his lady fair was any available wench."[9] Fighting and feuding among knights was often destructive, in many cases causing damage to churches, monasteries, and peasant's crops. In the tenth and eleventh centuries, the church tried to impose some order and discipline on knights. One way of doing this was to encourage knights to go on crusades to fight for the church in distant lands. Another was to try to establish peace in Europe. In the tenth century, the church pronounced the Peace of God, a measure that condemned all those who destroyed church property or attacked the poor. In the eleventh century, the church added the Truce of God, which attempted to limit knightly fighting to certain days and seasons of the year. Known collectively as the *Pax Ecclesiae* ("Peace of the Church"), these two edicts represented a religious attempt to limit warfare. The *Pax*

Ecclesiae was only partially successful but was significant in that it attempted to establish international peace in a turbulent world.

Serfdom and Manorialism

Feudalism had little direct impact on the 80 to 85 percent of the population who worked the land. Some medieval peasants were free to till their own soil, but most were *serfs*. Serfdom (from the Latin *servi* meaning "slave") originated late in the third century when the Roman Emperor Diocletian decreed that peasants had to remain on their land and continue farming it. Gradually, many peasants lost their freedom and came under the control of their owners.

Serfs worked within a form of agricultural organization known today as *manorialism*. The manor, or large estate, was a community of peasant-serfs who worked together under the authority of a lord (a member of the upper classes). The land of a manor was usually divided into several large fields, some belonging to the serfs and others to the lord. Within the serf fields (one for a winter crop, one for a spring crop, one to lie fallow), each serf household had one or more strips of land to farm and use for its own benefit. The produce of the lord's fields belonged to the lord, but the serfs were required to work his fields as well as their own. In addition to the cultivated land was a certain amount of common land (such as woods and pastures) available for use by everyone in the community. Also on large manors were buildings of varying sizes, including the lord's manorhouse, the peasants' huts, a blacksmith's barn, a chapel, and a mill to grind grain. The manor was similar in appearance to a small village, designed to be self-sufficient and, if necessary, cut off from the rest of the world.

Most serfs led a hard, laborious life. They were bound to their land, unable to sell or leave it. They had to perform a specified amount of labor for their lord, and they could not marry or otherwise change their manner of living without the lord's permission. But serfs were not slaves. They could not be bought or sold like slaves, and they had a right to a share of the manor's land and the produce derived from it. By the eleventh century, slavery had largely disappeared from Europe in part because Christian teachings stressed God's love for everyone (thus gradually undermining the attitudes that caused people to enslave others) and in part because the agricultural revolution produced a rising prosperity that made slavery unnecessary.

CONCLUSION

Despite the chaos of the early Middle Ages, it was one of the most creative epochs in Western history. Benedictine monks and nuns began to change

Western conceptions of time, education, and manual labor. Peasants began to use many new agricultural technologies that helped produce an agricultural revolution. The Carolingian dynasty marked the first political manifestation of a new European civilization. And, after the decline of the Carolingians, the growth of feudalism laid the foundation for a new legal and political order in Europe. These developments prepared the way for a fully developed medieval European civilization of the High Middle Ages—our focus in the following chapter.

THINGS YOU SHOULD KNOW

The Benedictine *Rule* and its significance
The moldboard plow
The three-field system
The shoulder harness and the horseshoe
Why the European peasants were so inventive
The Carolingian dynasty

Charlemagne
The Viking, Muslim, and Magyar invasions
The stirrup
Feudalism and its significance
Pax Ecclesiae
Serfdom
Manorialism

SUGGESTED READINGS

Francis Oakley, *The Medieval Experience: Foundations of Western Cultural Singularity* (New York: Scribner's, 1974) is an excellent survey of medieval history that stresses medieval contributions to Western cultural uniqueness. Christopher Dawson, *The Making of Europe* (New York: World, 1956) is a scholarly argument that the early Middle Ages were not a "Dark Age" but a creative epoch when European civilization was born. Good studies of more specific topics include Pierre Riche, *Daily Life in the World of Charlemagne* (Philadelphia: Univ. of Pennsylvania Press, 1978) and Johannes Bronsted, *The Vikings* (London: Harmondsworth, 1960).

Jacques Le Goff, *Time, Work, and Culture in the Middle Ages*, trans. Arthur Goldhammer (Chicago: Univ. of Chicago Press, 1980) includes important studies of time and work in the Middle Ages. Lynn White, Jr., has written several perceptive essays on technology and the connection between religion and technology in the Middle Ages that are collected in *Machina ex Deo: Essays in the Dynamism of Western Culture* (Boston: MIT, 1968), *Medieval Religion and Technology* (Berkeley: Univ. of California, 1978), and *Medieval Technology and Social Change* (New York: Oxford Univ. Press, 1962). Also good on medieval economic life is Georges Duby, *Rural Economy and Country Life in the Medieval West* (Columbia, S.C.: Univ. of South Carolina Press, 1968).

NOTES

[1] Georges Duby, *The Age of the Cathedrals: Art and Society, 980–1420,* trans. Eleanor Levieux and Barbara Thompson (Chicago: Univ. of Chicago Press, 1981), p. 3.

[2] L. S. Stavrianos, *The Promise of the Coming Dark Age* (San Francisco: W. H. Freeman, 1976), p. 2.

[3] Quoted in Christopher Dawson, *The Making of Europe* (New York: World, 1956), p. 171.

[4] Ibid., p. 177.

[5] Quoted in William R. Cook and Ronald B. Herzman, *The Medieval World View: An Introduction* (New York: Oxford Univ. Press, 1983), p. 171.

[6] Quoted in Richard Barber, *The Penguin Guide to Medieval Europe* (New York: Penguin, 1984). p. 126.

[7] Quoted in Francis Oakley, *The Medieval Experience: Foundations of Western Cultural Singularity* (New York: Scribner's, 1974), p. 143.

[8] Quoted in Cook and Herzman, *Medieval World View,* pp. 181–82.

[9] C. Warren Hollister, *Medieval Europe: A Short History* (New York: John Wiley & Sons, 1964), p. 136.

8

The High Middle Ages, 1000 to 1300

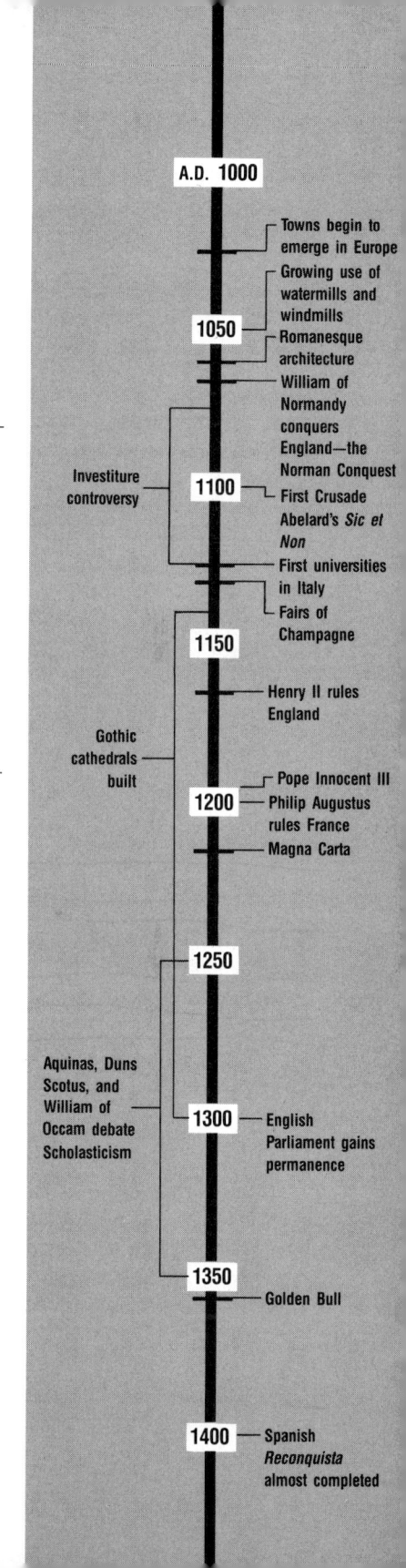

A.D. 1000	Towns begin to emerge in Europe
1050	Growing use of watermills and windmills Romanesque architecture
	William of Normandy conquers England—the Norman Conquest
1100	First Crusade Abelard's *Sic et Non*
	First universities in Italy Fairs of Champagne
1150	
	Henry II rules England
1200	Pope Innocent III Philip Augustus rules France Magna Carta
1250	
1300	English Parliament gains permanence
1350	Golden Bull
1400	Spanish *Reconquista* almost completed

Investiture controversy

Gothic cathedrals built

Aquinas, Duns Scotus, and William of Occam debate Scholasticism

E arly eleventh-century Europe was divided into five cultural areas. (1) In the north, Scandinavia and much of England were dominated by the Viking warriors and were just starting to be Christianized. (2) In eastern Europe, from the Black Sea to the Baltic, the Slavic peoples were being Christianized by the Byzantines. (3) In the southeast, Byzantine civilization prevailed in the Balkans, around the Aegean Sea, and in a few Italian trading cities. (4) In the southwest, Spain was a thriving outpost of Islamic civilization. (5) Only in the middle of Europe—the old heartland of the Carolingian dynasty—did Western Christian culture dominate.

Western Christian culture would eventually expand to cover most of Europe, but in A.D. 1000 it was backward and barbaric in comparison with the Byzantine, Islamic, Indian, and Chinese civilizations. A tenth-century Arab geographer described the Western Europeans with contempt:

> their bodies are large, their natures gross, their manners harsh, their understanding dull, and their tongues heavy . . . their religious beliefs lack solidarity . . . those of them who are farthest to the north are the most subject to stupidity, grossness, and brutishness.[1]

But these Europeans would soon become one of the most aggressive, innovative people in history. During the eleventh through the thirteenth centuries, they developed an energetic economic system, built new political structures, created new social, artistic, and educational concepts, and began to influence other regions. This period of creativity and expansion is known today as the *High Middle Ages*, so to distinguish it from the early Middle Ages. The High Middle Ages began with and sustained a surge of economic growth, and its achievements were greater than those of the early Middle Ages.

TOWNS, TECHNOLOGY, AND TRADE

The initial stimulus for economic growth during the High Middle Ages was the agricultural revolution of the seventh to tenth centuries. As agricultural productivity increased, populations grew. Between A.D. 1000 and 1300, the English population expanded from 2 to 5 million people, the French from 5 to 15 million, the German from 3 to 12 million, and the Italian from 5 to 10 million. Furthermore, agricultural surpluses stimulated short-distance commerce as the inhabitants of one region traded for products available in other nearby regions. To facilitate this trade, towns with a merchant class began to emerge.

TOWNS, TECHNOLOGY, AND TRADE   **163**

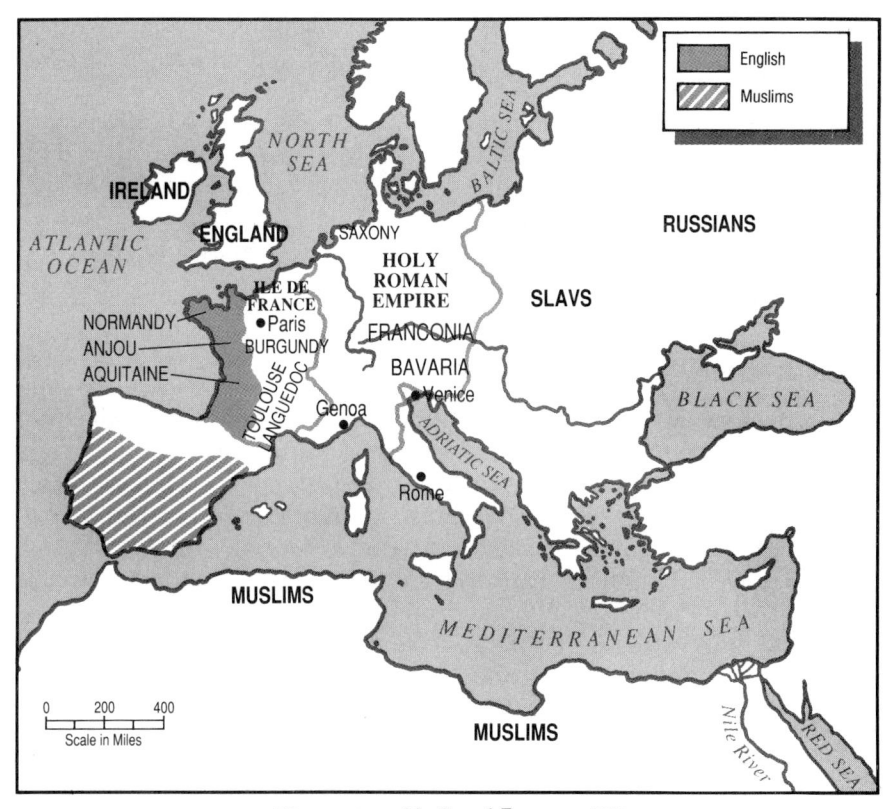

Figure 8.1 Medieval Europe, 1200

Towns

Most of the early medieval towns were clustered in northern France, the Low Countries (present-day Belgium and the Netherlands), and in northern Italy. Usually they were located on a crossroads, where two or more trading routes met, or alongside a river to take advantage of shipping traffic. The early towns were small, crowded areas of a few thousand people, often hidden behind walls and ramparts for protection. Inside the town walls, life was often chaotic and boisterous. A covered marketplace housed merchants selling meat, bread, cheeses, game, hay, wood, and so on. But often the markets overflowed with peddlars parading their wares through the streets and fishwives carrying their merchandise in baskets on their heads. Prostitution usually flourished in the marketplace, as tradeswomen and peasants' daughters sought to earn money.

These boisterous early towns were new to European life, for they were independent of the feudal hierarchy that dominated most of medieval politics and social life. The early towns usually had to pay feudal dues to a local lord, but they could make and enforce their own laws and collect their own taxes. Thus, many towns were bastions of local self-government, free to develop new political and social institutions and new ways of life. The towns developed a new type of economy, one that used currency and that gradually replaced the barter economy of the early Middle Ages. The towns also produced a new social class—a middle class of business people and merchants that was socially and economically below the feudal nobility but above the peasantry.

Technology

The early towns gradually became the centers of a small-scale industrial revolution, systematically using machinery to increase productivity. Some machines were borrowed from other parts of the world. The Persians, for example, were the original inventors of the windmill, and the Chinese the original creators of the canal lock gate, rotary fan, and wheelbarrow. Although the Europeans also invented some new devices, more important was their willingness and ability to use machines like the water mill and windmill on a large scale (see the Technology box). The widespread use of machines affected many aspects of European life, including dress and housing. The button was invented in the thirteenth century by someone who wanted tighter clothes to keep out the winter cold. Housing construction also changed to protect people from the weather. Fireplaces and chimneys were developed and used by some in early medieval Europe, but they became common in the eleventh and twelfth centuries (see the Technology box in Chapter 9).

The idea of creating new mechanical devices fascinated many medieval Europeans. The eleventh-century monk Eilmer of Malmesbury is considered a forerunner of modern aviation. He built a glider, took off in it from the top of Malmesbury Abbey, flew about six hundred feet, crashed, and broke both his legs because he forgot to put "a tail on the rear end."[2] Another example is Philip the Good, Duke of Burgundy in the fifteenth century and a practical joker who used machines to startle unwary visitors to his chateau:

> In the entrance, there are eight conduits for wetting women from below and three conduits which, when people stop in front of them, cover them with flour. When someone tries to open a certain window, a figure appears, sprays the person with water, and shuts the window.[3]

Eilmer of Malmesbury was particularly significant in that he was both a monk and an inventor, a man of God and a man of technology. Religion and technology were closely intertwined in the High Middle Ages, as

TECHNOLOGY
The Water Mill and Windmill

During the High Middle Ages, thousands of water mills—mills powered by river-driven waterwheels—were operated in northwestern Europe. The water mills provided a new source of energy that stimulated production and trade.

The Romans had used water mills on a small scale, but the availability of slaves in the ancient world undermined a strong commitment to labor-saving machinery. Also, the scarcity of rivers flowing year-round in the dry Mediterranean area limited the value of water mills. The northern Europeans faced neither of these difficulties, for slavery had all but disappeared and there were many rivers in northern Europe.

The first water mills used a rotary movement of millstones to grind corn and wheat. Gradually, the Europeans began to use a camshaft, which produced a reciprocal motion like that of a smith with a hammer. With the addition of the cam the mills could crush metal and perform various tasks in the cloth-making industry. Water mills were also used to power bellows at ironworks, to propel mechanical saws, and to pump water from mines.

Other mills were developed as well. Windmills began to appear in the twelfth century and were most often used in water-drainage projects. Tidal mills were constructed in some coastal areas.

A Windmill *In the foreground are peasants cutting hay. In the background to the right is a small town; and to the left is a windmill probably used for grinding corn or wheat. (Pierpont Morgan Library)*

many of the inventors and users of medieval technology were monks and priests. Technological advance was encouraged by the Christian teaching that nature should be used for human benefit. Historian Lynn White, Jr. describes the religious significance of medieval technology:

> The labor-saving power-machines of the later Middle Ages were produced by the implicit theological assumption of the infinite worth of even the most degraded human personality, by an instinctive repugnance towards subjecting any man to a monotonous drudgery which seems less than human in that it requires the exercise neither of intelligence nor of choice. . . . The chief glory of the later Middle Ages was not its cathedrals or its epics or its scholasticism [The medieval philosophy that attempted to make faith and human reason compatible]: it was the building for the first time in history of a complex civilization which rested not on the backs of sweating slaves or coolies but primarily on non-human power.[4]

Technology improved the lives of many in the lower classes, though it also had some less desirable side effects. With the emergence of a new working class came harsh treatment by employers. Workers were valued by only their output, so those who couldn't produce enough were often discarded into the ranks of the unemployed. Although serfs also lived a harsh life, unlike the workers they could expect to live their lives on the manor in which they were born. Furthermore, the upper classes were usually contemptuous of those who performed manual labor. One story tells of a vegetarian abbot who, unconcerned with the feelings of the masons whom he employed, threw away a pig they had killed and planned to eat. In addition, technology led to abuse of the natural environment. Millions of acres of forests were destroyed for the timber. By the thirteenth century, wood was so scarce in some areas that poor families could not afford wooden coffins for their dead relatives. At the same time, London was suffering from atmospheric pollution caused by burning coal.

Trade

The technological revolution stimulated the medieval economy and revived long-distance trade. By the eleventh and twelfth centuries, northern Italy and northern Europe dominated medieval commerce. In northern Italy, cities like Venice and Genoa organized trade across the Mediterranean and grew steadily wealthier. To facilitate trade, these cities developed (or borrowed from the Arabs) several business innovations, most notably banking and credit institutions and accounting methods to keep track of large sums of money. In northern Europe, specifically in the area of the Low Countries (the Flemish towns) and north Germany, over seventy towns organized the Hanseatic League, a

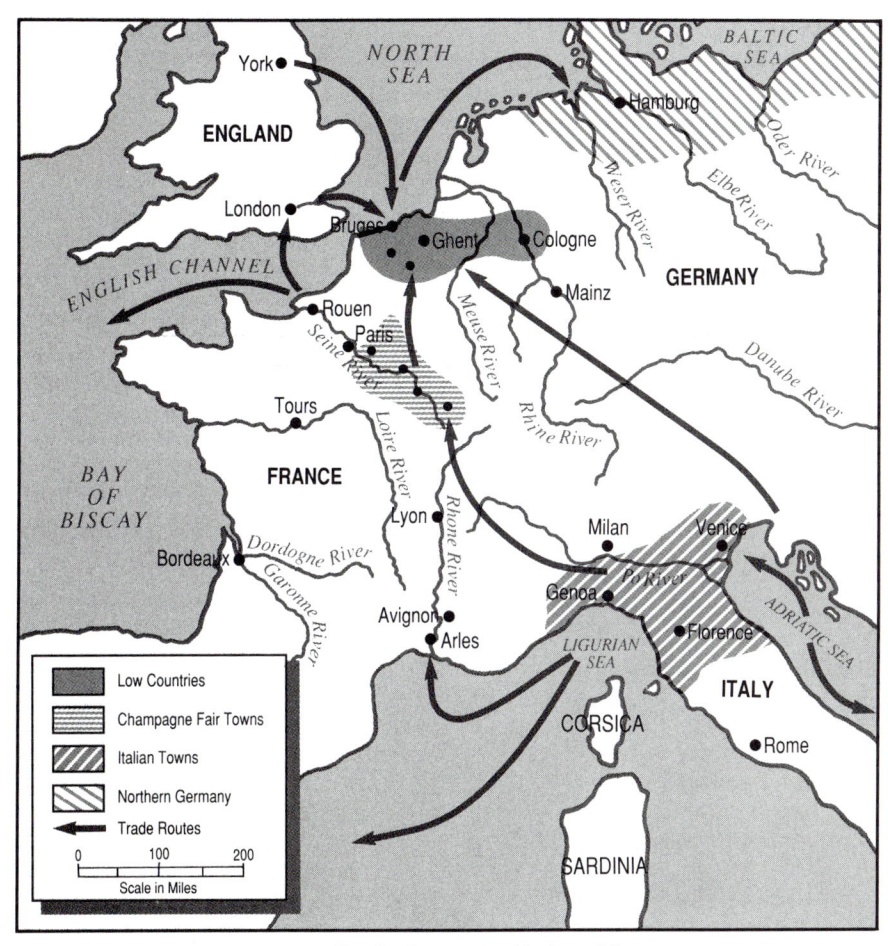

Figure 8.2 Trade Centers in Medieval Europe

confederation of cities that encouraged trade around the North and Baltic Seas.

The fairs of Champagne along the Seine River in France tied northern and southern Europe together and facilitated the replacement of the barter economy with a monetary economy. Fairs—wholesale markets where merchants from different areas met to do business—originated in the eleventh century in many parts of Europe. By the twelfth century, Champagne became the first European-wide fair that met throughout the year. It attracted all sorts of people—gamblers, musicians, traveling actors, peddlers, and prostitutes. But the real purpose of the Champagne fairs was to serve as a meeting place for the great merchant houses of northern Italy and the Hanseatic League. Available at the fairs were an elaborate credit system and an international money market where large accounts could be settled and loans arranged. They also provided an opportunity for trading in luxury goods, such as furs from northern Europe for silks purchased from China by the Italians.

Although the Champagne fairs declined in importance by the late thirteenth century, they were at this time the center of a European economy that included about three hundred trading cities and encompassed an area that extended from Lisbon (Portugal) to Alexandria (Egypt) to Novgorod (Russia) to Bergen (Norway). This wide-ranging economic network helped create a new economic system known as *capitalism*. Capitalism—whose aspects include a market economy, private wealth, or capital, managed by private businesspeople to generate more wealth, banks and international credit, and the use of accounting procedures—would rapidly become a driving force in European life.

THE CHURCH

Christianity was central to all aspects of medieval life. As noted earlier, the Christian perception of nature encouraged the agricultural revolution of the seventh to tenth centuries. Christian beliefs about the value of human life also helped to stimulate the technological breakthroughs of the eleventh to thirteenth centuries.

The Papacy

Most Europeans were Christians, born into the Roman Catholic church. (The only significant exception were the Jews, as we will see later in the chapter.) Structurally, the church was a hierarchy and the pope its head. During the early Middle Ages, popes were influential figures, but they became even more powerful in the High Middle Ages. A succession of strong-minded church leaders tried to turn the papacy into a monarchy, such that popes would not only govern the church but dominate secular kings and princes as well. In short, the claim was that popes should be the supreme rulers of "Christendom."

The first step was to free the church from secular control. Traditionally, secular rulers had often controlled appointments to church offices; for example, elections to the papacy were dominated by the aristocracy of the city of Rome. (Since popes had originally been bishops of Rome and bishops were customarily elected by local congregations, the Roman upper classes had slowly acquired the power to elect popes.) In 1059, a reform ended Roman control of papal elections by establishing the College of Cardinals, a select church group whose role was to choose successors to deceased popes.

Papal power increased markedly during the pontificate of Gregory VII (1073–1085). Gregory believed that the Roman Catholic church was the sole representative of God on earth and that the church's responsibility was to establish and lead a Christian society. He argued further that the pope was the supreme leader of all Christians, empowered by God to depose even emperors if they refused to follow papal direction. To institute these ideas, Gregory established several reforms. One imposed celibacy on the clergy, thus ending the practice whereby priests, but not monks, were allowed to marry. This change was supposed to ensure that priests and bishops would be loyal only to the church. In practice, though, it meant that women lost power in the church, since priests and bishops no longer had wives who could influence them. Another reform sought to eliminate the practice whereby kings and princes often appointed bishops who worked (and often had political influence) in their territories. This reform led to the titanic struggle known as the *investiture controversy* (discussed later in this chapter), but it eventually increased papal control over appointments to church offices.

The papal attempt to rule Christendom reached its peak during the pontificate of Innocent III (1198–1216). Innocent wanted to impose Catholic orthodoxy everywhere in Europe. Toward this end, he established the *Catholic Inquisition,* a church court empowered to uncover and interrogate heretics. In some cases, heretics were turned over to secular authorities to be executed by burning. Innocent also forced European Jews to wear a badge signifying their separation from Christian society. In 1204, he allowed a Crusader army to bypass the Muslims and attack Constantinople, so that Greek Orthodox Christianity might be destroyed. And, under Innocent's leadership, the Fourth Lateran Council (1215) strengthened papal authority by defining some church doctrines more strictly and approving several disciplinary rules that applied throughout the church. All of these measures were designed to increase the power of Roman Catholicism and of the popes. Innocent justified them by claiming that he was Christ's "vicar" on earth:

> I am he to whom Jesus said, "I will give to you the keys to the kingdom of heaven, and everything that you shall bind up on earth shall be bound up in heaven." See then this servant who rules over the entire family; he is the vicar of Jesus Christ and the successor of Saint Peter. He stands halfway between God and man, smaller than God, greater than man.[5]

The drive for papal power had an important result. By eliminating the practice of allowing secular rulers to appoint church officials, the popes insured the independence of the church as an institution. In this way, the popes unintentionally helped to create the principle that later ages would call the "separation of church and state" and to encourage *secularization,* the separation of worldly affairs from the sacred and religious.

Monasticism

The monastic tradition was also reinvigorated during the High Middle Ages. Over the centuries many monasteries had accumulated great wealth through donations of land and other gifts from the upper classes. As a result, many monks lived relatively luxuriously, in seeming contradiction to their vows of poverty.

One reform program began with the founding of a monastery at Cluny in central France in 910. Cluny eventually established over three hundred other monastic houses in Europe and imposed strict discipline on all. Gradually, however, monastic discipline again grew lax, so over the years several new religious orders sprang up to restore strict discipline among monks and nuns. The Cistercians, founded in the French town of Citeaux, were the most influential monastic order in twelfth-century Europe. They sought, successfully for a time, to renew the ascetic ideal of living a simple life in monasteries far removed from population centers. The most renowned of the Cistercians was Bernard of Clairvaux (1091–1153), a fiery mystic who was a model of Christian piety. His influence was so extensive that he helped launch crusades and lectured kings about their sins.

Two other religious orders—the Franciscans and the Dominicans—also adopted new practices. They lived communally among ordinary people rather than in isolated monasteries. They were also mendicants, meaning that they owned almost nothing and survived by receiving (begging for) charity from others. The Franciscans were founded by St. Francis of Assisi (c.1181–1226), to many in later years the personification of Christian sainthood. St. Francis consciously sought to make his life an imitation of the life of Christ. His love for the divine creation was so intense that he preached to nature—to "Brother Ant" and "Sister Fire"—on the assumption that animals and natural objects are just as much God's creatures as are humans. Thus, St. Francis revered nature for its own sake, a view significantly different from the attitude (also Christian) that nature should be used and even exploited. The Dominicans were established by St. Dominic (1170–1221) and also lived humbly and piously. The Dominicans believed that education in particular was a vital way of spreading the Christian message, so many became teachers in medieval universities.

The Common People's Christianity

For the common people, Christianity provided hope and a few bright spots in their otherwise harsh, short lives. The special occasions in life—birth, marriage, death—were all accompanied by church ceremonies. A new tradition focused on veneration of the Virgin Mary. Peasants especially regarded the mother of Jesus as a symbol of the gentleness and love that was all too often absent from their lives. Holy relics revealed the sometimes superstitious piety of ordinary people. The bones and hair of saints and slivers of wood supposedly from the cross on which Jesus died were reverently displayed in parish churches and peasant huts all over Europe.

Romanesque and Gothic Architecture

The most striking manifestations of medieval Christianity were the church buildings constructed between the eleventh and fourteenth centuries. During the early Middle Ages, most public buildings such as churches and palaces were small, crude, and made of timber. But the new wealth of the eleventh century allowed some Europeans, especially those in northern France, to build massive, finely decorated stone structures dedicated to the glory of God. The new *Romanesque* style of architecture was used in the building of many eleventh-century monastery churches, huge rectangular buildings designed to accommodate large congregations. Thick stone walls with narrow windows held up large roofs, the entire edifice giving an impression of great strength and solidity.

The Romanesque style soon gave way to *Gothic* architecture, one of the most splendid aesthetic achievements of Western history. Gothic architects used the pointed arch rather than the rounded arch of the Romanesque, allowing them to create taller buildings. The Gothic style was embodied in towering, graceful cathedrals with tall spires on the outside pointing toward heaven. In the walls were stained-glass windows through which the sun's rays sprayed a kaleidoscope of colors over the interior. To support the stone walls and high roof, architects invented the "flying buttress," a stone pier that supported the walls from outside the building.

The Gothic style was created in the years after 1130, largely by Suger, the Abbot of Saint-Denis monastery near Paris. Suger wanted to uplift human souls by using earthly beauty to point toward divine beauty. Believing that God is "light," he sought to create an art of light and radiance that would make the cathedral a symbol of the entire divine creation. He described his purpose in the inscription on the first Gothic church at Saint-Denis:

> The golden door foretells to you what shines here within; through palpable, visible beauty, the soul is elevated to that which is truly beautiful, and rising from the earth, where it was submerged, an inert thing, it is resuscitated in heaven by the radiance of its glory.[6]

Most Gothic cathedrals were built between 1150 and 1300 in towns in northern France and the Low Countries. They served as both religious and community centers for thriving urban communities. As religious

Notre-Dame-la-Grande, Poitiers, France The style pictured in this twelfth-century-facade is partially based on Roman architectural models, hence it's called *Romanesque*. Characteristics of Romanesque architecture include the use of stone rather than timber, rounded archways, and bell towers. (French Tourist Office)

centers they were monuments to Christian faith, many of them dedicated to the Virgin Mary and hence called *Notre Dame* (French for "Our Lady"). As community centers they were monuments to the civic pride produced by the freedom and prosperity of the new medieval towns. A significant point is that the cathedrals were financed and erected voluntarily by free people and, therefore, were the first large constructions in history to be built by free labor rather than by slaves or serfs.

It is equally significant that Gothic architecture displayed a new artistic attitude toward nature. In the early Middle Ages, nature was typically regarded as an elaborate set of symbols by which God communicated messages to humans (for example, the industrious ant symbolized God's opposition to laziness). Theologians and artists rarely considered nature to be important in itself. Gothic artists, however, cultivated a naturalistic art, decorating cathedrals with sculptures of flowers and trees that were exact replicas of natural objects. Because they thought of nature as God's creation, they believed that they should examine, copy, and understand it. Thus, Gothic art revealed a new

THE CHURCH 173

Chartres Cathedral, France The cathedral at Chartres is one of the most striking examples of Gothic architecture, characterized by tall spires pointing toward heaven, stained-glass windows, pointed archways, and flying buttresses (or building supports, not seen here). (Archives Photographiques)

THE JEWS

During the time of the Roman Empire, the Jews of Palestine had rebelled against Roman rule several times. Many Jews had voluntarily left Palestine or been driven out by the Romans. In what is called the *Diaspora* ("dispersion"), many Jews scattered to live in various parts of Asia, North Africa, and Europe. European Jews constituted about 2–3 percent of the medieval population and were the only significant non-Christian minority.

Many Christians regarded Jews as "Christ-killers" who were responsible for "murdering" Jesus (even though the crucifixion occurred under the auspices of the Roman government). Furthermore, many Christians considered Jews to be "heretics" who refused to accept the one true religion—Christianity. Consequently, European Jews were occasionally persecuted during the early Middle Ages. The persecution of Jews became more systematic during the High Middle Ages, as anti-Semitism prevailed throughout Europe. Intense religious feelings, evidenced by the Crusades, encouraged many Christians to perceive Jews as outsiders and even enemies. Jews were forbidden to own land and so were restricted to business or artisanal occupations. Crusader armies sometimes attacked Jewish communities and killed or drove away the inhabitants. One such episode was described by Albert of Aix (France):

> The slaughter of Jews was done first by citizens of Cologne. These suddenly fell upon a small band of Jews and severely wounded and killed many; they destroyed the houses and synagogues of the Jews and divided among themselves a very large amount of money. When the Jews saw this cruelty, about two hundred in the silence of the night began flight by boat to Neuss. The pilgrims and crusaders discovered them, and after taking away all of their possessions, inflicted on them similar slaughter leaving not even one alive.[7]

By the thirteenth century, those Jews who survived were usually required to wear a special identifying patch or cap and to live in special sections of towns called *ghettoes,* segregated from the rest of the community. In the fourteenth century, Jews were expelled from several countries and had no recourse but to migrate to and wander throughout eastern Europe.

The Jews endured and survived these persecutions largely because their religion bound them together as a community. But anti-Semitism reveals the intolerant side of medieval society, and that intolerance would continue in Western history.

THE RISE OF NATIONAL MONARCHIES

During the early Middle Ages, virtually all government and all politics were decentralized and, with the exception of the short-lived Carolingian dynasty, no large territorial states existed. This situation changed during the High Middle Ages when monarchs in England and France began to build states that slowly evolved into major European nations. German monarchs also tried to construct a centralized state, but their failure left Germany disunited. In eastern Europe, a powerful state did exist for a time in Poland.

England

During the great migrations of the fourth through the sixth centuries, England was settled by various Germanic tribes, including the Angles, Saxons, and Jutes. Although for a short time the area was divided into a number of kingdoms, by about the late ninth century much of England was controlled by Vikings. Only intermittently was England united under one native king during the tenth century. The turmoil caused by Viking incursions produced at least one enduring political officer—the sheriff. England was at this time divided into *shires*, or counties, in which local government was directed by an official *reeve*. The shire reeve eventually become known as the *sheriff*.

English history changed dramatically in 1066, when a dispute over the succession to the throne led to an invasion of England by William, Duke of Normandy (1027–1087). William defeated a Saxon army at the battle of Hastings and quickly overran the entire country. The *Norman Conquest*, as it is called, was important in several respects. First, by tying England to the ruling family of Normandy (northwestern France), it reoriented the island kingdom away from the Viking lands of Scandinavia and toward continental Europe. Second, the Norman Conquest enabled England to become the first centralized state in medieval Europe, since in feudal legal theory William the Conqueror was lord of all England and entitled to distribute all his land to vassals from whom he could expect absolute loyalty. In this connection, William conducted an inquest or inquiry to list all the wealth and land of the country he had conquered. The result was the *Domesday Book*, so named because the king's judgments in this matter were as final and absolute as God's. Finally, the Norman introduction of feudalism into England led to the establishment of a council of vassals to advise the king. This council later evolved into the English Parliament.

William the Conqueror ruled both England and Normandy, and in the decades after his death (1087) his successors accumulated even more territories. Henry II (reigned 1154–1189) inherited the French province of Anjou as well as Normandy and England. When he married Eleanor of Aquitaine, that rich area of southwestern France was added to his empire. By the late twelfth century, the English ruling family controlled most of the western half of France. Henry II sought to consolidate his power by developing new governmental and legal institutions. His predecessors had created an office known as the *Exchequer* to collect taxes, and Henry turned it into one of the most efficient state financial systems in Europe. (The Exchequer was so named because officials used counters on a checkered tablecloth to calculate accounts.) More significant in the long term were Henry's innovations in royal justice and law. He extended the practice of sending out circuit judges (who traveled a particular district or circuit) to hear legal cases throughout England. The judges began to develop the practice of calling together a jury of twelve local men who knew the facts of a case to determine guilt or innocence. (The word *jury* is derived from the French *jurer,* the oath of impartiality that the twelve men took.) Since royal justice was usually fairer than the decisions made by the nobility controlled local courts, the royal judges heard a growing number of cases and quickly created a large body of legal precedents that became the core of English *common law*—law common to the whole of England. By Henry's reign, then, the English had begun to form an elaborate legal tradition, and this tradition would eventually produce many principles of modern constitutional law.

Henry was an extraordinary ruler, and all his life he was involved with other extraordinary individuals. One was Thomas Becket, an old friend who became archbishop of Canterbury, the highest church official in England. Despite their friendship, Henry and Becket became embroiled in a power struggle over where clergy accused of crimes should be tried—in Henry's royal courts or in Becket's church courts. Their struggle was so intense that in a famous episode Henry angrily demanded why no one would rid him of his enemy. Taking him at his word, some of Henry's knights murdered Becket and thereby blackened their monarch's reputation. Another strong-willed rival was Henry's own wife, Eleanor of Aquitaine. Eleanor was influential in developing the courtly love tradition in her native Aquitaine and became an active participant in English politics after her marriage to Henry. Henry's and Eleanor's relationship gradually became acrimonious, however, and after Eleanor supported a revolt against Henry in 1173, he had her imprisoned for much of the last part of her life.

One of the few things that Henry and Eleanor agreed on was that their sons were disappointments to them. Richard the Lionhearted (reigned 1189–1199), to his parent's consternation, ignored his responsibilities in England and spent much of his life away on crusades. Their youngest son John suffered numerous political defeats and became portrayed in legend as an evil ruler taunted by the popular outlaw Robin Hood. (Many of the events mentioned here were so dramatic that they became the subject of twentieth-century films and dramas, notable examples being *Becket* and *The Lion in Winter.*) John (reigned 1199–1216) confronted and was defeated by powerful enemies, such as Philip Augustus, king of France. As duke of Normandy and Anjou (both provinces in France), John was a vassal to Philip, but as king of England he was not a vassal because kings could not be vassals. A dispute over feudal law enabled Philip to summon John to feudal court. But John refused to appear and, after a brief military conflict, Philip declared his vassal's fiefs—Normandy, Anjou, and some other areas—to be forfeited. The result was a major loss of English lands in France and the addition, notably, of Normandy and Anjou to French royal territory. The English monarchs still retained Aquitaine, however.

Many of the great English nobles also opposed John, in part because he demanded more taxes to finance his struggles with Philip Augustus. The nobles finally rebelled and, in 1215, in a peaceful meadow called Runnymede, forced their king to sign the Magna Carta, or "Great Charter." The Magna Carta was a feudal document in which John agreed to abide by various feudal laws and customs, such as not increasing taxes without the vassals' consent. Its long-term effect was to force the English kings to recognize that they had to respect the laws and could not rule arbitrarily. For this reason, the Magna Carta was a major step toward constitutionalism, the principle that traditional procedures of government cannot be changed without the consent of some lawful representatives of the kingdom.

A related development was the evolution of the English Parliament. As noted earlier, William the Conqueror formed a council of vassals to advise him, and by the thirteenth century the council's meetings were called *parliaments* (from the French *parler,* meaning to "converse"). At first the parliaments were simply adjuncts to royal administration, since their role was to support royal decisions and help collect royal taxes. As time passed, however, Parliament was increasingly recognized as an independent body representing the upper classes—nobles, upper clergy, knights from the shires, and wealthy townspeople. By the fourteenth century, it was accepted as a permanent institution and was beginning to acquire the right to approve or disapprove of new taxes proposed by the monarchs.

At the end of the High Middle Ages, two great issues dominated English politics. One was the continuing effort by the upper classes to use parliament, the Magna Carta, and the common law to limit monarchical power. The other issue was whether England could retain its remaining possessions (especially Aquitaine) in France. These issues were deeply affected by French politics.

France

The disintegration of the Carolingian dynasty left the area known today as France divided into several small principalities and medium-sized duchies. Each of these units tended to have its own laws and customs and its people often spoke a dialect of their own. During the next several centuries French monarchs asserted royal control over these political units and gradually united them into a centralized kingdom called France.

The first step toward unification occurred in 987, when Hugh Capet was elected by the leading nobles to the French throne. Hugh actually governed only the small area of Île de France centered in Paris, but the title of king gave him some prestige, if not authority, over the rulers of other French areas. Having male descendants over the next several generations, Hugh Capet became the founder of the Capetian dynasty that slowly gathered its resources and increased its power.

The first powerful Capetian ruler was Philip II Augustus (1180–1223). Paris at this time was one of the most exciting places in Europe. Its population was nearing 100,000 and it was the center of a thriving commercial and agricultural area. Furthermore, Paris was the home of Gothic architecture and the most prestigious medieval university. King Philip was a good match for this bustling, aggressive capital, for he was an ambitious ruler who intended to augment his power. It was he who seized Normandy and Anjou from King John of England and thereby expanded the French royal domains. Philip also began to expand royal power southward. In southern France there were a large number of people called Albigensians, who claimed to be Christian but believed in the eternal coexistence of God and Satan. When Pope Innocent III declared their belief in the eternality of Satan to be a heresy, Philip allowed his vassals to lead the Albigensian Crusade (1208–1213), in which many religious dissidents were killed. The destruction of the Albigensians created a political vacuum in some southern areas of France. Thus, during the thirteenth century, Philip's successors gradually added two new provinces, Toulouse and Languedoc, to the royal domains and extended royal power to the Mediterranean.

Philip and his successors also developed the royal administration, sending out officials to collect taxes and impose royal decrees in newly conquered territories. Louis IX (1226–1270), so pious that he was later canonized as St. Louis, was particularly effective at advancing royal power. He was such a fair and admired ruler that much of France was willing to ignore local customs and accept his legislation and royal courts. Slowly the French kings gathered political power, thus uniting a growing number of areas into one centralized system.

By the end of the High Middle Ages, most but not all of what is present-day France was under royal control. It wasn't until the Hundred

Years' War (1338–1453) that Aquitaine was absorbed into France. Burgundy (eastern France) was added still later. That war resulted in France finally being united geographically and England losing most of its last possessions on the continent and becoming an island nation. (The story of the Hundred Years' War is discussed in Chapter 10.)

Germany

The German monarchs, like their English and French counterparts, tried to unify their empire. They failed, however, and the result was a continuing disunity that had decisive consequences for German and European history.

Germany in the early Middle Ages was a frontier, a heavily forested area that was sparsely settled. In fact, only the western and southern parts of what is today Germany were inhabited by European Christians, the east being populated by pagan Slavic tribes. There was no German nation-state. The collapse of the Carolingian dynasty left western and southern Germany divided into several large duchies—Saxony, Bavaria, Franconia, and others—governed by powerful dukes. The dukes recognized the need for a strong leader who could protect Germany; thus, in the tenth century, they began the practice of electing a king. The strongest of the early monarchs was Otto I, the Great (reigned 936–973).

Otto the Great protected his kingdom by defeating the Magyars at the battle of Lechfeld in 955 and thereby ending Magyar attacks on Western Europe. He also began to extend his influence into northern Italy. Otto probably thought of himself as the political leader of all Western Christians (like Charlemagne before him) and, therefore, believed that he should control Italy, the home of the church. He invaded Italy in 962, and was crowned Roman Emperor by the pope. That coronation transformed German kings into emperors (a more prestigious title) of what came to be called the Holy Roman Empire (Germany and northern Italy). But the new imperial crown turned out to be a disaster for the German monarchy, since involvement in Italy led the monarchs into a conflict with the popes known as the *investiture controversy*.

The investiture controversy was a complex affair. German emperors, like English and French kings, traditionally had the right to appoint many church officials, since these officials often exercised legal and governmental power in the areas where they resided. (The term *investiture* refers to the ceremony in which a person assumed office and was "invested" with the symbols of that office.) By the eleventh century, the traditional practice was being challenged by the popes. In 1075, Pope Gregory VII prohibited investiture of church officials by secular rulers. Most of the European monarchs objected to Gregory's pronouncement, but the strongest reaction came from Henry IV, the German emperor who ruled some lands in northern Italy, near the pope. This was one reason the investiture conflict was more explosive in Germany than elsewhere. Another was that the German nobility had never been completely subdued by the monarchs.

For the next several decades, Gregory and Henry and their successors were embroiled in a titanic power struggle. Both sides believed that victory was essential to their cause—Emperor Henry assumed that he had to control church officials in order to govern effectively, while Pope Gregory argued that popes had to appoint church officials so as to ensure the independence of the church. Both sides assumed they were absolutely right and the other completely wrong, so compromise was impossible for a time. The upshot was that Gregory excommunicated Henry from the church, which according to official doctrine jeopardized the emperor's chances for eternal salvation and threatened to void the oaths of loyalty that vassals had sworn to Henry. The pope also encouraged the German nobles to revolt against their emperor, and many of them did. For his part, Henry invaded Italy, drove Gregory out of Rome to die in exile, and appointed a new pope.

Not until after Gregory and Henry died was order restored and the investiture controversy resolved. In 1122 at Worms (a city in Germany), representatives of the pope and the emperor agreed on the Concordat of Worms, which decreed that appointments to church offices in Germany had to be satisfactory to both emperor and pope. Although the issue was compromised, German politics had changed fundamentally in the intervening time. While the emperors were preoccupied with their struggle with the papacy, the German nobles had asserted their power to collect taxes, make laws, and control the territories in which they ruled. Consequently, real political power passed from the emperors to the nobility, from the centralized to the local level. Since Germany remained politically decentralized for the next eight hundred years, most historians designate the investiture controversy as one of the most decisive political developments in German history.

One monarch did make a last major attempt to build national unity in Germany—Frederick I (1152–1190), sometimes called Barbarossa (meaning "red-beard"). Frederick Barbarossa sought to impose unity by the sheer force of his will; specifically, he required the great nobles to become his vassals in the hope that feudal law would encourage loyalty to the emperor. His plan worked during his lifetime, but when Frederick drowned while on crusade in 1190, the German nobles were once again freed from centralized imperial control. (A legend quickly grew in Germany that Frederick Barbarossa did not really drown but was sleeping in a cave and would reappear to save Germany in some future time of great national distress.)

The final step in German political decentralization was the *Golden Bull* of 1356, issued by Emperor Charles IV. (A *bull* was an edict or formal pronouncement issued by the pope or an emperor.) German emperors were often elected, the electors being a few of the great nobles. The Golden Bull regularized this practice by providing that seven electors (the rulers of the seven most important German territories) had the sole authority to designate an emperor. In practice, this meant that the electors always tried to appoint a relatively weak emperor with limited power, so that each local German ruler would retain authority within his territory. The result, according to the historian Geoffrey Barraclough, was that "the monarchy was henceforward a nullity and . . . Germany advanced toward modern times divided and disunited."[8]

Decentralization ultimately brought great harm to Germany. There was in effect *no* Germany, only dozens of separate German territories, each of them theoretically a sovereign state. Some of the territories such as Bavaria and Saxony were large enough to contain several towns and vast amounts of farmland, but others consisted of only a few hundred acres presided over by an obscure prince who purported to be a supreme ruler in a small domain. None of the German states was large enough to protect itself from larger nations like France. Thus, over the centuries, Germany often became a battleground where foreign armies could intervene and dominate with impunity. Furthermore, each German state tended to guard its economic independence jealously, thus preventing the growth of a nationwide economic market and hindering economic development. The final, and perhaps greatest, penalty for Germany's failure to unify became apparent only in the nineteenth and twentieth centuries. Germany finally achieved national unification in 1871, and one outcome was the unleashing of long-dormant feelings of national pride and arrogance. That pride and arrogance was one of the factors that in the twentieth century spurred Germany into two world wars that devastated not only Germany but most of Europe as well.

Eastern Europe

Eastern Europe was lightly populated by Slavic peoples. By the late tenth century, some of these began to form enduring governments. Both a Hungarian and a Polish state were established at this time. The Hungarian state was especially significant because of its geographical position. Being in the middle of eastern Europe, it in effect separated the south Slavs in the Balkan peninsula from the north Slavs of Poland. One consequence was that when the Christian church split in the eleventh century into Roman Catholic and Greek Orthodox branches, many of the south Slavs remained Orthodox while the north Slavs—the Poles and some Czechs—gradually adopted the Catholic version of Christianity. In the long run, the Polish state became the most powerful political unit in eastern Europe, and it dominated the area by the fourteenth century.

The Significance of Medieval Political History

The political history of the High Middle Ages was significant for at least three reasons.

1. Many medieval political leaders—Charlemagne, the popes, the German emperors—tried to build a universal empire dominating all or most of Europe but were unsuccessful because Europe was divided into several nation-states. One result was a Europe chronically embroiled in warfare, since the various states competed with and often fought one another. Another was greater freedom, since, for example, private enterprise and economic freedom could develop partly because there was no single political authority to restrict them.
2. Medieval politics helped create the principle of separation of church and state. On the one hand, the church sought to establish primacy over the secular states, but ultimately it was unable to do so. On the other hand, various secular rulers (like Henry IV of Germany) tried to assert control over the church, but the church usually maintained its independence from the secular states and insisted that secular rulers should not interfere in its affairs. This church-state division would become the foundation for the modern conception of a secular state uninvolved with religious matters.
3. Medieval political conflicts led to the creation of representative political assemblies in England (the Parliament), Sweden, Portugal, Spain, France, some parts of Germany, and several other places. The idea of representation had at least three roots: the Germanic belief that the people were the source of law, the feudal right of vassals to advise their lord, and the church teaching that rulers could not demand whatever they wanted but had to govern in accordance with God's commands. Thus, even though monarchy was the dominant form of governance in the High Middle Ages, medieval political practices developed ideas that would later lead to modern notions of the right of the people to govern themselves.

EUROPEAN EXPANSION: THE CRUSADING SPIRIT

Western European civilization has expanded aggressively throughout most of its long history, and that pattern began during the High Middle Ages. One reason Europe began to expand was economic, as the growing population and surging economy provided the material strength for expansion. Another was religious, as Europeans often saw themselves as God's vassals fighting to impose the divine will on others.

Crusades to the Holy Land

The most prominent aspect of medieval expansionism were the Crusades, a prolonged attempt to conquer the Holy Land (Palestine) from the Muslims. The Muslims first captured the Holy Land in the seventh century. For several hundred years they allowed a few Christian pilgrims to visit religious shrines without interference. In 1070, however, the Seljuk Turks (who were Muslim converts) conquered Jerusalem and quickly began to harass Christian visitors. In 1071, they defeated a Byzantine army at the battle of Manzikert in present-day eastern Turkey, thus weakening the eastern Christian empire and opening Asia Minor to Turkish influence. These events produced in Europe a growing hatred and fear of Muslim infidels.

Fear led to the Crusades, a mixture of four elements: holy war against a religious enemy, pilgrimage to shrines in the Holy Land, an assertion of papal leadership in Europe, and conquest of land and other economic prizes. Eight major crusades occurred between 1095 and 1270. The First Crusade reached Jerusalem in 1099 and resulted in a massive slaughter of the Muslim population. An account, probably exaggerated, by Fulcher of Chartres (France) describes the brutality:

> Many of the Saracens who had climbed to the top of the Temple of Solomon in their flight were shot to death with arrows and fell headlong from the roof. Nearly ten thousand were beheaded in this Temple. If you had been there your feet would have been stained to the ankles in the blood of the slain. What shall I say? None of them were left alive. Neither women nor children were spared.[9]

The Crusaders controlled much of the Holy Land for several decades after 1099, but sporadic fighting between Christians and Muslims continued. By the late twelfth century, the Turks were led by Saladin, a powerful and relatively enlightened, humanitarian ruler as well as an able military commander. Saladin recaptured Jerusalem in 1187 and treated the captured population much more leniently than had the First Crusaders. The Europeans felt compelled to launch another Crusade, but it was a failure even though it was led by such powerful monarchs as Frederick Barbarossa of Germany and Richard the Lionhearted of England. More successful from the Crusader perspective was the Fourth Crusade of 1202–1204, in which Europeans attacked fellow Christians—the Byzantines—and sacked Constantinople. The irony was that the undermining of the Byzantine Empire made it easier for the Turkish "infidels" to expand into Asia Minor, eventually destroy the Byzantines, and then threaten Western Europe. The Fourth Crusade was followed by the Children's Crusade. Two German boys, in what was probably the origin of the legend of the Pied Piper, persuaded thousands of children to march to Mediterranean ports in the belief that the waters would part and allow the Crusaders to get to the Holy Land. Many of the children perished on the way or were sold into slavery by Mediterranean pirates. Several other Crusades were launched during the thirteenth century, one of which briefly retook Jerusalem for the Christians. But the Crusaders were far from home and continually weakened by shortages of men and supplies. In the late thirteenth century, the Muslims once again defeated the Christians, and the Crusades, but not the crusading spirit, came to an end.

The Crusades were in one sense a massive failure. Not only were the Crusaders unable to control the Holy Land permanently but their efforts also led to the deaths of unknown numbers of people. Christians and Muslims slaughtered each other for two centuries, attacked and hastened the demise of the Byzantine Empire, and within Europe produced increased persecution of Jews and religious dissidents such as the Albigensians. In another sense, though, the Crusades were a source of power and wealth. North Italian cities like Venice grew rich from the trade that developed between Europe and the eastern Mediterranean. Many European monarchs used the period of the Crusades to enhance their power, since many nobles expended their money and energy on crusading expeditions and were thus unable to oppose the continuing growth of monarchical strength.

Crusades in Europe

Despite the failure of the Crusades to the Holy Land, the crusading spirit thrived and produced Christian expansion within Europe itself. A military monastic order, the Teutonic Knights, led German expansion into eastern Europe. This expansion was partially a religious crusade to convert those Slavs who were still not Christian and partially a military and economic colonization of sparsely populated lands. One result was that Prussia (east of Denmark along the Baltic coast) was conquered and settled by Germans, moving German boundaries eastward. Another was the gradual conversion of Slavic Poland to Catholicism.

The crusading mentality lasted longest in Spain, because Christians and Muslims encountered each other face to face there. Spain had been conquered by Muslims in the eighth century, and for the next two or three centuries Christian Europe and Muslim Spain coexisted peacefully. The concept of Christian holy war originated in the eleventh century, when Christians began the *Reconquista*, the religious war for the reconquest of Spain. By the late twelfth and early thirteenth centuries, much of northern Spain was taken by Christians, and the city of Toledo became a transmission point from which Muslim knowledge of ancient Greek culture, particularly many works by Aristotle, began to filter into Christian Europe. The final unification and Christianization of Spain occurred in the late fifteenth century, when King Ferdinand of Aragon and Queen Isabella of Castile married and thus brought the two major sections of the country under one ruling family. Ferdinand and Isabella drove out the last Muslims in 1492, and in the same year commissioned Christopher Columbus's first voyage across the Atlantic. Both events were caused in part by the crusading spirit. The spirit that expelled Muslims from Spain would by the sixteenth century impel Spanish *conquistadores* to conquer much of the New World and convert or exterminate many of the pagan natives of the Americas.

SOCIAL CHANGE

The economic and political transformations of the High Middle Ages were accompanied by significant social changes. Some of the more important were (1) the emergence of the aristocratic ideals of chivalry and "courtly" or "romantic" love; (2) a decline in the status of women; and (3) a growing sense of individualism.

Aristocratic Ideals

Chivalry was a code of conduct for medieval knights. It stipulated that knights were to be brave, loyal, honest, and above all honorable. They were to serve God and their king by fighting infidels and other enemies of Christian society. They were to honor their women (who were usually not their wives) by performing great deeds and daring exploits. In theory, the chivalric relationship between a knight and his lady was an adulterous affair between a married man and his mistress. No one really knows how much this chivalric conception actually affected social practice.

The chivalric code became the subject of many stories, the most famous being those written in the twelfth century by Chretien de Troyes about King Arthur and his knights of the round table. (There probably was a King Arthur in early medieval England, but he was an obscure prince who was later immortalized as a chivalric hero.) These stories describe an ideal of conduct, never the mundane reality of bawdy, boisterous knights who usually fought and caroused wherever they went. Yet, the stories did encourage medieval aristocrats to behave in a more civilized manner, to try to become "gentlemen" (meaning a man distinguished by his ancestry, or *gens* in Latin).

Another new aristocratic ideal was "courtly" or "romantic" love, so named because it originated in aristocratic courts and glorified romance between man and woman. The courtly love tradition was created in southern France, where it was to some degree stimulated by Muslim romantic literature imported from Spain. Particularly in Aquitaine, a series of troubadour poets began to idealize love as the supreme virtue in male-female relationships, though it was more often the love of a man for a woman who was not his wife. Originally, troubadour poetry was bawdy and sensual. William IX, duke of Aquitaine, wrote: "Let my hands 'neath her mantle meet / And I'll have done with sorrowing." The poetry became more spiritual and idealized as it developed in the twelfth century at the court of Eleanor of Aquitaine and at that of her daughter, Marie of Champagne. Bernart de Ventadorn wrote: "By nothing is a man so worthy as by the love and courting of women, for thence arises delight and song and all that pertains to excellence. No man is of value without Love."[10] Gradually, the poets defined the male-female relationship in a new way. In the ancient world and the early Middle Ages, marriage was usually thought of as a legal partnership with little romance involved, and other male-female relationships like prostitution were perceived in sexual terms. In contrast, the courtly love tradition of the High Middle Ages held that marriage should result from a man and a woman "courting" each other and "falling in love."

The Status of Women

Despite its long-term influence, the courtly love tradition had little practical impact on medieval society. In particular, it did not help the status of women. In the early Middle Ages, female status was relatively high, since a frontier society needed women's labor and managerial skills. Female power increased in some instances during the Crusades, as women managed property while men were off on their travels. Historian David Herlihy puts it this way:

> the social impact of Europe's great waves of military and geographic expansion, combined to raise the women to a position of prominence. . . . The great, external dramatic events of the day, the wars and crusades, are the work of active men. But their accomplishments were matched and perhaps made possible by the work of women no less active.[11]

The status of women began to decline during the High Middle Ages, however. The church fostered two stereotypes—Eve and the Virgin Mary—of female behavior, neither of which helped women. Eve was portrayed as the source of evil in the world, while the Virgin Mary was pictured as a pure, ethereal figure removed from and uninterested in worldly matters. In addition, political and legal developments decreased the political influence of women. Women were not allowed to enter the new universities. The church became increasingly male dominated because of the prescription of clerical celibacy. The rise of monarchical power reduced the power of aristocratic women who had previously influenced local politics through their families.

By the late Middle Ages most upper-class women had little political or economic influence, their primary roles being to produce heirs. A few middle-class married women were respected for their ability to manage a large urban household. But unmarried women in the cities suffered, many of them known as "spinsters" because spinning thread was their only way of making a living. Peasant wives were the only women who worked beside men (their husbands) in a position of equality, but this was an equality in poverty.

It is difficult to judge whether the actual lives of women in the late Middle Ages were worse than before. Women had greater opportunities during the early Middle Ages, but they also worked hard and often died young. In the later Middle Ages, women's social and political status was lower than in the early Middle Ages, but middle-class women in particular worked less and lived longer than before.

Growing Individualism

The High Middle Ages also witnessed a growing sense of individualism among people. Individualism was encouraged by the greater career choices open to at least some upper- and middle-class men. The more diverse economy and the availability of university education meant that men could choose to become knights, monks, bishops, teachers, or administrators for either the church or the new monarchies. Greater educational opportunities also helped encourage independent thought and individual self-expression. Often this self-expression was critical of the established authorities, especially the church. One example is this student parody of the Apostles' Creed:

> I believe in wine that's fair to see
> And in the tavern of my host
> More than in the Holy Ghost
> The tavern will my sweetheart be,
> And the Holy Church is not for me.[12]

More biting criticism came from young satiric poets, the most important known as the Archpoet. In the 1160s, he wrote a "Confession" that expressed his disenchantment with the society of his day:

> Boiling over inwardly
> With anger unconfined,
> Now in deepest bitterness
> I will speak my mind.
>
> I go down the primrose path
> As most young men do;

Am addicted much to vice,
Thoughtless of virtue.
I am more for merriment
Than renouncing sin,
And, being dead in soul, I take
Good care of my skin.[13]

The words of the Archpoet reveal that not everyone in the High Middle Ages was piously religious, that at least some social criticism and freedom of expression were possible.

INTELLECTUAL DEBATE AND CREATIVITY

The University and Scholasticism

The center of intellectual activity in the High Middle Ages was the university, another creation of the period. During the early Middle Ages, monastic schools were the only source of formal education. Many monks and nuns contemplated the scriptures, copied a few books, and sometimes taught neighboring children (the boys, rarely the girls) to read and write. New educational institutions appeared only after the year 1000, when a few Italian cities organized municipal schools and bishops in northern France formed cathedral schools to educate men for the church. Gradually, the students in these schools came to be collectively called the *universitas,* a Latin word that in this context meant only "group of people."

The university as a distinct institution first emerged in Italy during the twelfth century. The University at Bologna stressed the study of law, an appropriate orientation since knowledge of Roman law and of Justinian's Code had never completely dried out in Italy. In Sicily, the University of Salerno taught primarily medicine and mathematics, partly because Sicily was favored by geographical proximity to the Muslim world that at this time was a leading source of scientific and mathematical knowledge. Thus, Italian universities taught practical subjects, and students came to the universities to prepare for careers. Most of the students were in their twenties and thirties, old enough to be mature and to demand good instruction from the "masters," or teachers. In fact, Italian students often did the actual hiring of masters and sometimes refused to pay instructors who did not complete a course of study in the allotted time.

Other universities appeared by the late twelfth and early thirteenth centuries at Paris, Salamanca (Spain), and Oxford (England). The University of Salamanca was an early European center for the study of Arabic culture. But Paris was the most renowned of the medieval universities and attracted students and masters from all of Europe. The Paris masters taught the liberal arts curriculum inherited from ancient Greece and Rome. The liberal arts consisted of a *trivium* (grammar, rhetoric, and logic) that stressed verbal communication and a *quadrivium* (mathematics, astronomy, geometry, and music) that focused on mathematical communication. Liberal arts education was designed to be preparatory study for the ultimate goal—the study of theology that would qualify students for careers in the church.

The most important part of the liberal arts curriculum was the study of logic, which in practice meant the study of Aristotle. Aristotle's logical and scientific works, which were being transmitted from Spain into France during the twelfth century, were causing great intellectual excitement, particularly in Paris, because they contrasted so sharply with the traditional deductive thought of Plato. The theologians at Paris sought to use Aristotelian logic to support Christian theology, specifically to employ rational analysis to examine and clarify scriptural passages and theological propositions. The result was *Scholasticism,* the name given to the medieval attempt to combine reason (Aristotle) and revelation (Christian faith).

Abelard

One of the most prominent early Scholastics was Peter Abelard (c. 1079–1142), a renowned teacher and logician. Abelard's *Sic et Non* ("Yes and No") was a compilation of seemingly contradictory statements that he found in the Bible and other church writings. He sought to use rational analysis to examine the statements and perhaps dispel the contradictions involved. Thus, he believed he was employing intellectual methods to strengthen and fortify Christian theology. But his intellectualism and his willingness to debate and argue brought him many enemies, particularly those who thought Christian faith should be based on emotion and church authority. Adding to Abelard's notoriety was his famous love affair with his student Heloise. Abelard and Heloise had a child and married even though he was supposed to remain celibate; in the resulting furor, Heloise's irate relatives had Abelard castrated and at Abelard's urging Heloise became a nun. For the rest of their lives, the two lovers could only write affectionate letters to each other.

Abelard was one of the first participants in an extraordinary theological and philosophical debate that obsessed Christian theologians during the twelfth to the fourteenth centuries. Before it ended, that debate formed the philosophical foundation for modern natural sciences that emerged in Europe in the sixteenth and seventeenth centuries. For this reason it was of crucial importance to the history of Western Civilization and indeed to the history of the world. The major issue of the debate was the relationship between reason and revelation. Some of the most prominent debaters were St. Thomas Aquinas (1225–1274), John Duns Scotus (1265–1308), and William of Occam (1285–1349).

St. Thomas Aquinas

Aquinas, like Abelard, sought to combine reason and revelation. In his *Summa Theologica*, he argues that both forms of knowledge come from God. Reason provides humans with logical and empirical knowledge of this world, while revelation gives knowledge of the spiritual realm. Revelation (or faith) is ultimately the final authority, but there can be no conflict between reason and revelation, since God's creation is rational and can be understood rationally. Hence, Aquinas believed that such things as the immortality of the soul and the freedom of the human will could be proven on rational grounds. His *Summa* was a majestic synthesis of the medieval belief that Greek rational thought (personified by Aristotle) was consistent with and complemented Christian faith. His thought, often called *Thomism*, became basic to Catholic theology for centuries.

Some of Aquinas's contemporaries believed that he placed too much emphasis on the rationality of the universe. John Duns Scotus, a Franciscan and teacher at Oxford, argued that many Christian truths are not rational. The existence of God, for example, cannot be proven on rational grounds and has to be accepted on faith. Thus, he challenged the harmony of faith and reason that was the basis of Aquinas's thought. Another challenge emanated from the Council of Paris (1277), in which the church condemned many of Aristotle's philosophical propositions and thereby deemed Aristotelian rational thought as incompatible with Christian faith.

William of Occam

The philosophical dispute continued with the English philosopher William of Occam, also a Franciscan and a student of Duns Scotus. Occam insisted that the most basic fact about God is that he is absolutely free and omnipotent. Therefore, God can create any kind of world he chooses, either rational or irrational. God's creation might be rational if he chooses to make it so, but there is no guarantee of rationality. In short, God's freedom is superior to reason. For example, Occam agreed that the world *appeared* to be rational and would presumably have accepted the law of gravity—that objects always fall toward, not away from, the earth—as an illustration of the fact that natural objects always act in accordance with rational laws of nature. But he would have argued that

God, if he so chooses, can override the law of gravity, although he may never have actually done so.

Occam's ideas may sound like abstruse philosophizing, but they had significant implications. If the world was completely rational, then intelligent humans like Aristotle could by rational analysis come to understand how the world operates. This is why science was a thinking activity rather than a form of experimentation for the ancient Greeks; through rational thought a person could penetrate the mysteries of the universe and then *deduce* why natural objects behave the way they do. (Deduction is a form of thinking in which a person begins with general assumed principles and reasons from there to truths.) But if, as Occam argued, there is no guarantee that the world is rational, then rational thought cannot lead to reliable knowledge of how nature operates. The only way to attain scientific knowledge is to *observe* nature, to study it empirically and see how it actually functions in reality. In short, science must be *empirical* rather than *speculative*.

The shift in thought that came to fruition in Occam's philosophy was a major turning point in Western history. If Occam was, and is, right, then purely abstract thought is of little use to humans and they can hope to attain knowledge only in two radically distinct ways: (1) religious faith and the acceptance of certain unprovable truths, such as the existence of God; and (2) scientific observation of the world as created. In other words, faith and the belief in God constitute one form of knowledge, science another. Thus, Occam turned the study of nature in an empirical direction and separated it from religious knowledge. Too much emphasis should not be placed on Occam's thought, for Aquinas's philosophy, which Occam opposed, continued to have great influence, particularly within the Catholic church. It remains true, however, that Occam helped prepare the way for modern secular science.

It is significant that both Occam and Duns Scotus were Franciscans, for it was St. Francis who provided an emotional basis for the study of nature. During the early Middle Ages, nature was rarely studied as such, partly because it was perceived as a collection of symbols expressing God's messages. The rainbow, for example, was a symbol of hope. St. Francis refused to accept this interpretation, which implied that nature exists only for the spiritual benefit of humans. He insisted that nature is fully a part of God's world and should be appreciated as a divinely created reality, not just as a series of symbols. His enthusiasm for nature carried over into the religious order he founded, and the English Franciscans in particular began to study and observe nature. Robert Grosseteste (1169–1253), for example, said nothing about the rainbow as a symbol of hope but examined it in an empirical manner as a way of studying optics. Roger Bacon (1214–1294) theorized that nature, being a divine creation, is a source of knowledge about God and thus created the idea of natural theology. Many of the early scientists who created the scientific revolution of the sixteenth and seventeenth centuries considered themselves to be natural theologians who studied God through his creation.

CONCLUSION

During the European High Middle Ages, Western Civilization became a dynamic force, more energetic and aggressive than other civilizations of the world. Some of the most important features of this dynamism were the following:

1. *The rise of cities.* Medieval European cities were different from most other cities in the world, in that they were largely free to govern themselves. Freedom allowed the unhindered development of a new merchant class that would slowly create the aggressive economic practice of capitalism.
2. *Technological development.* Medieval Europeans were more mechanically minded than most other peoples and by the fifteenth century had developed the beginnings of a technological civilization. Examples of medieval technology are the water mill, the windmill, and the mechanical clock, which first appeared in Europe late in the thirteenth century.
3. *Secularization* (the separation of worldly ideas or institutions from the sacred and religious). The increasing separation of church and state created an institutional tension that prevented any one organization from dominating Europe and thereby possibly suppressing creativity. The growing secularization of nature (that is, the presumption that the study of nature is a different form of knowledge than the study of theology) helped create the basis of modern science.
4. *Representative political institutions.* The Europeans, like many other peoples, were traditionally governed and continued to be governed by monarchies. But by the late Middle Ages, many parts of Europe had developed political institutions through which at least some part of the populace had a voice in governmental decisions. These institutions would gradually become the most innovative and even revolutionary element in Western politics.
5. *Territorial expansion.* European civilization began in Western Europe, then expanded into Scandinavia and eastern Europe, gained domination of the northern seas (the Baltic and North Seas), and during the Crusades wrested control of the Mediterranean from the Muslims.
6. *Intellectual development.* The rise of the university provided a permanent base for continued thought and research. Medieval thought, particularly Thomism and Scholasticism, became a basic philosophical-theological perspective for the Catholic church.

THINGS YOU SHOULD KNOW

Early towns
The emergence of a merchant class
The growth of trade
The importance of water mills and windmills
The fairs of Champagne
Pope Gregory VII
Pope Innocent III
Cistercians
Franciscans
Dominicans
Romanesque and Gothic architecture
The status of Jews in the Middle Ages
William the Conqueror
Henry II (England)
Eleanor of Aquitaine
Magna Carta
Evolution of the English Parliament
Philip Augustus
Otto the Great
Investiture controversy
Golden Bull of 1356
The Crusades
Reconquista
Chivalry
Courtly love
Decline in the status of women
Growing sense of individualism
Rise of the university
Scholasticism
Peter Abelard
St. Thomas Aquinas
William of Occam
Late medieval natural theology

SUGGESTED READINGS

The works by Francis Oakley and Lynn White, Jr., cited in the Suggested Readings section of Chapter 7, are also excellent sources for the High Middle Ages. Georges Duby, *The Age of the Cathedrals: Art and Society, 980–1420,* trans. Eleanor Levieux and Barbara Thompson (Chicago: Univ. of Chicago Press, 1981) is a superb study of medieval art and architecture and is particularly good on the social and spiritual background of that art. Willis B. Glover, *Biblical Origins of Modern Secular Culture: An Essay in the Interpretation of Western History* (Macon, GA: Mercer Univ. Press, 1984) is useful on the philosophical debate that helped lay the foundations for modern science and modern secular culture. Jean Gimpel, *The Medieval Machine: The Industrial Revolution of the Middle Ages* (New York: Penguin, 1976) summarizes medieval technological developments and the industrial revolution. Renate Bridenthal and Claudia Koonz (eds.), *Becoming Visible: Women in European History* (Boston: Houghton Mifflin, 1977) includes several good essays on women in the Middle Ages, as does Susan Mosher Stuard (ed.), *Women in Medieval Society* (Philadelphia: Univ. of Pennsylvania Press, 1976). On the Crusades, see Jonathan Riley-Smith, *The Crusades: A Short History* (New Haven: Yale Univ. Press, 1987). On the development of the new national monarchies, see Sidney Painter, *The Rise of the Feudal Monarchies* (Ithaca, N.Y.: Cornell Univ. Press, 1951).

NOTES

[1] Quoted in Bernard Lewis, *The Arabs in History,* rev. ed. (New York: Harper Torchbooks, 1966), p. 164.

[2] Lynn White, Jr., "Eilmer of Malmesbury, An Eleventh Century Aviator," in *Medieval Religion and Technology* (Berkeley: Univ. of California Press, 1978), p. 68.

[3] Quoted in Richard Barber, *The Penguin Guide to Medieval Europe* (New York: Penguin, 1984), p. 237.

[4] Lynn White, Jr., "Technology and Invention in the Middle Ages," in *Medieval Religion and Technology* (Berkeley: Univ. of California Press, 1978), p. 22.

[5] Quoted in Georges Duby, *The Age of the Cathedrals: Art and Society, 980–1420*, trans. Eleanor Levieux and Barbara Thompson (Chicago: Univ. of Chicago Press, 1981), p. 137.

[6] Ibid., p. 89.

[7] Quoted in William R. Cook and Ronald B. Herzman, *The Medieval World View: An Introduction* (New York: Oxford Univ. Press, 1983), p. 236.

[8] Geoffrey Barraclough, *The Origins of Modern Germany* (New York: Capricorn, 1963), p. 319.

[9] Quoted in Cook and Herzman, *Medieval World*, p. 234.

[10] Quoted in Francis Oakley, *The Medieval Experience: Foundations of Western Cultural Singularity* (New York: Scribner's, 1974), p. 199.

[11] David Herlihy, "Land, Family, and Women in Continental Europe, 701–1200," in *Women in Medieval Society*, ed. Susan Mosher Stuard (Philadelphia: Univ. of Pennsylvania Press, 1976), p. 34.

[12] Quoted in C. Warren Hollister, *Medieval Europe: A Short History* (New York: Wiley, 1964), p. 229.

[13] Quoted in Colin Morris, *The Discovery of the Individual, 1050–1200* (New York: Harper & Row, 1972), pp. 131–32.

9

The Countryside and the City, 1200 to 1700

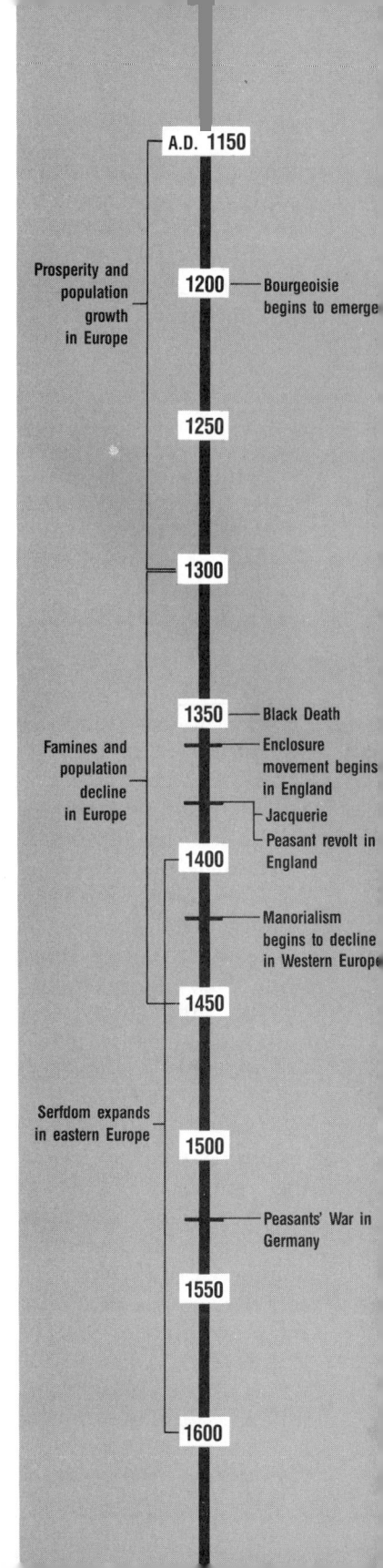

A.D. 1150	
1200	Bourgeoisie begins to emerge
	Prosperity and population growth in Europe
1250	
1300	
1350	Black Death
	Enclosure movement begins in England
	Jacquerie
	Peasant revolt in England
1400	
	Famines and population decline in Europe
	Manorialism begins to decline in Western Europe
1450	
1500	Serfdom expands in eastern Europe
	Peasants' War in Germany
1550	
1600	

The study of history traditionally focuses on great events and great people—the most famous battles, the most powerful political leaders, the most creative artists and philosophers. Yet, only a few men and women attain this status of greatness; most are ordinary people whose lives rarely, if ever, gain the attention of historical study. As B. H. Slicher van Bath once said,

> the life of almost all men consists chiefly of small, daily happenings. Not every day does one set out on a campaign or voyage of discovery; it is but seldom we are called upon to hold the barricades or man the battlements. The greater part of mankind was not actively affected by the mighty events of history books, or if affected at all, only passively, by enduring patiently the distress they caused. Ordinary people worked, ate, slept. For them birth, marriage, and death, their own or those in the circle of their families and friends, were the important events that stood out above the common routine.[1]

Social history is the term usually applied to the study of ordinary people who lived routine lives in the past. In this chapter, we interrupt our survey of great events to examine the social history of Western Civilization from late medieval to early modern times, a period extending roughly from the thirteenth to the eighteenth centuries.

During this five-hundred-year period, European society was overwhelmingly rural and agricultural. Most people—over 80 percent of the population—were peasants who worked the land and lived in poverty. Dominating the peasants was a small upper class—the aristocrats—whose wealth and power was derived from military and legal power, land ownership, and the ability to get food and other supplies from the lower classes. Although peasants and aristocrats were separated both socially and economically, they were bound together by a rural life-style dominated by tradition and only gradual change—a sort of "culture of the countryside."

During the High Middle Ages there emerged another way of life—the "culture of the city." Life in the city was significantly different from life in the countryside. In the countryside, wealth came from the land. But in the city, it came from artisans, who made products with their hands and rudimentary machinery, and from merchants, who engaged in trade and commerce. Furthermore, the city fostered a different attitude toward life, one that welcomed change rather than tradition, aggressiveness rather than acceptance, and economic growth rather than stability. The European city was not just an urban extension of the countryside. Rather, it was a rival culture that offered a different way of life and fostered a different attitude toward life.

THE PEASANT'S LIFE-STYLE

We do not know much about how peasants lived, since most of them were illiterate and thus did not write about their thoughts, feelings, and beliefs. Most literary accounts of the time (books, diaries, memoirs) that describe the peasantry were written by members of the upper classes, who rarely sympathized with the peasants and usually regarded them with a mixture of contempt and fear. One such writer, for example, described a peasant as having "huge limbs, eyes a hand's breadth apart, broad shoulders, an enormous chest, bristling hair, and a face black as coal. He went six months without washing. The only water that ever touched his face was rain."[2] Another source—a collection of comic stories entitled *Nouvelles Nouvelles*—ridiculed peasants by portraying them as grasping and greedy; in one story, a peasant finds his wife having intercourse with a friend and allows the lovers to continue when he is promised a gift.

The literary works of the time are usually biased in favor of the upper classes and thus are unreliable sources of information on the lower classes. For a more accurate account of the peasant life-style, historians often turn to nonliterary sources such as marriage records, monastic chronicles, and birth and death registers (which can indicate, for example, when a famine occurred or when the population rose or fell). These sources strongly indicate that the life of the typical European peasant was hard at best. Indeed, peasants of preindustrial times probably lived in much the same way as the poverty-stricken people of Third World countries do today.

Material Conditions of Peasant Life

Most European peasants were poor because agricultural productivity was low, such that food shortages existed even in what were considered good harvest years. In addition, peasants rarely got to keep all their crops—*usually* about 10 percent went to the church as a tithe, 20–40 percent to the lord for taxes, and another 10 percent to seed grains for the next year's crop. Thus, most peasants were left with only 40–50 percent of a small harvest to support their family throughout the year. But even then bad weather or a marauding army might destroy the crops, in which case peasants had to beg for food or eat roots and bark from trees just to survive.

Food, then, was the typical peasant's first priority. Since bread was the cheapest, hence the most common food, grains were the primary crops. Many European peasants would consume two or three pounds of bread a day. There were many different types of bread. The darker kinds were most available and white bread was so rare that it was considered a luxury reserved primarily for the upper classes. The old German proverb "man is what he eats" meant that a person's social position was indicated by the color of the bread they ate. In addition to bread, the peasant diet occasionally included vegetables mixed into a porridge, some cheese, and some fish for those who lived near the sea.

The peasants' struggle to get enough to eat was so pervasive that displays of food were symbolic of good times. Offering food to a visitor was a sign of respect and generosity. The village banquet—where food was available in large quantities—was the distinctive mark of festive occasions such as weddings and christenings. Also symbolic was the physical difference between the peasantry and upper classes. Since food was readily available to the rich, they tended to be heavier in weight than the poor. Thus, being overweight was considered good, symbolic of one's well-being and high status.

Peasants lacked other things besides enough food. Cloth was expensive, so most peasants had only one or two changes of clothes. Even the clothing they had didn't fit well and was usually dirty and uncomfortable to wear. Their undergarments, for example, were often made of scratchy wool. Even when peasants could afford some new piece of clothing, they had to lessen the cost by settling for short cloaks that reached only to the waist or knees. Since the rich could afford longer garments, the length of a person's clothes also came to distinguish the rich from the poor.

Peasant housing was crude. The typical abode was a wooden or stone hut of one or two rooms. A fireplace was used for cooking and heating, though it provided little heat. (Heating was difficult even for the upper classes. One account of a dinner at the French royal palace at Versailles tells of how the water froze in the drinking glasses.) Furniture was scarce as well. The peasant usually had a storage chest, a table, a bench or two, some straw mats for sleeping, and a few cooking utensils. Often, livestock stayed in one of the rooms.

The living conditions of peasants caused most of them to be malnourished and vulnerable to disease. The death rate among peasants was high and even higher for their children. The average peasant life span in normal times was about thirty-five years, in part because of high infant mortality rates. Although some peasants reached the age of fifty or more, most did not live long enough to see the birth of their grandchildren.

Villages

The material conditions just discussed characterized most of the thousands of villages that dotted preindustrial Europe. (Until the late Middle Ages, most villages were part of the manorial system—see Chapter 7.) A typical village contained 500–700 people, most of them subsistence farmers. The few nonfarmers in a village might include a

Village Street This drawing shows a typical village street, including a village gate in the background, a cobble-stoned road, and houses packed tightly together. In order to get as many buildings as possible inside the city walls for protection, the buildings in a village were constructed in clusters. (Pierpont Morgan Library)

miller to grind grain, a smith to make and repair farm implements, an innkeeper, a parish priest, and perhaps a few local "gentlemen" who owned large farms but hired others to work the land. In appearance, the village was a collection of huts centered around a church building and a cemetery. Outside the inhabited area were the fields—some pastures, a few orchards, a pond perhaps for fishing, and, most important, the cultivated land. The main crops were cereals—oats, wheat, and barley—that fed both people and livestock. Small livestock were more numerous than large, since they were easier to support. A peasant might own several pigs, chickens, and ducks, but only one or two horses or cows.

Each village was expected to be self-sufficient, to produce everything it needed. There was usually a lot of activity on local rural roads—peddlars going to local fairs, herdsmen driving sheep or cattle to local markets, pilgrims walking to religious shrines. But long-distance travel was difficult, so most villages were isolated from the rest of the world. This isolation made peasants suspicious of strangers and discouraged attitudes other than those dominated by local custom and the farming way of life. Routine was the norm, unless a calamity struck. Sons and daughters lived as their parents did before them, often cultivating the same fields and living in the same huts. The nineteenth-century English poet and novelist Thomas Hardy describes well the spirit of peasant life:

> Only a man harrowing clods
> In a slow silent walk
> With an old horse that stumbles and nods
> Half asleep as they stalk.
>
> Only thin smoke without flame
> From the heaps of couch-grass;
> Yet this will go onward the same
> Though dynasties pass.[3]

In many villages, local noble families were usually comparatively well-off, and peasants were expected to respect and submit to them. One parish church, for example , expected peasants to follow this rule: "When the Lord or Lady de Bretennières or their family are entering or leaving the church, all the inhabitants and parishioners of the said place shall keep silence and make their respects."[4] The most unfortunate peasants were the landless. They were usually desperately poor and survived only by hiring out their labor or by begging.

Customs and Attitudes

The majority of European peasants had a little land and a few animals; their goal in life was to wrest a living from the land and then pass the property on to the next generation. The peasant family was more than a personal or sexual relationship; it was also an economic partnership in which property was considered more important than sentiment or physical attraction between husband and wife. Two French proverbs indicate this importance: "Love may do much, but money more" and "Never trust a nice arse or a starry sky."[5]

Marriage customs usually allowed peasant women to choose their husbands. Many peasant women waited until their mid-twenties to choose a partner. One reason for this was that chronic malnutrition delayed their reaching puberty before their late-teens. Another reason was that delayed marriages resulted in fewer children and thus kept family sizes down. (In some parts of the world, peasants tried to have as many children as possible so as to have more people to help in the fields. Many Western European peasants, however, preferred to keep family size down so that more land and wealth could be passed on to each member of the next generation.) After marriage, the wife and children worked alongside the husband, sometimes laboring in the fields but more often spinning cloth or doing other household chores. If the husband died before the wife, the widow was sometimes left in an unfortunate situation. Peasant women had few legal rights, and inheritances passed through the male line, so a widow was dependent on the good will of her children. If the children refused to support her, she was forced to live alone, and it was not uncommon for single women to be suspected of witchcraft.

Peasant life did have some positive aspects. Most villages held numerous festivities throughout the year to celebrate church holidays, saints' days, and special events like weddings. The church was the social center of the community, a place not only for religious services but also for meeting neighbors, exchanging gossip, and discussing business. It might also serve other purposes, such as a place to store grain or a fortress to which villagers could retreat for protection.

Virtually all European peasants considered themselves Christians. They usually attended church services on Sunday, occasionally went on short pilgrimages, and tried to bury their dead in consecrated ground. But most peasants knew little about the formal theological doctrines of Christianity. Many distrusted the priests and bishops, who often lived more comfortably than peasants. One peasant said, for example, that "priests want us under their thumb, just to keep us quiet." He also asserted that Masses for the dead were pointless: "What are you doing giving alms in memory of these few ashes?"[6] His skepticism resulted in his being burned at the stake. Another peasant blamed God for poor harvests: "Old man God is too old, he does not know what he is doing anymore. He spoils everything. Our vineyards and our pear orchards are lost. We'll have to make another God."[7] Although most peasants were not so outspoken, historians agree that a considerable number of peasants did not submit meekly to religious authorities. Peasants were Christian, but their beliefs were not necessarily orthodox and their attitudes were not always respectful.

Some peasants either left voluntarily or were forced out of the tightly knit village community. (Leaving voluntarily was, of course, not an option for serfs.) The more adventuresome joined a king's army or found work on a merchant sailing vessel. Those considered troublemakers were often driven away and left to survive by begging, banditry, smuggling, or piracy. For women, a respectable route out of the village was to find work as a domestic servant in a nearby city. The wealthier nobility employed dozens of cooks and maids; in some cities, domestic servants constituted 10–20 percent of the population. Another respected female occupation was that of wet nurse. Abandoned children and the illegitimate offspring of upper-class men were often cared for by wet nurses, who thus performed an essential social service. A less respectable but common means of survival for women was prostitution. Virtually every city contained large numbers of prostitutes, many of them peasant women who had come to the city in search of work. A popular saying in southern France illustrates this point: "On the bridge at Avignon you are always certain to encounter two monks, two asses, and two whores."[8]

TIMES OF FAMINE

Our discussion has thus far focused on peasant life in normal times, when harvests were reasonably good and external threats such as army attacks were absent. But not all times were normal. Famine and plague constantly threatened the peasants' existence, and when these calamities struck, peasants quickly became desperate and miserable.

Famines were usually regional phenomena, occurring whenever two or more bad harvest years followed successively in one particular area. Famine led to malnutrition, which, in turn, led to epidemics like cholera and the bubonic plague as well as smallpox, typhoid fever, and diphtheria. The devastation of famine and disease occurred at different times in different places, but virtually every area of Europe endured them sporadically for centuries. For example, famine afflicted the region of Languedoc (southern France) for twenty years between 1302 and 1348. Four bad harvest years occurred from 1302 to 1305, and then in 1310 torrential rains produced several more crop failures. The years 1322 and 1329 were also bad, and the poor had to survive on raw herbs through the winter of 1332. In 1348, the Black Death (bubonic plague) swept through Europe, decimating the population in what one historian calls the "holocaust of the undernourished."[9] At a religious community in Montpellier, only 7 out of 140 friars survived the plague. The depopulation of Languedoc was so severe that forests and wild game reappeared on abandoned farmland.

The following account reveals on a more personal level how crop failures drove up the price of bread and destroyed what had been a reasonably fortunate family:

> There was a family in Beauvais in the year 1693 named Cocu: Jean Cocu, weaver of serges, and his wife with three daughters, all four spinning wool for him, since the youngest daughter was already nine years old. The family earned 108 sols a week, but they ate 70 pounds of bread between them. With bread up to 0.5 sol a pound, their livelihood was secure. With bread at one sol a pound, it began to get difficult. With bread at 2 sols, then at 3.2, 3.3, and 3.4—as it was in 1649, in 1652, in 1662, in 1694, in 1710—it was misery.
>
> They went without; they pawned their things; they began to eat unwholesome food, bran bread, cooked nettles, mouldy cereals, entrails of animals picked up outside the slaughter-houses. . . . The family was registered at the Office of the Poor in December 1693. In March 1694, the youngest daughter died; in May the eldest daughter

The Black Death In a fifteenth-century written account of a Catholic religious service known as the *Office of the Dead,* the illustration shows a goldsmith, a victim of the bubonic plague, being carried off by Death. The first outbreak of bubonic plague lasted from 1347–1351 and killed nearly a third of Europe's population. (Pierpont Morgan Library)

and the father. All that remained was a widow and an orphan. Because of the price of bread.[10]

Another poignant account simply quotes from the 1623 death register of Greystoke (England):

27th March: A poor hungerstarved beggar child, Dorothy, daughter of Henry Patteson, Miller.

19th May: At night James Irwin, a poor beggar stripling born upon the borders of England. He died in Johnby in great misery.

11th September: Leonard, son of Anthony Cowlman, of Johnby, late deceased, which child died for want of food and maintenance to live.

12th September: Jaine, wife of Anthony Cowlman, late deceased, which woman died in Edward Dawson's barn of Greystoke, for want of maintenance.

27th September: John, son of John Lancaster, late of Greystoke, a waller by trade, which child died for want of food and means.

4th October: Agnes, wife of John Lancaster, late of Greystoke, a waller by his trade, which woman died for want of means to live.[11]

When famine struck, many peasants left their homes in search of food. They often wandered to cities to beg, but they were usually met with hostility and punished by the authorities. One eyewitness account describes the punishment of peasant beggars in Languedoc in the famine year of 1595:

> They imprison them, they nail them down by their outstretched arms and hands; others force their mouths open and inflate them until they burst, hanging them by the feet. Oh, poor peasants. Be consoled in your misery. Help us to bear the cross of Our Lord.[12]

PEASANT REBELLIONS

Peasants rarely had any political power or influence. In addition, the upper classes expected peasants to bear their burdens without complaint. German nobles likened peasants to dumb beasts: "A peasant is just like an ox, only he has no horns."[13] Rebellion and war were the only means by which peasants could vent their rage and express their opposition to the forces that dominated them.

Peasant rebellions usually were not revolutionary attempts to overthrow the existing social order. Most peasants were conservative, and their rebellions were aimed at correcting some specific abuse of traditional peasant rights. The most common peasant grievance was increased taxation. In most areas, the upper classes paid little if any taxes and the peasantry assumed most of the tax burden. Peasant resistance to both state and church taxation was chronic, as indicated in the following conversation among peasants in a village square:

> "We're going to have to pay the bishop's tax on new born lambs," says one of five peasants sitting under the elm tree in the village square in the year 1320.
> "Don't let's pay anything," answers another. "Let us rather find one hundred *livres* to pay two men to kill the bishop."
> "I'll willingly pay my share," replies a third man. "Money could not be better spent."[14]

Some peasant outbursts were actual wars in which well-organized peasant armies were able to sustain long military campaigns. These wars were usually defensive struggles waged to protect peasants' land from predatory princes and aristocrats. They occurred during the thirteenth and fourteenth centuries in northern Germany and Switzerland, where peasants who controlled their own land were able to form peasant republics. The legend of William Tell grew out of the Swiss peasant wars.

More common than wars, though, were badly organized relatively spontaneous peasant rebellions that usually lasted only briefly. These rebellions were numerous and occurred throughout Europe. In Aquitaine (southern France), for example, there were nearly five hundred peasant insurrections between 1590 and 1715. Roughly two hundred rebellions occurred in Germany between 1301 and 1550. In all of Europe between 1300 and 1800, tens of thousands of peasant outbursts occurred. The most famous of these rebellions include the Jacquerie around Paris in 1358, the Peasants' Revolt of 1381 in England, and the German Peasants' War of 1525.

The Jacquerie derived its name from a French nickname—Jacques—for peasants. In 1358, peasants around Paris rebelled against increased taxes imposed by the government to support the Hundred Years' War fought between France and England (see Chapter 10). The rebels plundered several noble estates and killed a few people. The nobility reacted with vengeance, executing over twenty thousand people, including some children, priests, and monks.

The Hundred Years' War also caused turmoil in England, as the political instability and increased taxation produced by the war helped precipitate the Peasants' Revolt of 1381, inspired in part by Biblical ideals. For several years before 1381, an itinerant preacher named John Ball traveled through northern English villages proclaiming that all men were equal and that church lands should be given to peasants. A popular rhyme was associated with Ball:

> When Adam delved, and Eve span,
> Who was then a gentleman?[15]

In 1381, an army of peasants, inspired by Ball and led by Wat Tyler, marched into London, burned some houses, and forced the king to agree to reforms. The peasants beheaded one of their enemies, the archbishop of Canterbury, and then played football with his severed head. But the king's forces quickly recovered, dispersed the peasants, and executed Ball and Tyler. English folklore still remembers the two peasant leaders as spokesmen for the lower classes.

The German Peasants' War of 1525 was caused in part by the religious upheavals of the Reformation in which Protestant churches in some parts of Europe split from the Catholic church (see Chapter 11). German peasants, in addition to their usual grievances against the upper classes, began to believe that scriptural teachings sanctioned rebellion against oppression. Thus peasants rose in revolt. But, just as in England and France, the upper classes destroyed the rebellion and killed over 75,000 peasants in the process.

As these three examples indicate, most peasant rebellions were quickly crushed. Yet peasant rage continued to explode sporadically, and the aristocracy and urban classes lived in constant fear of peasant reprisals. This fear was often depicted in artwork created for or by the upper classes. Many paintings of the time portray peasants as brutish, dirty, drunken people usually engaged in fighting or rioting.

CHANGES IN PEASANT LIFE

Peasant life was not the same at all times in all places. Indeed, there was both variety and similarity among the European peasantry. For instance, while most peasants lived in tightly knit villages, some peasants lived in isolation on separate homesteads such as in mountainous areas. Mountain peasants tended to engage more in cattle grazing than in farming, and the need to guide cattle to distant pastures meant that they had to live near the pastures rather than in the villages.

Other differences in peasant life resulted from economic and social changes that developed over long periods of time. The most important of these changes were in the peasant standard of living, the decline of the medieval manorial system in Western Europe, and the expansion of serfdom in eastern Europe.

Peasant Standard of Living

The peasant standard of living varied greatly, depending on the general condition of the European economy. From 1150 to 1300, Europe enjoyed sustained agricultural prosperity and population growth, so most Europeans were relatively well-off. Gradually, though, population expansion outstripped food supplies, causing famines, plagues (the Black Death), population declines, and agricultural depression from 1300 to about 1450. A slow recovery began in the mid-fifteenth century, and some agricultural prosperity and population growth occurred between 1450 and 1600. After this came another depression, as both food production and population remained the same from about 1600 to 1750. At this point began a long agricultural boom and rapid population growth that continued into the twentieth century (See Table 9.1.) The basic economic "law" of preindustrial Europe was that food production was sharply limited by inferior farming technologies, so famines and hard times resulted whenever population expanded beyond the available food supplies. Only with the agricultural and industrial revolutions of the eighteenth and nineteenth centuries did Europe break through the old

TABLE 9.1 VARIATIONS IN THE GENERAL CONDITION OF THE EUROPEAN ECONOMY, 1150–1950

1150–1300	General prosperity
1300–1450	Economic depression
1450–1600	Some renewed prosperity
1600–1750	Economic depression
1750–1950	Continued economic growth

A Farmyard A drawing of a typical peasant farmyard, with small but well-constructed buildings. However, many peasant dwellings were more crude and less comfortable than portrayed here. (Pierpont Morgan Library)

limits on food production and create the conditions for a continually improving standard of living.

The Manorial System Declines in Western Europe

The decline of the manorial system in Western Europe began during the hard economic years between 1300 and 1450. Previously, most Western European peasants were serfs, unfree laborers who worked for and obeyed a lord in exchange for protection and access to some land. But the population decline of 1300–1450 created a severe labor shortage, and peasants were thus able to demand better working conditions, a reduction in the labor services they owed, and even some wages for work performed. Gradually, a growing number of serfs either bought or were given their freedom and became peasants who owned or rented land. This change in the legal status of serfs occurred at different times in different places. In northern France and the Low Countries (Belgium and the Netherlands), for example, serfdom largely disappeared by the sixteenth century. Other, more economically backward areas—southern

Spain, southern Italy, Ireland, the Highlands of Scotland—retained serfdom until well into the eighteenth century. In these areas, the landowning classes were so conservative that they fought any attempt to modify the practice of serfdom.

When serfs became free peasants, their lives were fundamentally transformed. They could now make contracts, buy or sell land, and borrow money from a moneylender. In short, their destiny was in their hands, for their well-being depended on their ability to manage property and income. Some peasants prospered in their new freedom. Others, however, lost more than they gained. They lost first the economic and psychic security provided on a manor that was guided and protected by an able lord. Then, some free peasants lost access to land because of a change in land organization known as the *enclosure movement*. Medieval manors usually divided land into three cultivated fields and common land—one field was for a fall crop, another for a spring crop, and the third lay fallow (see Chapter 7). Farming was communal, as each villager controlled several plots of land scattered among the three fields and also used the common land for grazing cattle and gathering nuts and berries. The enclosure movement sought to combine the landowners' cultivated land and their share of the common land into one united area, thus "enclosing" the land into one large farm. The reality was that the large landowners usually initiated the request that legal authorities grant permission to enclose in a given area. They, unlike illiterate serfs, had the legal documentation and political power to claim most of the land for themselves whenever a village was subjected to the enclosure process. One result was that some landowners acquired increasingly larger, privately owned farms, on which they could graze large herds of cattle or raise cash crops. Enclosure was one source of the new concept of *private property*. Another result was that many peasants lost their land and many peasant villages simply disappeared. One peasant complaint said bitterly that the large landowners "leave no grounde for tillage, thei enclose al into pastures, thei throw downe houses, thei plucke downe towns, and leave nothing standynge, but only the churche to be made a shepehowse."[16]

The enclosure movement began in England during the mid-fourteenth century. First one village and then another was enclosed, so that gradually over a four-hundred-year period (1350–1750) much of English farmland passed into the hands of large landowners. A similar process began in other countries in the sixteenth and seventeenth centuries. In some parts of Italy, Spain, and Germany, large landowners began to annex common lands, drive many peasants off the land, and create larger farms for themselves.

Serfdom Expands in Eastern Europe

A very different process occurred in eastern Europe. Whereas in the west many serfs became free peasants, in the east, particularly in Poland and

Russia, many formerly free peasants were forced into serfdom during the fifteenth and sixteenth centuries. One reason for this difference between the west and east lay in political factors. In Western European countries, monarchs often used financial help from the urban business classes to assert their authority over the nobility (see Chapter 10) and put an end to serfdom. The monarchs were not consciously trying to help the serfs; rather, they were seeking to weaken the nobility by decreasing their control over the peasantry and to strengthen themselves by forcing free peasants to pay taxes directly into royal purses. In Poland the nobility remained more powerful than the monarchs, and in Russia the monarchs received their strongest political support from the nobility. The result was that eastern nobles were more influential than their counterparts in the west and thus free to force serfdom on the peasants.

Another reason for the divergence between east and west was the gradual evolution of *capitalism* in Western Europe. Capitalism encouraged the development of a monetary economy. The availability of coinage made it easier to transform the lord-serf relationship based on labor services into a noble-free peasant relationship based on a peasant's paying cash to buy or rent land.

The living conditions of eastern European serfs varied greatly. Some serfs were little different from slaves, being completely controlled and sometimes physically abused by their lords. Others were relatively well-off, particularly those who were protected by good lords and had steady access to some land. But all serfs were unfree, subject to the will of their owners. The only difference between a serf and a slave was that the law recognized the serf as a human being with some legal rights (sometimes only the dubious right of paying taxes), while the slave was considered property.

By the seventeenth century, significant variations existed in the legal and economic status of European peasants. In the east, most peasants were enserfed. In the west, most peasants were free. However, in some Western countries like England, the free peasants were losing their land and sinking deeper into poverty; in others like France, large numbers of small peasant farms survived and an independent peasantry endured for centuries. Despite these variations, most peasants shared a life of poverty, a closeness to the land, and subjection to the relatively wealthy landed class—the aristocracy.

THE ARISTOCRACY

The word *aristocracy* means "rule by the best," specifically rule by a small, privileged group presumed to be best qualified to govern. For over a thousand years—from the early Middle Ages to the beginning of the twentieth century—European nations were governed by aristocracies of various kinds. Monarchs were usually the actual rulers, but they were in a sense the greatest of the aristocrats. Furthermore, monarchs governed through the aristocratic elite, since aristocrats usually served as royal advisors and often assumed the responsibility of implementing royal decisions on the local level.

The European aristocracies were a varied group. Some aristocrats claimed to be descended from the knights of the Middle Ages and professed to be able to trace their lineage back over the centuries. Others, particularly in commercial areas like Holland, were descended from urban merchants who were wealthy enough to buy a noble title. The common denominator among almost all types of aristocrats was ownership of land, since land was a source of both wealth and prestige. Actually, some aristocrats were quite poor, owning only small tracts of land and living little better than the peasants around them. But a few in each country controlled vast areas, usually divided into small farms rented by tenants. These few great landowners were the "real aristocracy," the less than 1 percent of the population that held most political and economic power. (The one exception is Poland, where nearly 10 percent of the population was aristocratic.) The most powerful aristocrats usually numbered only a few thousand in each country, but they seemed to be everywhere. The Duke of Norfolk (England), for example, at one time owned ten residences, including castles in four different areas and an enormous townhouse in London.

Aristocrats used a variety of means to distinguish themselves and to assert their superiority over the rest of the population. One was the display of wealth—wearing fine clothes, maintaining great residences, and employing large numbers of servants. Another was the use of violence to intimidate people. Aristocrats were trained to use both sword and pistol, so upper-class violence was a customary part of everyday life. An extreme example of this violence is the case of Lord Rich, who directed twenty-five retainers to attack a man in broad daylight while he stood yelling "Cut off his legs" and "Kill him!"[17]

Most aristocrats were acutely aware of their social rank and status. Their prestige and power resulted in part from the appearance of superiority, so appearances mattered. Who bowed first to whom was important, as was who sat where at dinner parties. An elaborate system of rules governed the relationships among the various ranks within the aristocracy. One episode, although ludicrous to twentieth-century readers, illustrates the importance attached to rules of etiquette. In this episode, a fifteen-year-old duchess became socially superior to her mother because she married a powerful duke. The young duchess was outraged and threw a fit when both leaves of a door were opened for her mother to enter a room, because her mother as an inferior was entitled to have only half the door opened for her.

For the wealthiest aristocrats, life was filled with good things and good times. Compare with the earlier analysis of peasant ways of life the following description of a young nobleman of the late Middle Ages who attended the university at Montpellier (France):

> He had a room on the first floor, paintings on the wall, a gilded easy chair to study in. . . . The distractions multiplied; suppers of partridge, drinking bouts of muscatel and hippocras, masked balls. . . . [He] watched the nobles, their plumed mounts adorned with multicolored panoplies, tilting at the ring; the defenses of academic theses that invariably drew a crowd; the fine autopsies; the popular spectacle of criminals being tortured or executed in public in the presence of young girls and entire families. Innocent gaiety, cruel pleasures, money, sadism, luxury.[18]

Only a few lived so luxuriously, but even they lacked many things. Heating was scarce, so aristocratic residences were cold and drafty. Toilet facilities, even in the richest palaces, were never more than narrow passageways with holes in the floor. Food was often available in great quantities, but aristocrats, like peasants, ate a monotonous diet—the same breads and meats every day. Although the upper classes ate meat regularly, the meat had to be heavily salted in order to preserve it, and so large amounts of wine and beer were consumed to quench the thirst produced by the salt. The lack of certain technologies—central heating, indoor plumbing, refrigeration—meant that in many ways aristocrats lived little better than peasants. Of course, most twentieth-century Americans and Europeans live much more comfortably than the aristocrats of preindustrial Europe.

THE CULTURE OF THE CITY

Life in the city was significantly different from life in the countryside. The cities were more crowded. Most of them had populations of 20,000–30,000, but a few like Paris and Naples contained more than 200,000 by the sixteenth century. Many citizens of cities were more free than peasants in the countryside, since cities were basically independent political entities that governed themselves. The cities derived their income from business and commerce rather than from land, and in many cases the people of the cities were wealthier than those of the surrounding countryside. Finally, the people of the cities were more inclined than peasants and aristocrats to welcome social change and economic growth. In describing life in the cities, we focus on four groups (1) the bourgeoisie, (2) the artisans, (3) women, and (4) the poor.

The word *bourgeoisie* means "townsmen" (from the French *bourg*, meaning "town"). More precisely, the term was used in preindustrial Europe to refer to a member of a commune, since the bourgeoisie was the

TECHNOLOGY
The Chimney

Material comfort slowly began to increase, particularly for the wealthy, with the development of the chimney. During the early Middle Ages, buildings were heated by a fire in a central hearth. The smoke simply went out through a hole in the roof. The central-hearth approach was very inefficient in producing heat, and gradually people began to understand the physics of updraft and downdraft, which enables the fire both to keep going and to carry away smoke. As a result, the first well-developed chimney stacks to vent smoke out of the building appeared in the eleventh and twelfth centuries.

As time passed, improved chimney construction allowed placement of several fireplaces throughout a building. Thus, people could live and sleep in separate rooms, and some privacy was created, at least for the rich. Previously, everyone—parents, children, servants—had lived, eaten, and slept in one large room where the central fire was located. The new privacy fostered a growing sense of individuality, a sense of being apart from the group. Belief in the importance of privacy and of individualism would slowly become a major influence in European political and social history, though some in the Middle Ages disliked the general decline in communal association. William Langland in the *Vision of Piers the Plowman* (written in three versions between 1362 and 1387) lamented the fact that rich and poor no longer lived together in the great hall:

> Woe is in the hall each day of the week.
> There the lord and lady like not to sit.
> Now every rich man eats by himself
> In a private parlor to be rid of poor men,
> Or in a chamber with a chimney,
> And leaves the great hall.[19]

The Chimney A middle-class man and boy warm their hands by the fire, while another man and woman prepare for a meal. (Pierpont Morgan Library)

dominant voice in the communal city governments. They were the merchants and businesspeople who controlled the cities. Their social status lay somewhere between the aristocracy and the peasantry, so they were sometimes termed a *middle* group or class.

The distinctive feature of the bourgeoisie was that they derived their livelihood from business and commerce, from manipulating money rather than cultivating land. Some of them eventually became quite wealthy. This account describes the home of a rich merchant in the sixteenth century:

> A circular staircase leads to seven rooms in the upper stories; there is a reception hall, a kitchen, an attic, and a cellar. . . . His strongbox is filled with money. He owns gold rings, precious stones, jaspar, bracelets. . . . There are dozens of chairs, stools and footstools, and banks and benches, all of walnut, the rich man's wood.[20]

A few of the bourgeoisie became wealthier than all but the greatest aristocrats. Their wealth enabled them to buy titles of nobility and to marry their children into the aristocracy. It also enabled them to acquire the education and expertise that made them valuable to monarchs as advisors and administrators. In short, the wealthiest of bourgeoisie gradually began to compete with the aristocracy for positions of political power and social prestige.

The artisans were craftspeople who used tools to make things like clothing, shoes, and jewelry. Most of them worked in small workshops and marketed their wares through a local merchant. Their wages were usually inadequate and their standard of living far lower than that of the bourgeoisie. Some artisans—the "journeymen"—had to travel from city to city to learn and practice their craft. To protect their employment and wages, artisans usually organized *guilds*, associations of all those engaged in a particular craft. Thus, in each city there might be a clothier's guild, a jeweler's guild, and the like. The purpose of the guilds was to guarantee stable employment and wages, a policy that seemed desirable to artisans who feared unemployment more than anything else. So, the guilds were licensed to control entry into a craft, thus ensuring that a city had only as many craftspeople as were needed. They also controlled pricing in an attempt to guarantee that the artisans received a fair price for their products. Finally, the guilds sought to provide certain social services for their members, such as charity for the needy and some education for the children. What they did not do, and never desired to do, was to foster economic competition.

Urban women, like peasant women, were not equal to men and were excluded from universities and professions like law and medicine. But some urban women had opportunities unavailable to their counterparts in the countryside. The wife of a well-to-do bourgeois had to manage a

The Hunt of the Unicorn Many Europeans believed in the existence of imaginary creatures. This fifteenth-century painting shows the unicorn, a mythical horse with one long horn. (Metropolitan Museum of Art, NY)

large household of family and servants and thus had access to some wealth and power. Furthermore, many cities established municipal schools through which middle-class girls and boys could acquire some education. Lower-class women were less well-off. Particularly vulnerable were unmarried servant women, who worked from dawn to dusk and ate table scraps in the hope of saving enough dowry money to attract a husband. That hope was sometimes destroyed when the master of the house seduced and impregnated the woman and then drove her out into the streets to join the ranks of the poor.

The poor—those who were chronically unemployed and lived in abject poverty—constituted 10 to 20 percent of most urban populations. Usually the poor were classified into two categories: (1) *paupers*, local poor who were considered deserving of some charity; or (2) *beggars*, who wandered into a city from other areas and were driven out as quickly as possible. The presence of large numbers of paupers and beggars had undesirable consequences for a city. Babies abandoned by the poor were common, and large cities employed a number of people to pick up abandoned children every morning and transport them to orphanages. The adult poor might live and die in a crowded poorhouse. Every day in a large city a number of pathetic funeral processions carried the dead from the poorhouse to unmarked graves in the pauper's cemetery.

CRIME, PUNISHMENT, AND DEATH

Crime was always present in both the countryside and the city. Peasants stole from other peasants. Politicians and businesspeople engaged in fraud, bribery, and even assassination. The poor often tried to survive by stealing.

Greatly feared were the hordes of vagrants who moved from place to place and stole or extorted what they could. These hordes often included those who were unwilling or unable to find a place in stable society: orphans, cripples, defrocked priests, war victims, ex-soldiers, discharged servant-girls, and the like. The more enterprising hordes turned to banditry, and a few became folk heroes famed for daring exploits. One Spanish robber was said to be "the most courteous bandit . . . never did he dishonor or touch churches, and God aided him."[21] Less resourceful vagrants lived as best they could until they died of malnutrition or were executed by the authorities.

Governments sought to control crime by decreeing harsh punishments. Relatively minor crimes were punished by physical disfigurement—the chopping off of a hand or an ear, for example. Major crimes—murder, treason, heresy, witchcraft, robbery of a significant amount—were punished by execution. Those convicted of religious crimes such as heresy were burned at the stake; others guilty of secular crimes were hanged or beheaded. Executions were usually public, the theory being that public torturings and executions would deter others from a life of crime. Yet many spectators enjoyed the spectacles—one town went so far as to buy a convicted thief so that the citizens could watch him being drawn and quartered (his body forcibly spread out and then hacked into four pieces). Executions were a form of entertainment in which the crowds participated. Once, in Brussels, a young murderer addressed his spectators just before his execution and "so softened their hearts that every one burst into tears and his death was commended as the finest that was ever seen."[22] On another occasion, in Paris, the criminal, a nobleman, was berated:

> At the moment when he is going to be executed, the great treasurer of the regent appears on the scene and vents his hatred against him; he climbs the ladder behind him, shouting insults, beats him with a stick, and gives the hangman a thrashing for exhorting the victim to think of his salvation. The hangman grows nervous and bungles his work; the cord snaps, the wretched criminal falls on the ground, breaks a leg and some ribs, and in this condition has to climb the ladder again.[23]

Why did so many people flock to executions? One reason may be that people in traditional Europe were so accustomed to death that they were often callous about it. The severed heads of executed criminals were sometimes kept on display for weeks. The church, both Catholic and Protestant, used torture and burnings to suppress enemies. The poor and the weak were usually treated harshly. Little attention was paid to the children who regularly died of malnutrition or disease. The great essayist Montaigne commented: "I lost two or three children as nurslings not without regret but without great grief."[24] Montaigne was not a cruel man, but he lived in an age when brutality and death were common and life was easily lost.

CONCLUSION

An analysis of social history from 1200 to 1700 reveals two major themes. The first is that even in the best of times most Europeans were impoverished, constantly threatened by possible famine and disease. The second is that some factors—the growth of trade, the gradual emergence of the bourgeoisie and capitalism—were slowly laying a foundation for a rising standard of living in Europe.

THINGS YOU SHOULD KNOW

The material conditions of peasant life
Peasant villages
Peasant customs and attitudes
Times of famine and plague
The Jacquerie
The Peasants' Revolt of 1381 in England
The German Peasants' War of 1525
The decline of the manorial system in Western Europe

The expansion of serfdom in eastern
  Europe
The enclosure movement
European aristocracies
The bourgeoisie

The artisans
The position of women, both in the
  countryside and the cities
The poor in the cities
Crime and punishment by execution

SUGGESTED READINGS

An excellent introduction to the study of peasant life is Natalie Zemon Davis, *The Return of Martin Guerre* (Cambridge, Mass.: Harvard Univ. Press, 1983), the true story of a peasant who disappeared from his native village and returned years later to expose the imposter who had assumed his identity. A more traditional but still excellent survey of European social history before the Industrial Revolution is Carlo M. Cipolla, *Before the Industrial Revolution: European Society and Economy, 1000–1700*, 2nd ed. (New York: Norton, 1980). Another very readable survey with much information on specific people and places is George Huppert, *After the Black Death: A Social History of Early Modern Europe* (Bloomington: Indiana Univ. Press, 1986). On the material condition of everyday life in preindustrial Europe, see Fernand Braudel, *Civilization and Capitalism, 15th–18th Century*, vol. 1: *The Structures of Everyday Life: The Limits of the Possible*, trans. Sîan Reynolds (New York: Harper & Row, 1979). For the history of agriculture, see B. H. Slicher van Bath, *The Agrarian History of Western Europe, A.D. 500–1850*, trans. Olive Ordish (London: Edward Arnold, 1963). Two excellent works that focus on Languedoc (France) and England, respectively, are Emmanuel LeRoy Ladurie, *The Peasants of Languedoc*, trans. John Day (Urbana: Univ. of Illinois Press, 1974), and Peter Laslett, *The World We Have Lost*, 2nd ed. (New York: Scribner's, 1971). Johan Huizinga, *The Waning of the Middle Ages* (New York: Doubleday, 1969) provides a revealing analysis of the pessimism that engulfed much of Europe near the end of the Middle Ages. Finally, Rosalind and Christopher Brooke, *Popular Religion in the Middle Ages* (London: Thames Hudson, 1984) is a good source on the religion of the common people.

NOTES

[1] B. H. Slicher van Bath, *The Agrarian History of Western Europe, A.D. 500–1850*, trans. Olive Ordish (London: Edward Arnold, 1963), p. 3.

[2] Quoted in Michel Mollat, *The Poor in the Middle Ages: An Essay in Social History*, trans. Arthur Goldhammer (New Haven: Yale Univ. Press, 1986), p. 70.

[3] Quoted in Jerome Blum, *The European Peasantry from the Fifteenth to the Nineteenth Century* (Washington, D.C.: American Historical Association, 1960), p. 22.

[4] Quoted in Marc Bloch, *French Rural History: An Essay on Its Basic Characteristics*, trans. Janet Sondheimer (Berkeley: University of California Press, 1966), p. 149.

[5] Natalie Zemon Davis, *The Return of Martin Guerre* (Cambridge, Mass.: Harvard Univ. Press, 1983), p. 1.

[6] Quoted in George Huppert, *After the Black Death: A Social History of Early Modern Europe* (Bloomington: Indiana Univ. Press, 1986), pp. 136, 138.

[7] Ibid., p. 154.

[8] Quoted in Emmanuel LeRoy Ladurie, *The Peasants of Lanquedoc*, trans. John Day (Urbana: Univ. of Illinois Press, 1974), p. 112.

[9] Ibid., pp. 13–14.

[10] Quoted in Peter Laslett, *The World We Have Lost*, 2nd ed. (New York: Scribner's, 1971), pp. 118–19.

[11] Ibid., pp. 121–122.

[12] Quoted in LeRoy Ladurie, *The Peasants*, p. 199.

[13] Quoted in Slicher van Bath, *Agrarian History*, p. 189.

[14] Quoted in Huppert, *Black Death*, pp. 56–57.

[15] Quoted in Slicher van Bath, *Agrarian History*, p. 192.

[16] Ibid., pp. 165–66.

[17] Quoted in Huppert, *Black Death*, p. 58.

[18] LeRoy Ladurie, *The Peasants*, pp. 152–53.

[19] Quoted in Lynn White, Jr., "Technology Assessment from the Stance of a Medieval Historian," in *Medieval Religion and Technology* (Berkeley: Univ. of California Press, 1978), p. 271.

[20] LeRoy Ladurie, *The Peasants*, p. 155.

[21] Quoted in Huppert, *Black Death*, p. 109.

[22] Quoted in Johan Huizinga, *The Waning of the Middle Ages* (New York: Doubleday, 1969), p. 11.

[23] Ibid., p. 25.

[24] Quoted in Carlo M. Cipolla, *Before the Industrial Revolution: European Society and Economy, 1000–1700*, 2nd ed. (New York: Norton, 1980), p. 156.

10

The Renaissance and the European Discovery of the Americas, 1300 to 1600

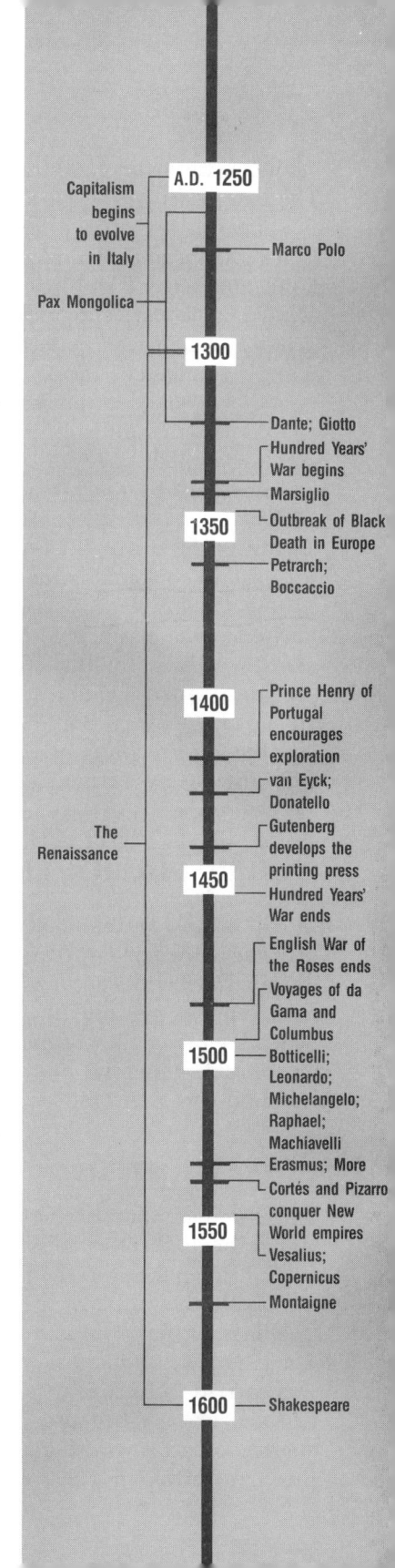

A.D. 1250	Capitalism begins to evolve in Italy
	Marco Polo
	Pax Mongolica
1300	
	Dante; Giotto
	Hundred Years' War begins
	Marsiglio
1350	Outbreak of Black Death in Europe
	Petrarch; Boccaccio
1400	Prince Henry of Portugal encourages exploration
	van Eyck; Donatello
	Gutenberg develops the printing press
1450	Hundred Years' War ends
	English War of the Roses ends
	Voyages of da Gama and Columbus
1500	Botticelli; Leonardo; Michelangelo; Raphael; Machiavelli
	Erasmus; More
	Cortés and Pizarro conquer New World empires
1550	Vesalius; Copernicus
	Montaigne
1600	Shakespeare

The Renaissance spans approximately 1400–1550.

The period from 1300 to 1600 was a time of both decline and rebirth. The early part of the period was one of the most devastating times in European history. Crop failures and famines, the plague known as the Black Death, and several prolonged wars brought misery and death to large numbers of European people. Population declined precipitously. Many people were convinced that the end of the world was near. Fear of death and hell was pervasive. Artwork sometimes portrayed skeletons doing death dances and tombstones were occasionally decorated with the image of a naked corpse crawling with worms.

Yet, in the midst of great hardship and death, Europeans were creating and discovering anew. The *Pax Mongolica*—the peaceful era administered by the Mongols across much of Eurasia—allowed some Europeans to travel to China and develop trade there. That trade encouraged the growth of *capitalism* in Italy and later in other areas. Italy was also the original home of the intellectual and cultural revival known as the *Renaissance*, which eventually spread to northern Europe. Portugal and Spain were the initiators of a European drive into the world's oceans, finding both a sea route to Asia and two continents previously unknown to Europeans—North and South America. This was an age of discovery. Some of the discoverers were merchants developing new business techniques, others were artists creating new art forms, and still others were adventurers exploring unknown parts of the globe.

FAMINE, PLAGUE, AND WAR

Much of Europe was relatively prosperous during the High Middle Ages because increased crop production supported its growing population. By the late thirteenth century, however, population growth began to outstrip food supplies, and the inevitable results were famine, malnutrition, and death for many Europeans. Population continued to decline as Europe was struck with two more calamities—plague and war—over a two-hundred-year period.

The Black Death

The famines that occurred throughout Europe made people more vulnerable to disease and particularly to the *Black Death,* which struck in 1347. Known today as the bubonic plague, the Black Death was a disease in which the afflicted person suffered high fever, large buboes or swellings in the groin and armpits, and death within two or three days. The plague spread across much of Eurasia in the fourteenth century and was carried to Europe by rats living in ships. (The rats spread rapidly in Europe, in part because many Europeans thought cats—the natural enemies of rats—were agents of the devil and killed them.) It spread through Europe quickly, intensified by the unsanitary conditions of the

FAMINE, PLAGUE, AND WAR   **221**

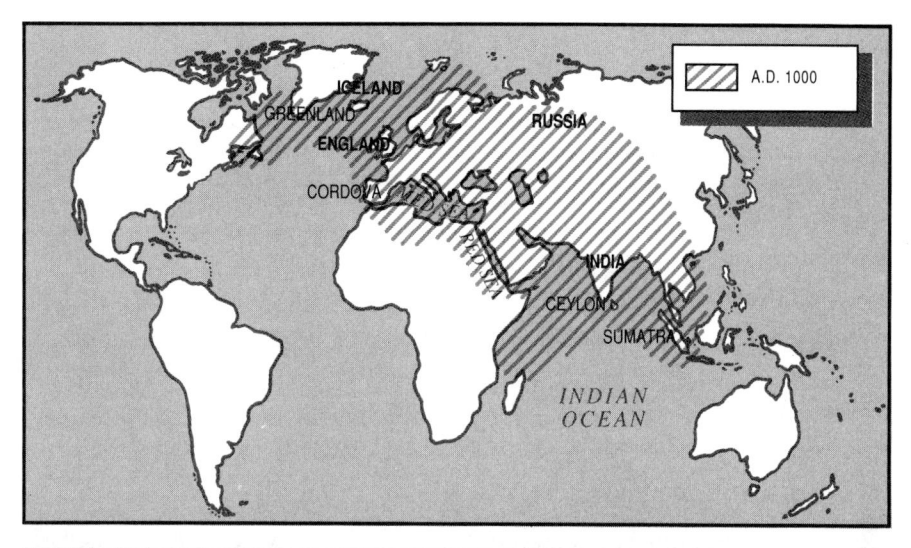

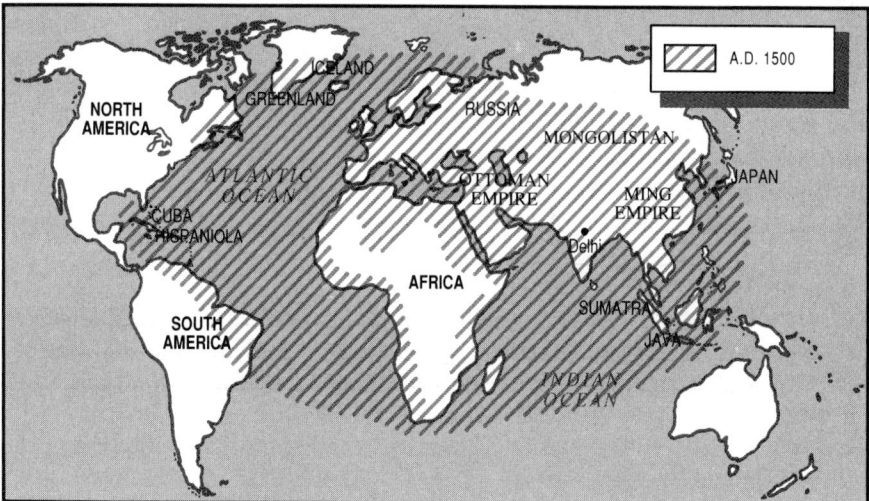

Figure 10.1 The Known World, 1000–1500

time and the general vulnerability of a population already weakened by famine and malnutrition.

Since the real source of the plague was not known at the time, most Europeans interpreted it as a divine punishment and called the buboes "God's tokens." The result was growing fear and despair. In the *Decameron*, the Renaissance writer Giovanni Boccaccio (1313–1375) describes the consequences of the Black Death:

> many died daily or nightly in the public streets; of many others, who died at home, the departure was hardly observed by their neighbors,

until the stench of their putrefying bodies carried the tidings . . . one and the same bier carried two or three corpses at once . . . one bier sufficing for husband and wife, two or three brothers, father and son . . . nor, for all their number, were there obsequies honored by either tears, or lights, or crowds of mourners; rather it was to come to this, that a dead man was then of no more account than a dead goat would be today.[1]

The Black Death killed nearly a third of Europe's population between 1348 and 1351. Although it then became dormant for a time, there were several more outbreaks of the plague over the next four hundred years. It was not until the eighteenth century that the disease was finally eliminated from most of Europe.

The Hundred Years' War

It was as if the Four Horsemen of the Apocalypse were galloping across Europe, for famine and plague were accompanied by war. (In the New Testament Book of Revelation, the Four Horsemen of the Apocalypse—Famine, War, Pestilence, and Death—personify the evils of the world.) In the fourteenth and fifteenth centuries, there were Mongol attacks on Hungary and Poland, incessant conflicts among the city-states of northern Italy, and the continuing battles of the Christian reconquest of Spain. But the most devastating war was the *Hundred Years' War* (1337–1453) centered in France.

The Hundred Years' War was precipitated by three primary factors: (1) a dispute over the succession to the French throne, which was claimed by both English and French monarchs; (2) a dispute over the boundaries of some lands in France owned by the English king; and (3) the English nobility's desire to capture some rich land in France. These factors led to a series of intermittent conflicts, known collectively as the Hundred Years' War. The war was particularly terrible for France, not only because many French died in the fighting but also because the armies often burned entire towns and destroyed the crops needed to feed the population. For a time the English won most of the major battles, but they were disadvantaged by being in a foreign land far from home. The French also had the good fortune to find in their midst a heroine—Joan of Arc—who became their inspiration and rallying point in the war.

The French ultimately drove the English out and in the process gained control of the rich province of Aquitaine (southwestern France). Aquitaine had belonged to the English crown since the twelfth century (see Chapter 8), but with the end of the Hundred Years' War it became a permanent part of France. One result was the establishment of most of France's national boundaries along lines that would last for many centuries; in short, France was now largely unified. Another was that

The Four Horsemen of the Apocalypse This drawing, from a woodcut by the German artist Albrecht Dürer (1471–1528), portrays Famine, War, Pestilence, and Death galloping across Europe in the fourteenth and fifteenth centuries. (Museum of Fine Arts, Boston)

England was left an essentially island kingdom with no significant territories on the continent. In the future, the English would seek to gain territory, not on the continent, but in other worlds across the oceans.

The War of the Roses

The English endured another calamity, as the turmoil of the Hundred Years' War helped produce a civil war in England. The *War of the Roses* (1455–1485)—so named because each side adopted a different colored rose as its symbol—was a struggle between two noble families, the Lancasters and the Yorks, for control of the English throne. The war was filled with brutality, murder, and treachery, with much of the English nobility being destroyed. Not until 1485 did a strong monarch—Henry VII—restore peace and stability in England. A century later, William Shakespeare would use the War of the Roses as the subject of many of his historical dramas.

Reactions to the Calamities

The combination of famines, plague, and wars produced feelings of despair, hysteria, and anger among many Europeans. One reaction to the chaos of the times was peasant revolt, such as the Jacquerie and the English Peasants' Revolt discussed in Chapter 9. Another reaction was the practice of flagellation, by which some especially pious people whipped themselves as penance for the sins that they believed had caused the plague. A third reaction by some people was the feeling that humanity had been abandoned by God and so had no choice but to seek happiness on earth. This attitude helped precipitate the Renaissance. A contrasting reaction led to a revival of the mystic tradition, as some sought consolation in a direct spiritual experience with God. One noted mystic was Meister Eckhart of Germany (1260–1327); another was Catherine of Siena (1347–1380), who once saw a vision in which "Christ appeared clothed in a pure white garment . . . and he smiled at the young girl and there issued from him, as from the sun, a ray which was directed at her."[2] In their desire for a more personal and individual relationship with God, the mystics were expressing the attitudes that would help initiate the Reformations of the sixteenth century.

PAX MONGOLICA AND THE GROWTH OF CAPITALISM IN ITALY

While Europe was enduring the torments of famine, plague, and war, momentous events were occurring across Eurasia. The Mongols, a group of east Asian nomadic tribes, were building an enormous empire after they were united by their great leader, Genghis Khan (reigned 1206–1227). Genghis Khan was one of the greatest military conquerors in history, and during his lifetime he extended Mongol power across much of central Asia. After his death, his successors increased Mongol influence by leading armies northward into Russia and westward into Germany and Poland. By the mid-thirteenth century, the Mongol Empire stretched from the Pacific Ocean through much of China all the way west to the Black Sea and from the Baltic Sea and Siberia in the north to the Persian Gulf in the south.

The Mongols were tolerant, able rulers, who allowed most of their subjects to live in peace. By the time of Kublai Khan, who ruled the Mongol Empire from 1260 to 1294, a Pax Mongolica (Mongolian peace) prevailed across most of Eurasia. It lasted several decades—until the Mongol Empire splintered into several Mongol states—and fostered both cultural interaction and trade. One example of such exchange is the astronomical observatory in Persia, where Chinese astronomers compared notes with Arab scientists from Spain.

European Trade with the East

The Mongolian trade routes connected Europe with a prosperous and creative China. During the Sung dynasty (960–1279), the Chinese built a thriving commercial economy that engaged in trade and shipping throughout the entire Indian Ocean area. In addition, by the end of the tenth century, they had developed several new inventions—the compass, gunpowder, and the printing press—that would eventually be transported to Europe. But it was spices and silks that first attracted European traders to China. These products were so eagerly sought by the European upper classes that eventually ambitious Europeans would invade and dominate much of Asia in order to get them.

In *Science and Civilization in China*, the historian Joseph Needham points out the irony of the Pax Mongolica—that this time of peace and toleration stimulated the European desire for Asian products and thereby encouraged the later European conquest of Asia: "No nomad horseman, watching from his shaggy red pony a quiet caravan amble by, could have imagined that it was the distant forerunner of conquerors more merciless than the four hounds of Temujin."[3] (Temujin was the original name of Genghis Khan, and the four hounds symbolize the powerful military forces of the Mongol conqueror.)

The first Europeans to profit from trade with Asia were from northern Italy. Several north Italian cities—Venice, Milan, Florence, Pisa—first enriched themselves during the Crusades, when they supplied ships to crusading armies and developed trading networks in the eastern Mediterranean. By the thirteenth century, they were the main contacts in the Asian–European trading system. A noteworthy example of Italian enterprise is the Venetian merchant Marco Polo, who in the 1270s traveled across Asia to the court of Kublai Khan. Polo lived and worked there for nearly twenty years before returning to Venice with his vast knowledge of and experience in Asia.

Capitalism

Long-distance commerce between Europe and Asia hastened the development of a new economic mentality in Europe—*capitalism*. Although capitalism has its roots in late medieval cities, it wasn't until the twelfth to the thirteenth centuries that the word *capital* was first used in northern Italy to mean the accumulated wealth of a person or company that was then invested to produce more wealth. (The terms *capitalist* and *capitalism* did not appear until much later.)

The essence of the new idea of capitalism was a more aggressive and more calculating attitude toward business and commerce. Those who used capital were consciously seeking economic gain—to make profits rather than just live day to day as the feudal nobility and the peasantry usually did. They calculated their monetary resources, assessed business opportunities, and then invested in whatever projects seemed most likely to produce wealth. Since most investments were risky endeavors at that time, merchants had to be willing to gamble.

The north Italian cities adapted several new methods of operation to aid business and commerce and the creation of wealth. One was double-entry bookkeeping, borrowed from the Arabs, which enabled businesspeople to maintain accurate records of profits and losses. Another was banking, which allowed wealthy merchants to make more money by lending at interest to others. The new banks also offered a substitute for monetary exchange—a bill of exchange or a "check." The bill of exchange made it easier to exchange large sums of money over long distances, since bulky sacks of coins didn't have to be transported. Also during this time was the gradual evolution of a new type of business firm, the joint-stock company, in which capital could be raised by selling shares in the firm to the public.

THE RENAISSANCE

The term *Renaissance* (meaning "rebirth") is used to refer to an era of intellectual and artistic creativity that began in Italy during the fourteenth century and gradually spread northward to France, the Low Countries, and England. What produced this outburst of creativity? The people of the time believed that the Renaissance was stimulated by the rediscovery of ancient Greek and Roman writings. They argued that the ideas contained in the classics caused a rebirth of intellectual life. This is partially true, since some ancient writings were recovered and did create great intellectual excitement during this time. But the argument is overstated, for intellectual life was not "dead" during the Middle Ages and so could not have been "reborn" in the fourteenth century. It is more accurate to say that the Renaissance was stimulated by a fundamental transition in European society and thought. European society was gradually becoming more urbanized (see Chapter 9), and Renaissance creativity was in many ways a response to the new urban culture. The people of the Renaissance gradually defined a new attitude toward life that was more humanistic (in terms of its focus on life on earth) than the scholasticism of the Middle Ages. This new attitude was congenial to many of the merchants and artisans in the thriving cities.

Italy during the Renaissance

The Renaissance is considered to have begun in Italy early in the fourteenth century and continued there until the mid-sixteenth century. Renaissance Italy was a tumultuous place. External foes—the Ottoman

TECHNOLOGY
The Printing Press

The invention of the printing press was particularly important in spreading Renaissance ideas. Its invention was made possible by two new techniques. One was the use of flexible paper, which was more supple than parchment and could be used with machinery. Paper was probably developed first in China, but by the thirteenth century, linen paper was being produced in Europe. The other new technique important to the invention of the printing press was movable type, in which letters of the alphabet were fashioned on separate pieces of metal that could be arranged to form words and then reused. Movable type may have been invented by the German printer Johan Gutenberg (1398–1468) in the 1440s, and he is usually regarded as the designer of the first modern printing press. Prior to Gutenberg, printers had used the woodblock method, in which entire pages of text were carved into blocks of wood and then imprinted on paper.

The printing press had a revolutionary impact on Europe and eventually on the world. Gradually, printers were able to produce books that were sufficiently inexpensive to be bought by large numbers of people. The result was to "democratize" knowledge by making it available to more people. In particular, the expanding amount of printed material encouraged literacy, scholarly research and publication, and education, as more people attended schools and universities.

The Gutenberg Press
An 1869 engraving of Johan Gutenberg examining the first page produced by his new printing press. (The Granger Collection)

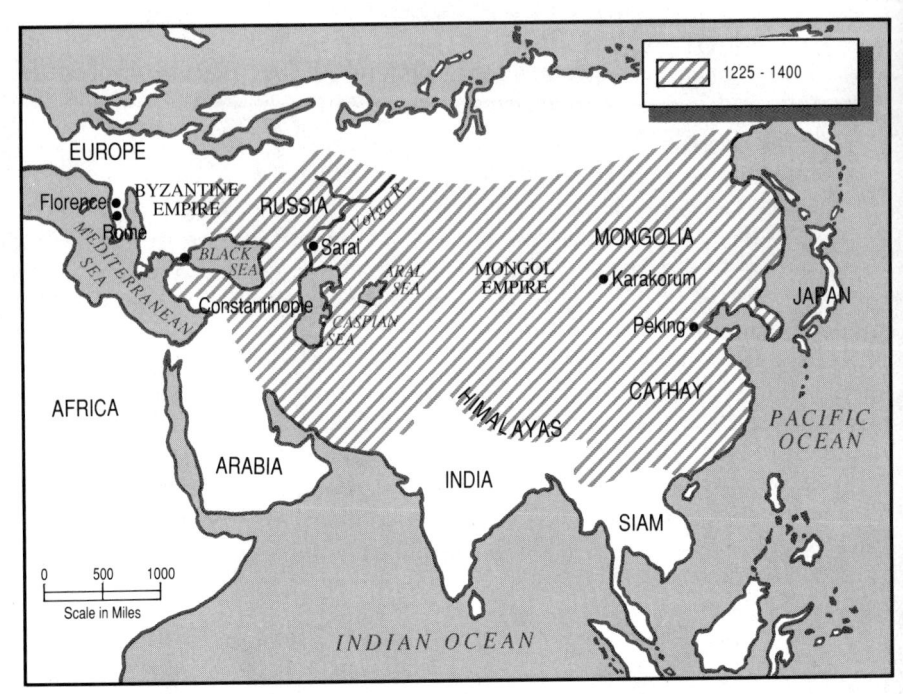

Figure 10.2 The Old World, 1225–1400

Turks, Barbary pirates from North Africa, and the French—periodically attacked the Italian peninsula. Furthermore, Italy itself was disunited, since there was no central Italian state. In southern Italy, there was a conservative kingdom centered on the city of Naples; in central Italy, there were Papal states controlled by the Catholic church; and in northern Italy, there were several small duchies as well as city-states dominated by merchants.

It was the north Italian city-states—Florence, Venice, Milan—that were the first centers of Renaissance thought and art. These cities were controlled by a merchant upper class that often used violence to dominate the governments. Each city was controlled by one or more merchant families, a notable example being the Medici family that led Florence during much of the fifteenth century. Renaissance Italy was a class-ridden place in which women had little influence on the great art and literature of the time and the lower classes were excluded from most everything except their obligation to pay taxes, some of which supported artistic projects.

The Italian Renaissance began with a gradual reorientation of thought, one that placed less emphasis on eternal life and more emphasis on life on earth. Even so, the majority of Renaissance people were still devout Christians who felt certain that their ideas and beliefs were just as pious as the ideas and beliefs of medieval thinkers. The nature of Renaissance thought is revealed in the writings of four Italians of the late thirteenth and early fourteenth centuries: Dante, Petrarch, Boccaccio, and Marsiglio.

Dante Dante Alighieri (1265–1321), author of the *Divine Comedy*, is often regarded as the last great literary representative of medieval culture. The *Divine Comedy* is a poetic representation of a journey through hell, purgatory, and paradise. In this imaginary tour, Dante speaks with the souls of both the damned and the saved, and in the process creates images of what it is like to be in hell or heaven. The subject of the *Divine Comedy* is typically medieval, in that it expresses an obsession with the afterlife. Dante's writing style is also medieval, for the *Divine Comedy* is an allegory (a story in which the actions are symbolic of something else) describing the Christian's pilgrimage from darkness to light, or from sin to blessedness. Yet, as distinctly medieval as he was, Dante was also a forerunner of the Renaissance. He wrote in Italian, the everyday language of the northern Italian people, rather than in Latin, the traditional language of medieval intellectuals.

Petrarch More clearly oriented to the new age of the Renaissance was the poet and essayist Francesco Petrarca (1304–1374), usually regarded as the first Renaissance humanist. Petrarch's poems and essays helped initiate the enthusiasm for the ancient Greek and Roman classics. He explored old libraries in search of long-forgotten ancient manuscripts and then used them as models for his own writing. For Petrarch, the ancient manuscripts were much more than old pieces of paper; they were sources of wisdom. He believed that they taught a new and stimulating way of life, one that stressed human happiness and human accomplishments on earth.

Boccaccio and Marsiglio Some of the implications of that new way of life were developed by Giovanni Boccaccio (1313–1375) and Marsiglio of Padua (c. 1275–1343). Boccaccio wrote the *Decameron*, a collection of stories purportedly told by a group of young people who had gone into rural exile to escape the Black Death. The stories satirize priests, monks, and other "respectable" people and are often raucously humorous. One, for example, tells of a virile young man who satisfies sexually an entire convent of sex-starved nuns. The *Decameron* is significant in terms of the Renaissance because it expresses a love of life, of the beauty and joy to be found in this world.

Marsiglio of Padua was a political thinker whose *Defensor Pacis* marks a radical break from the medieval assumption that the church should be directly involved in political affairs. Marsiglio argued that the church should concern itself only with spiritual matters and leave politics to the secular state. He argued further that within the secular state the people should be the ultimate source of authority. In his words, "the legislator, or the primary and efficient cause of the law, is the people or the whole body of the citizens, or the weightier part thereof, through its election or will expressed by words in the general assembly of citizens."[4] Although Marsiglio's ideas were far too radical to have much influence in the fourteenth century, they presaged Machiavelli's theory of a secular state and would have great influence in the sixteenth and later centuries.

Other Renaissance Humanists Petrarch, Boccaccio, and Marsiglio were early Renaissance humanists, in that they put people at the center of intellectual inquiry and looked to the ancient classics for inspiration. Other humanists established the classics as the basis of educational programs for the upper classes in Italian cities. One example is the Platonic Academy founded in Florence by Cosimo de Medici, head of the prominent family that dominated Florence. At the Platonic Academy, the scholar Marsilio Ficino fostered neo-Platonism, reviving the Platonic contention that human knowledge is based on knowledge of spiritual concepts. Ficino believed that the study of Platonism was the best way to teach political and ethical ideals to Florentines. One of Ficino's disciples, Pico della Mirandola, wrote the "Oration on the Dignity of Man"; another, Gianozzo Manetti, wrote the book *On the Dignity and Excellence of Man*. The phrase *the dignity of man* was popular in fifteenth-century Florence, for it not only expressed the Renaissance humanists' faith in the freedom and power of people, but it was also considered to be a Christian idea.

Giotto, Donatello, Ghiberti, and Botticelli The close relationship between humanism and Christianity was portrayed by early Renaissance artists. Art became more realistic and naturalistic than the symbolic religious art of the Middle Ages, and Christianity provided much of the subject matter for artists. Giotto di Bondone (1266–1337), for example, painted the New Testament story of Mary and Jesus, but he portrayed human figures in a much more naturalistic, full-bodied fashion than had medieval artists who pictured humans as flat figures.

Another example is the statue of *David* produced by Donatello (1386–1466), the first great Renaissance sculptor. Although David is an Old Testament folk hero, Donatello used the humanistic perspective to present him in a new light. The statue was the first freestanding nude sculpted since ancient times, and its realistic portrayal of the human body celebrates humanity.

Lorenzo Ghiberti (1378–1455), also a sculptor, received a commission from a secular organization—the Guild of Cloth Merchants—to cast two bronze doors for the Baptistery of the cathedral at Florence. The

THE RENAISSANCE

The Madonna of the Magnificat (1483) by *Sandro Botticelli* The Renaissance painter Botticelli depicts the Virgin Mary and Jesus naturalistically, unlike medieval artists who tended to portray humans as flat figures. (Firenze Museum)

two doors, on which Ghiberti worked for nearly forty years, depict the Old Testament story of Abraham's sacrifice of Isaac in such realistic terms that Michelangelo later called them the "Doors of Paradise."

Not all Renaissance art was religiously inspired, though. The painter Sandro Botticelli (1444–1510), for instance, used classical mythology as the subject for his *The Birth of Venus,* one of the greatest works of the Renaissance era.

The Renaissance fascination with art and beauty had an unintended but significant influence on manual labor. Many art patrons were merchants and businesspeople who admired and mixed easily with sculptors and painters. As they became familiar with the workings of artists' workshops, they gained a new respect for the labor that went on within them. The result was an appreciation of the manual labor that went into the artistic creation of something beautiful. Thus, the association of manual labor with beauty helped to elevate the status of those who worked with their hands.

Savonarola Not everyone in Italy was enraptured by Renaissance humanism. In the late fifteenth century, a Dominican friar named Girolamo Savonarola (1452–1498) persuaded the people of Florence that the Renaissance was an anti-Christian, upper-class movement. He gained control of Florence for a time and directed a program of Christian repentance that included the destruction of humanist books and paintings in gigantic bonfires. Savonarola was so uncompromising, however, that he had many enemies and was eventually executed as a heretic.

Leonardo, Michelangelo, and Raphael Despite the brief influence of Savonarola, the last flowering of the Italian Renaissance occurred during the latter decades of the fifteenth century and the early decades of the sixteenth. This was the time of Leonardo da Vinci (1452–1519), Michelangelo Buonarotti (1475–1564), Raphael (1483–1520), and Niccolo Machiavelli (1469–1527).

Leonardo da Vinci was so versatile that it is difficult to identify him with any one field of endeavor. He was a military engineer and inventor who often supported himself by working for rulers in northern Italy. He was also an anatomist who was fascinated by the human body and spent many hours dissecting cadavers. His most enduring fame resulted from his artistic work. His *Mona Lisa* is still considered one of the greatest portraits ever created, and his *The Last Supper* immortalizes the last meal shared by Jesus and his disciples.

Both Michelangelo and Raphael did their greatest work in Rome. A succession of popes began to rebuild and rebeautify many of the church buildings in the old imperial city. Pope Sixtus IV (1471–1484) built the Sistine Chapel in the Vatican Palace (the papal headquarters), and Pope Julius II (1503–1513) commissioned the construction of a new St. Peter's Basilica to serve as the centerpiece of Western Christendom. Julius called Michelangelo and Raphael to Rome. Michelangelo, a painter, sculptor, and architect, carried out several artistic and architectural projects, including planning the future St. Peter's. His most renowned achievement was the decoration of the walls and ceiling of the Sistine Chapel. (See Chapter 3 for three examples of Michelangelo's work.) On the ceiling, he painted what art historian Kenneth Clark calls "a poem on the subject of creation":

> Man, with a body of unprecedented splendour, is reclining on the ground in the pose of all those river gods and wine gods of the ancient world who belonged to the earth and did not aspire to leave it. He stretches out his hand so that it almost touches the hand of God and an electric charge seems to pass between their fingers. Out of this glorious physical specimen God has created a human soul.[5]

Two decades later, Michelangelo painted the Last Judgment on one of the walls of the Sistine Chapel. The artist thus told the entire story of humanity—from beginning to end.

At the same time that Michelangelo was painting the Creation, Raphael was decorating the papal apartments. There he painted the *School of Athens*, which illustrates the Greek influence on the Renaissance. Raphael portrayed Plato, Aristotle, and the other ancient philosophers seeking to understand and interpret the world.

Machiavelli The Renaissance ended in Italy during the sixteenth century, in part because Italian political and economic power was

The Virgin and Child with St. Anne (c. 1502) by Leonardo da Vinci In this painting, Leonardo shows the Virgin Mary and Jesus in the company of St. Anne. Leonardo's brilliant style, which focused on the beauty of the human form, captured the essence of the Renaissance in Europe. (Musée National du Louvre)

declining. The discovery of the Americas and the development of Atlantic sea routes by Portugal and Spain gradually undermined the Mediterranean commerce that was the source of Italian wealth. Furthermore, early sixteenth-century Italy became an international battlefield where Spain, France, and others fought for influence. The resulting chaos weakened Italy, but it also stimulated Niccolo Machiavelli to write *The Prince*, one of the most important political treatises of European history.

Machiavelli, like Marsiglio before him, developed a theory of the secular state distinct from the church and Christian ideology. He argued that a ruler should not be bound by traditional moral precepts and should do whatever is necessary to preserve the power and independence of the state:

> how we live is so far removed from how we ought to live, that he who abandons what is done for what ought to be done, will rather learn to bring about his own ruin than his preservation. . . . Therefore it is necessary for a prince, who wishes to maintain himself, to learn how not to do good, and to use this knowledge and not use it, according to the necessity of the case.[6]

Machiavelli became most famous for advocating that rulers ignore moral standards (hence the word *machiavellian* came to mean "ruthlessness"). However, more significant was his theoretical basis for a new politics, by which European monarchs would concentrate their attention on expansion of state power.

The Northern Renaissance

The ideas of Renaissance Italy spread to parts of northern Europe during the fifteenth and sixteenth centuries. The greatest artist of the northern Renaissance, Jan van Eyck (1390–1441), came from the urbanized, commercial areas of the Low Countries (present-day Belgium and the Netherlands). Van Eyck was a painter and a realist. His work celebrates humanity in a realistic sense rather than in a religious or philosophical sense. In a portrait of his wife, for example, van Eyck portrayed her not as a glamorous or brilliant figure but as she was—an ordinary person in ordinary clothes.

Also from the Low Countries was Desiderius Erasmus (1466–1536), though he was actually an international man who lived and traveled throughout much of Western Europe. Erasmus was the most renowned learned man of his time and often gave advice to popes and kings. One source of his fame was his *Praise of Folly*, a satire of what he considered the stupidities of his world—wars, political maneuverings, and the like. Erasmus also studied and wrote theological treatises, for he considered himself a Christian humanist—one who combines Christian teachings with an appreciation of human abilities.

Another Christian humanist of the northern Renaissance was Sir Thomas More (1478–1535), an English statesman whose *Utopia* describes an ideal society. (Depictions of ideal worlds have since been called "utopias" or "utopian.") In *Utopia*, More portrays a world in which everyone has enough to eat and a decent place to live, because society is organized so that all material goods are shared equally. Since everyone has what they need, there is no crime and no war. Obviously, such a place does not exist, but More was using an ideal to criticize the realities of poverty and crime in England. In many ways, More was arguing against progress, particularly against the kind of progress in which enclosure movements, for example, destroyed the livelihood of many peasants. He was saying, in effect, that life could be better, and that Christian and humanist teachings about the dignity of the individual should be taken more seriously.

Some northern Renaissance humanists were more skeptical than More and Erasmus. The Frenchman Michel de Montaigne (1533–1592) expressed his ideas in a new form of writing—the personal essay. His *Essays* analyze a number of fundamental human problems—such as education, superstition, marriage, and death—and characterize Mon-

William Shakespeare (1564–1616) A nineteenth-century engraving of the English poet and dramatist. Shakespeare is considered by many to be the greatest writer of all time. All together, more than thirty-six major plays are attributed to him as well as many sonnets. (The Granger Collection)

to foretell earthly events by the positions of heavenly bodies.) Paracelsus, a sixteenth-century German chemist and alchemist, tried to use secret methods to transmute base metals into gold. (Alchemy was popular during the Renaissance, since it promised to reveal how to create gold as well as how to prolong life.) There also was the sixteenth-century German alchemist and astrologer who became known in history as Dr. Faust. Exactly who Dr. Faust was is uncertain, but according to European legends he sold his soul to the devil in exchange for forbidden knowledge. As a personification of the willingness to pay any price to learn the unknown, Dr. Faust was celebrated in some European literature and his name was symbolic of the drive for power and knowledge in Western Civilization.

The study of nature also led in the direction of modern science. Renaissance humanists rediscovered or received from the Arabs a number of Greek scientific writings and thus helped increase the fund of scientific knowledge. Furthermore, the business classes of northern Italy supported those scientific studies that promised to lead to greater use of natural resources. It was, therefore, no coincidence that several major works in the history of science were produced during the Renaissance. In 1543, Andreas Vesalius published *On the Fabric of the Human Body*, a detailed work that originated modern anatomical studies. In the same year, Nicolaus Copernicus posited a heliocentric (sun-centered) conception of the universe in *On the Revolutions of the Celestial Bodies*. Copernicus's work eventually revolutionized the study of astronomy and helped launch a scientific revolution. In the late sixteenth and seventeenth centuries, Tycho Braehe, Johannes Kepler, Galileo Galilei, and others gathered the scientific data needed to prove that the Copernican conception of the universe was right.

THE CONQUEST OF THE OCEANS BY PORTUGAL AND SPAIN

During the fifteenth century, European explorers began to lead sailing expeditions far out into the Atlantic Ocean. Some pushed into the South Atlantic and eventually found a sea route around Africa to the Indian Ocean and Asia. Others drove westward across the Atlantic and unexpectedly found the continents that would become known as North and South America. These explorers in a sense conquered the oceans, such that the waters gradually became a vast highway for European commerce and exploration.

The Europeans pushed out into the oceans because they wanted to acquire gold and slaves from Africa and to find a new route to the east—to Cathay (China) and the Spice Islands (present-day Indonesia). For a thousand years, an overland trading system had brought Asian luxury goods to Europe—Chinese and Persian silks, Indian cottons, emeralds from India and rubies from Burma, and various kinds of spices, food preservatives, perfumes, and drugs. The luxury trade peaked during the Pax Mongolica but then began to decline with the erosion of Mongolian power. In addition, the fall of the Byzantine Empire in 1453 left the Muslims in control of eastern Mediterranean lands and the trade routes to the east. Thus, the Europeans hoped to bypass the difficulties associated with the overland trade routes by finding a new sea route to Asia. The potential rewards were enormous, for at times a merchant could ship six cargoes from Asia to Europe, lose five, and still make a profit when the sixth was sold.

The Europeans had not only the desire but also the ability to conquer the oceans. They had, most importantly, an aggressive attitude, fed both by the Renaissance impulse to seek new knowledge and by the Reformation enthusiasm for gaining new converts to Christianity (the Reformation is discussed in Chapter 11.) They also had several new technologies in the areas of navigational equipment, ship construction, and armaments (see the Technology box). The first to use these technologies to travel the oceans were the Portuguese and the Spanish.

The Portuguese Voyages

Portugal began the conquest of the oceans. The Portuguese had several advantages: (1) geographically, they were ideally situated to drive either out into the Atlantic or down the coast of Africa; (2) they knew the benefits and perils of long-distance trade because of their economic contacts with Muslim Africa; (3) they had a stable government during the fifteenth century, at a time when other European states—England, France, Spain—were plagued with internal conflict; and (4) they had Prince Henry the Navigator (1394–1460), a member of the royal family who encouraged and sponsored oceanic voyages.

Prince Henry organized a sailor's school where the latest navigational and shipbuilding techniques were taught. He also launched the first voyage of discovery in 1416. Henry never went on any of the voyages, but his voyagers soon found their way to the Azores and, by 1444, were down the African coast as far as Cape Verde. Portugal began to receive sugar from the Azores and gold and black slaves from Africa. The Portuguese voyages continued after Henry's death. Sailors crossed the equator in 1471, found the mouth of the Congo River in 1482, and reached the southern tip of Africa in 1487. Vasco da Gama established a sea route to Asia in 1498, when he sailed around Africa into the Indian Ocean and to India.

During the sixteenth century, the Portuguese dominated the seas across much of Asia. They sailed into Goa (India), Hormuz (the Persian Gulf), Macao and Canton (China), Nagasaki (Japan), and Malacca

(Indonesia) and brought rich cargoes back to Europe. But the Portuguese did not have enough sailors and resources to maintain their dominant position for long. In 1580, the Spanish ruling dynasty, after inheriting rights to the Portuguese throne, seized control of Portugal. By the end of the sixteenth century, the Dutch were expanding into Asia and taking over many of the best trade routes. The Portuguese finally regained their independence from Spain in the mid-seventeenth century, but by then their empire was enmeshed in a slow, lingering decline.

The Spanish Discoveries

The Portuguese explorations inspired others, especially the Spanish, to search for another sea route to Asia. (Though the Portuguese tried to prevent others from following them around Africa by refusing to share their hard-earned geographical and navigational knowledge.)

The man who led the Spanish quest was a Genoese sea captain, Christopher Columbus (1451–1506). Columbus, like most educated people of his time, believed that the earth was round and that it was thus possible to get to Asia by sailing west. In 1492, the Spanish monarchs Ferdinand and Isabella commissioned Columbus to undertake a westward voyage. They provided him with a letter of introduction to the Great Khan of China and an interpreter who spoke Arabic. When Columbus found some islands after a journey of several months, he thought he was sailing between Cipangu (Japan) and Cathay (China). He was actually among the Caribbean Islands, but even after several more voyages he still half-believed that the islands were somewhere off the coast of Asia.

A succession of other explorers quickly followed Columbus. The Spanish took control of Hispaniola (modern Haiti and the Dominican Republic) before 1500, Jamaica in 1511, Cuba in 1511–1514, and moved into Panama in 1519. The Portuguese commander Pedro Alvarez Cabral accidentally found the coast of Brazil in 1500, when he strayed off course on his way around Africa. Amerigo Vespucci made two voyages in 1499 and 1501, respectively, during which he mapped much of the Atlantic coast of South America. Since his mapping finally convinced Europeans that they had found a "New World," his name in the form of "America" became attached first to the southern continent and later to the northern as well.

Yet, for a time, the Spanish continued to think of America as nothing more than a barrier between Europe and Asia. In 1519, they sent Ferdinand Magellan to find a way around South America. Magellan's fleet returned to Spain in 1522, after circumnavigating the entire globe. The dangers faced by these and other early explorers are illustrated by what happened to Magellan's fleet. Magellan was killed in the Philippines during a small battle with natives. As for his crew, only fifteen survived to

TECHNOLOGY
Improvements in Navigation

During the early Middle Ages, the ships that sailed the Mediterranean were propelled either by oars or by the old Roman square sail. Early ships lacked the freedom to sail any place at any time, since the square sail forced them to go only in the same direction as the prevailing winds. This situation changed in the late Middle Ages with the development of the *lateen sail*. The lateen, a triangular-shaped sail fitted to a mast and a movable boom, could catch the wind from any direction and thus allow sailors to leave port at any time. The Europeans got the lateen from the Arabs, who either invented it themselves or received it from the Chinese.

A number of other developments in navigation were also occurring in the late Middle Ages. Shipbuilders along the Atlantic and North Sea coasts were learning how to construct strong ships that could withstand oceanic weather. They were producing new instruments—an improved astrolabe and the quadrant—to measure the altitude of heavenly bodies and thus give sailors more accurate ways of calculating their positions on the seas. The magnetic compass, invented in China probably in the eleventh century, appeared in Europe by the late twelfth century. Also from China came knowledge of gunpowder, which the Europeans began to use in cannons. (See Chapter 11 for a detailed discussion of the importance of gunpowder.)

By the late fifteenth century, the Portuguese, Spanish, and others were using a new ship called the *caravel* that could withstand harsh oceanic weather, catch the wind from any direction, and carry cannon. The caravel allowed the Europeans to overpower navies in all other parts of the world.

The Lateen Sail *This drawing illustrates the versatility of the lateen sail. The sail was attached to a boom, which could move around the mast and was fastened to the flooring of the ship. (The Granger Collection)*

return to Spain and most of the others died of scurvy during the voyage. Scurvy, a deficiency disease caused by a lack of vitamin C and clean water, sometimes turned ships on long voyages into floating cemeteries. The English later eliminated the disease by having their sailors eat citrus fruits, particularly limes; hence, English sailors were often called "limeys."

The Spanish in the Americas

The Spanish, of course, were not the first people to come to America. Thousands of years earlier Asian peoples had come to the Americas probably via a land bridge from northeastern Siberia to Alaska. The Europeans called these native Americans *Indians*, because they first thought they had found Asia and sometimes referred to Asia as India. Some of the native Americans had built large civilizations (see Chapter 1). The first Indians encountered by the Spanish were the Aztecs of central Mexico. One Spaniard, seeing the Aztec capital for the first time, was greatly impressed by what he observed:

> With such wonderful sights to gaze on we did not know what to say, or if this was real that we saw before our eyes. On the land side there were great cities, and on the lake many more. The lake was crowded with canoes. At intervals along the causeway there were many bridges, and before us was the great city of Mexico.[7]

In 1519, Hernando Cortés (1485–1546) led an expedition of six hundred troops into Mexico. Cortés was a complex man, driven both by the desire to perform great deeds and by the wish to Christianize the heathen. His small army defeated the much more numerous Aztecs by 1521, in part because the Spanish had firearms and horses, while the Aztecs had neither; in part because the Spanish allied with other native Americans who hated the Aztecs; and in part because the Aztec ruler Montezuma at first welcomed the arrival of Cortés as the return of the god Quetzalcoatl.

Other Spanish *conquistadores* (conquerors) pushed further into the two continents. In the south, Francisco Pizarro conquered the Incas in Peru during the 1530s. Pedro de Mendoza founded the city of Buenos Aires in 1536. In the north, the coasts of lower California were explored, and Acapulco soon became a port from which Spanish ships sailed to Asia. Hernando de Soto led an expedition from Florida west to the Mississippi in 1539, and in 1541 Francisco Vásquez Coronado marched into the great prairies west of the Mississippi and found large herds of buffalo, which he called "cows." Other nations began to emulate the Spanish. The French, for example, directed Jacques Cartier to find a northwest passage to Asia, but he ended up exploring much of the Canadian coast.

By 1540, the Spanish held a large empire centered in Central America with its capital at Mexico City. The Spanish conquerors expected the native Americans to work for them just as peasants worked for their masters in Spain. Usually, this meant laboring on farms or in mines. Forced labor killed many native Americans, while many more died from smallpox or typhus. These diseases were previously unknown in the Americas, so the native Americans had no immunity to them when the Spanish carried them across the ocean. The native American population of Mexico dropped from about twenty-seven million in 1519 to around one million in 1600, and in Peru the native American population fell during the same period from seven million to less than two million. The Spanish destruction of the native Americans was not completely deliberate, but it was nonetheless devastating.

The Spanish received many things—good and bad—from their new empire. They brought back to Europe syphilis, a disease that would plague many Europeans for centuries. They also brought many products—gold, silver, sugar, the potato—that temporarily made Spain a wealthy nation. The Spanish were unable, however, to use their imperial wealth to build a strong, competitive economy that could sustain Spanish power. Too many wars consumed the wealth from the Americas (as we will see in Chapter 11). Too many people refused to learn business and technical skills, since the Spanish nobility thought of labor as demeaning and the educated preferred to seek employment in government or church bureaucracies rather than in business. The result was a chronically weak economic base. Although the Spanish were able to retain their overseas empire, their political and economic strength began to dissipate in the seventeenth century.

Indeed, both exploring nations—Portugal and Spain—were unable to sustain their power for very long. Yet they had inaugurated a new era in history—one in which the full geographical contours of the globe would become known and Europe would dominate much of the world.

CONCLUSION

The period from 1300 to 1600 was a time of great change in Europe. Europeans lived through the gradual weakening of the old medieval order, the beginning of a transition from a rural to an urban way of life, the creation of new forms of art and literature, and the expansion of European power into overseas areas. They also lived through a religious upheaval, the Reformation, in the sixteenth century—our focus in the next chapter.

THINGS YOU SHOULD KNOW

Famines in Europe	Machiavelli
The Black Death	The Northern Renaissance
Hundred Years' War	van Eyck
War of the Roses	Erasmus
Pax Mongolica	More
Capitalism	Montaigne
The printing press	Shakespeare
The Renaissance in Italy	Nostradamus
Dante	Paracelsus
Petrarch	Dr. Faust
Boccaccio	Vesalius
Marsiglio	Copernicus
Giotto	The lateen sail
Donatello	Prince Henry the Navigator
Ghiberti	da Gama
Botticelli	Columbus
Savonarola	Vespucci
Leonardo da Vinci	Magellan
Michelangelo	Cortés
Raphael	

SUGGESTED READINGS

A good introduction to late medieval pessimism is Johan Huizinga, *The Waning of the Middle Ages* (New York: Doubleday, 1969). One cause of that pessimism was the Black Death, for which see William H. McNeill, *Plagues and Peoples* (New York: Doubleday, 1977) and Robert S. Gottfried, *The Black Death: Natural and Human Disaster in Medieval Europe* (New York: Free Press, 1985). Fernand Braudel, *The Wheels of Commerce*, vol. 2: *Civilization and Capitalism, 15th–18th Century*, trans. Siân Reynolds (New York: Harper & Row, 1986) is useful on the growth of capitalism. The classic work on the Italian Renaissance, written in the mid-nineteenth century, is Jacob Burckhardt, *The Civilization of the Renaissance in Italy* (New York: Modern Library, 1954). It is still worth reading. Other good works on the Renaissance include Wallace K. Ferguson, *The Renaissance* (New York: Henry Holt, 1940) and Denys Hay, *The Italian Renaissance in its Historical Background* (Cambridge, Eng.: Cambridge Univ. Press, 1977). Two good surveys of European expansion and exploration are J. H. Parry, *The Age of Reconnaissance: Discovery, Exploration and Settlement, 1450 to 1650* (New York: Praeger, 1963) and G. V. Scammell, *The World Encompassed: The First European Maritime Empires, c. 800–1650* (Berkeley: Univ. of California Press, 1981).

NOTES

[1] Quoted in Jean Gimpel, *The Medieval Machine: The Industrial Revolution of the Middle Ages* (New York: Penguin, 1976), p. 209.

[2]Quoted in Donald J. Wilcox, *In Search of God and Self: Renaissance and Reformation Thought* (Prospect Heights, Ill.: Waveland Press, 1975), p. 241.

[3]Joseph Needham, *Science and Civilization in China*, vol. 1: *Introductory Orientations* (Cambridge, Eng.: Cambridge Univ. Press, 1954), p. 189.

[4]Quoted in George Holmes, *Europe: Hierarchy and Revolt, 1320–1450* (New York: Harper Torchbooks, 1975), p. 146.

[5]Kenneth Clark, *Civilisation* (New York: Harper & Row, 1969), p. 129.

[6]Quoted in Wilcox, *In Search of God*, p. 165.

[7]Quoted in C. C. Lamberg-Karlovsky and Jeremy A. Sabloff, *Ancient Civilizations: The Near East and Mesoamerica* (Menlo Park, Calif.: Benjamin Cummings, 1979), p. 305.

11

The Reformations and Subsequent Conflicts, 1500 to 1715

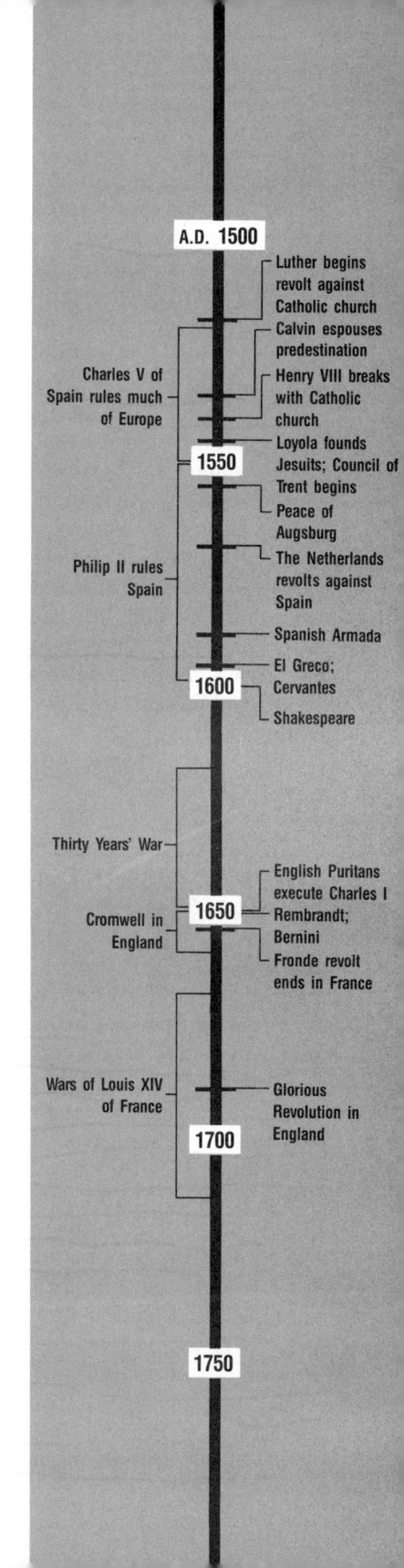

A.D. **1500**
- Luther begins revolt against Catholic church
- Calvin espouses predestination

Charles V of Spain rules much of Europe
- Henry VIII breaks with Catholic church
- Loyola founds Jesuits; Council of Trent begins

1550
- Peace of Augsburg

Philip II rules Spain
- The Netherlands revolts against Spain
- Spanish Armada
- El Greco; Cervantes

1600
- Shakespeare

Thirty Years' War

- English Puritans execute Charles I

Cromwell in England **1650**
- Rembrandt; Bernini
- Fronde revolt ends in France

Wars of Louis XIV of France
- Glorious Revolution in England

1700

1750

During the sixteenth and seventeenth centuries, much of Western and central Europe was dominated by two interconnected developments. One was the *Reformation*, a complex upheaval that included both the *Protestant Reformation*, in which many Christians left the Roman Catholic church to establish independent churches, and the *Catholic Reformation*, in which the Catholic church sought to reform and rejuvenate itself. The other was the gradual emergence in Spain, France, and England of strong monarchical states, in which monarchs increasingly dominated the politics of their countries.

The Reformations and the emergence of strong monarchical states were connected in various ways. Sometimes monarchs used the religious struggles of the Reformation to increase their political power. At other times, religious leaders used monarchical armies to support their religious causes. At still other times, aristocrats in various areas used the religious conflicts to oppose the growth of monarchical power, which usually undermined the power of the aristocracy.

One result of the religious and political struggles was war. There were civil wars within countries as well as international conflicts. Most significant were the Spanish wars with various countries, particularly the Netherlands; the Thirty Years' War in the Germanies; the long English civil war in the seventeenth century; and the wars of the French monarch, Louis XIV.

THE PROTESTANT AND CATHOLIC REFORMATIONS

Several underlying factors helped produce the Reformations that split the Catholic church. First, resurgence of religious belief and emotions encouraged many Europeans to take their religious loyalties more seriously and to refuse compromise with those who disagreed with them. Second, a growing emphasis on individualism impelled many Christians to reject the organizational discipline of the Catholic church. Third, the constant traveling of people engaged in commerce helped break down traditional loyalties to the Catholic church. Finally, the growth of literacy, aided by the printing press, and the rise of universities helped create ways of learning and thinking that were often independent of traditional religious institutions.

Divisions within Christianity had begun well before the sixteenth century. The first division was the Greek Orthodox-Roman Catholic split of 1054. Then, in the late Middle Ages, there was a political split within Roman Catholicism. French monarchs acquired strong influence over the papacy for a time and, from 1305 to 1378, the popes resided in Avignon (present-day France) rather than in Rome. This was the so-called Babylonian Captivity of the papacy, named after the Babylonian defeat of the Hebrews during Old Testament times. Then followed the Great Schism (1378–1417), during which one line of popes continued to live in Avignon while another was established in Rome. The Avignon papacy eventually disappeared, leaving only the popes in Rome. But while the Schism lasted, Europe witnessed two successions of popes, each denouncing and excommunicating the other. The Schism created many dilemmas for the ordinary believer. According to Catholic doctrine, only legitimate priests can administer the sacraments—baptism and the eucharist, for example—through which Christians receive divine grace. With the Schism, it was difficult for Christians to know which priests to approach in order to receive the sacraments.

Another problem for the medieval church was the growth of several heretical movements, such as the Hussite rebellion in Bohemia (present-day Czechoslovakia). Early in the fifteenth century, John Hus initiated a religious reform designed to free the Bohemian church from papal control. Hus was burned at the stake, but Bohemian anger against the papacy and against the German kings of Bohemia kept the rebellion alive for a time. The church and the German rulers finally had to organize a crusade to regain control of the area.

Still another difficulty for the church was a growing anticlericalism among many ordinary people. One reason was a slowly emerging sense of nationalism in some areas, which fostered resentment of papal money-raising activities that took wealth from all over Europe to Rome. Another was the amount of land and other resources already owned by the church. By the late fifteenth century, the church owned almost 25 percent of the land in England and 20 percent in Sweden. Land-hungry peasants often perceived the clergy as parasites who accumulated land and lived off the labor of others. One peasant ridiculed the vows of poverty and chastity taken by clergy: "They go to the houses of rich, young, and beautiful women. They take their money and, if they consent, they sleep carnally with them, putting on appearances of humility the while." A young shepherd had an equally low opinion of monks: "Instead of saving the souls of the dead and sending them to Heaven, they gorge themselves at banquets, after funerals. . . . They are wicked wolves! They would like to devour us all, dead or alive."[1]

Martin Luther and the Reformation in Germany

Certainly not everyone in Europe was anticlerical or antipapacy, but there was enough opposition to the church to spark protest. The spark came from a German friar, Martin Luther (1483–1546), and signals the beginning of the Protestant movement. As a young man, Luther was obsessed by a fear of God as a stern judge who condemned most people to perdition. In his anxiety, he joined a monastery in an effort to find spiritual satisfaction and peace. During his years as a monk, Luther

Martin Luther A 1529 portrait of the Protestant reformer Martin Luther, by Lucas Cranach the Elder (1472–1553). (The Granger Collection)

constantly pondered the phrase "the righteousness of God" and gradually came to believe that salvation was possible for humans only because God imparted righteousness to them. The Biblical passage that inspired Luther is from the Book of Romans—"The just shall live by faith"—meaning people cannot earn salvation by their own efforts but only through God. The implication was that the center of the Christian experience is an individual's personal relationship with God through which God grants righteousness to the person. The institutional church, though, was not that important.

Luther's views might have led him into a conflict with the church under any circumstances, but the actual conflict began over the relatively minor issue of the sale of *indulgences*. Indulgences were monetary payments to the church by means of which, the church said, people could reduce the penalties (but not the guilt) for their sins. In 1517, a German indulgence seller named Johann Tetzel began to preach, wrongly, that indulgences would remove a sinner's guilt as well as his penalty. Luther immediately protested Tetzel's errors and, according to tradition, posted "Ninety-five Theses" (a challenge to a debate) on the door of a church in Wittenberg, Germany. His protest was quickly supported by many Germans who resented the church's wealth and power. Luther was emboldened, and by 1518 he was attacking the church on a number of issues, including the claim that the pope had final authority to interpret the scriptures. As a result, he was soon excommunicated by the pope and outlawed by the German emperor.

Originally, Luther did not intend to split from the Roman Catholic church, but several factors soon encouraged him to start what became the *Lutheran church*. One was his growing conviction that the Roman Catholic church was so overly organized and wealthy that it hindered the individual Christian in his or her quest for a personal relationship with God. Another factor was the support he received from evangelical preachers in Germany, who carried Luther's message to ordinary people. In addition, Luther was supported by many German princes, in part for religious reasons and in part for the opportunity to expropriate church property and wealth. Some of the princes also saw Luther's revolt as an opportunity to enhance their political power in the areas they governed. They supported Luther against the German Emperor Charles V, who sought to increase his power over the princes and was supporting the Catholic church against Luther. (The princes stood for decentralized politics in Germany so they would control their own small areas, while the emperor stood for centralized power in imperial hands.)

During the 1520s and 1530s, Germany was embroiled in constant religious and political conflict. Luther encouraged the revolt against Rome by preaching, writing hymns, interpreting the Bible, and training missionaries. Evangelical preachers carried the revolt into many German cities, where Lutheran churches were often established. Religious wars between Lutherans and Catholics erupted several times. The German Peasants' War of 1525, caused both by religious emotions and the peasant complaints, exploded and was savagely repressed by the princes, who had Luther's support.

The eventual result was that much of north Germany became Lutheran while south Germany remained predominantly Catholic. Then, in 1555, the Peace of Augsburg formulated a truce that allowed each German prince to establish which church he wanted in his realm. The Peace of Augsburg both recognized Lutheranism as permanent and contributed to the religious and political fragmentation of Germany.

The Peace of Augsburg recognized only Lutherans and Catholics; it did not tolerate the other sects that emerged in Germany during Luther's revolt. One new sect was the *literalists*, who sought to live by the exact words of the Bible. A particularly notorious literalist got so carried away that he imitated the prophet Isaiah in throwing off his clothes and running through the streets to look for a sign from God. More numerous were the *Anabaptists*. Anabaptism was an evangelical movement that flourished primarily among poor townspeople and peasants. It had no central organization, but its defining characteristic was a belief that baptism should occur only when a person reaches adulthood. Both

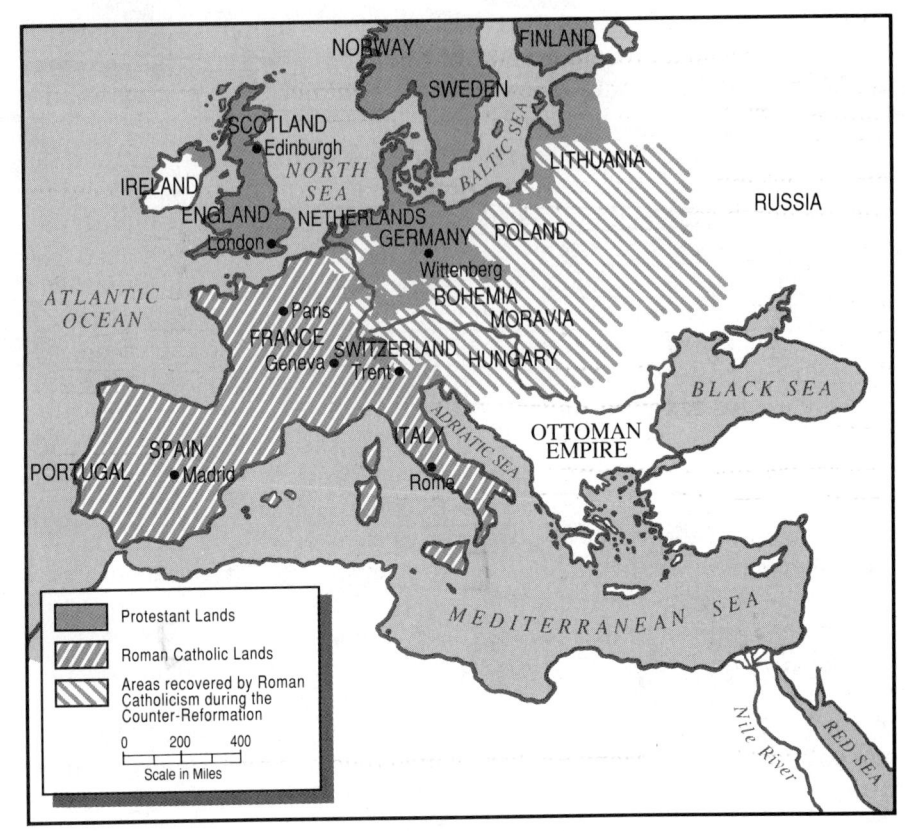

Figure 11.1 The Religious Division of Europe, 1517–1648

Lutherans and Catholics regarded the Anabaptists and other sects as radicals who should be persecuted and destroyed. Many of the persecuted eventually migrated to North America.

John Calvin and the Reformation in Switzerland

The *Protestant* movement (which "protested" against and split from Catholicism) spread to Switzerland in the 1520s. Huldrych Zwingli (1484–1531) established a reformed church in Zurich, but more significant was the work of John Calvin in Geneva.

Calvin (1509–1564) was a Frenchman who wrote *The Institutes of the Christian Religion* in 1536. His belief in the absolute power of God led him to espouse a doctrine of *predestination*, which stipulated that God has foreordained the ultimate destiny of all people. Those who are chosen for salvation are the elect, and, according to Calvin, they should live rigorously disciplined lives in conformity with God's laws. The logic and clarity of Calvin's writings were so persuasive that in 1541 he was invited to Geneva to lead a Protestant reform. Under his guidance, the Genevans established a theocracy, a government dominated by ministers and churches. The government promulgated numerous regulations to control behavior: card playing and dancing were prohibited, children were strictly disciplined to obey their parents, and everyone was expected to attend church services regularly. A number of people were executed for heresy, blasphemy, or adultery.

John Calvin may seem to have been a harsh, demanding figure who took all the fun out of life. It is important to remember, though, that most Genevans accepted his leadership willingly, because they too believed that a morally disciplined life was a sign of their salvation. Others outside of Geneva also followed Calvin's leadership. Switzerland, being in the middle of Europe, was ideally positioned to spread the Reformation, and Geneva became a haven where religious exiles could learn from Calvin and then carry his message back to their home countries. As a result, Calvinism rather than Lutheranism took root in the Netherlands, France (the Huguenots), Scotland (the Presbyterians), and England (the Puritans).

The Reformation in England

In England, religious change was caused by a combination of religious and political factors. Many English wanted religious reform for the same reasons as people elsewhere, but the issue that precipitated a split with the Catholic church was Henry VIII's marital problems.

Henry VIII (reigned 1509–1547) was obsessed with wanting a son to succeed him. He believed that a secure succession would prevent the kinds of conflicts that had plagued England in the preceding century (such as the War of the Roses). But he and the queen, Catherine of Aragon, were unable to produce a son. By the 1520s, Henry was convinced that their marriage was invalid because of Catherine's earlier marriage to Henry's deceased elder brother. So, Henry requested that the pope grant an annulment of his marriage to Catherine. The pope refused and later excommunicated Henry when he married Anne Boleyn in 1533. In his rage, Henry appealed to the English Parliament, which in 1534 passed the Act of Supremacy that made the monarch the head of the English church and stipulated that the English owed no allegiance to the Roman pope. This political action was supported by many English for religious reasons; they were already anti-Rome and wanted religious reform.

Henry soon had Anne Boleyn beheaded because of her alleged plotting against him. His desire for a son drove him to marry again, and his third wife, Jane Seymour, gave birth to a boy. (After Jane Seymour died, Henry married three more times.) It is ironic that what Henry

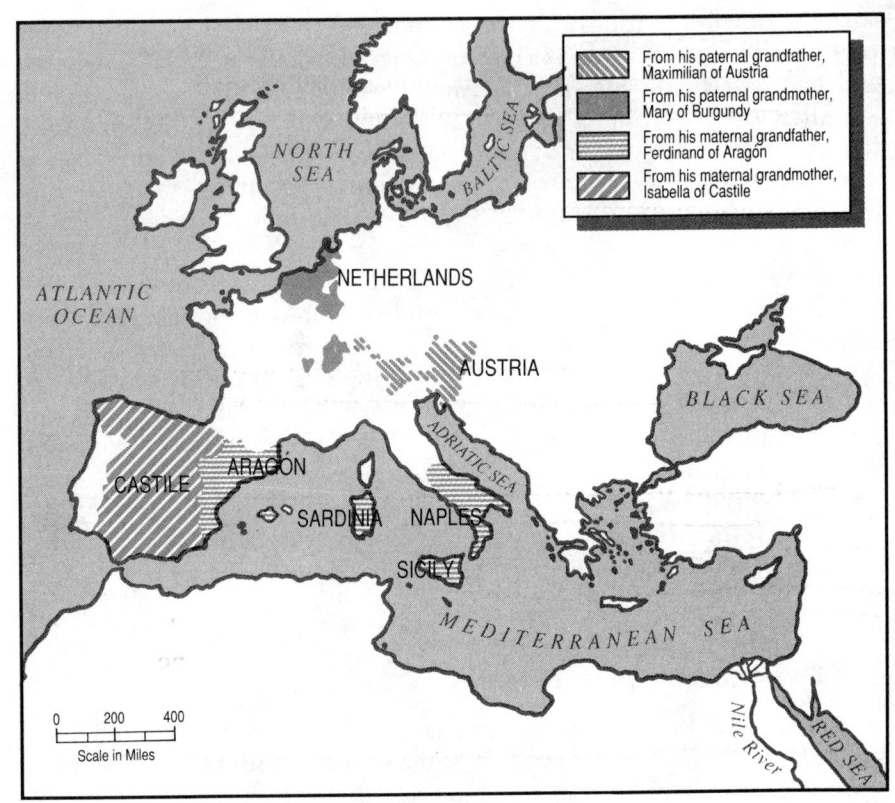

Figure 11.2 Lands Ruled by Charles V, 1514

wanted most, a strong successor, turned out to be, not his son, who died after a brief reign, but the daughter he had by Anne Boleyn. She became Queen Elizabeth I (reigned 1558–1603) one of the greatest rulers in English history.

The Catholic Reformation

During the early years of the Protestant Reformation, the Catholic church was too confused and disorganized to respond effectively to the Protestant challenge. Gradually, however, the Catholics launched a reform of their own—the *Catholic Reformation* (sometimes called the *Counter-Reformation*).

The Catholic Reformation began with individuals seeking a closer relationship with God, particularly in Spain, one of the most loyal Catholic nations. St. Teresa of Avila (1515–1582) was a mystic who reinstituted monastic discipline in the Carmelite convents in Spain. (The

Carmelites were a mendicant order originally founded in the twelfth century.) St. John of the Cross (1542–1591) was a follower of St. Teresa's, and he helped reform the Carmelite monasteries in Spain.

The most prominent of the Spanish reformers was Ignatius Loyola. Loyola (1491–1556) was a boisterous soldier as a young man and became intensely religious only after being seriously wounded. He began to practice spiritual exercises—various forms of meditation and contemplation—and to teach the spirituality so prevalent in his day: "Love ought to manifest itself in deeds rather than in words."[2] Loyola gradually acquired some followers, and in 1540 the pope designated his group as a new religious order—the Company of Jesus, or *Jesuits*. The Jesuits were committed missionaries. Some became scholars and founded schools and colleges; others went to the New World and even to China to convert non-Christians. Thus, the Jesuits were instrumental in reviving Catholicism.

The Catholic Reformation also included a variety of measures more directly intended to block the spread of Protestantism. One was the *Index*, a list of books (mostly Protestant writings) that Catholics were forbidden to read. Another was the Inquisition, a church court created during the Middle Ages, which the Catholics used to identify and punish heretics. In addition, the Catholic response to Protestantism included the calling of a church council. The Council of Trent met off and on for eighteen years (1545–1563) and had two primary goals: (1) to institute reforms to strengthen the church internally and (2) to respond to Protestantism on a doctrinal level. The Council clarified Catholic thought in a number of areas, including the matter of indulgences that had initially precipitated the Protestant revolt. It also established a better training system for priests, required stricter discipline with regard to the behavior and morality of clergy, and prohibited the practice of a bishop's holding more than one bishopric. Basically, the Council of Trent refused any compromise with Protestantism, but it clarified Catholic doctrines and made church organization more efficient. Thus, it helped prepare the Catholic church for the future.

Art during the Reformation

The heightened religious feelings of the Reformation era helped inspire several great artists. Some of these were Hans Holbein, Pieter Brueghel, and Peter Paul Rubens. Two of the most influential were Rembrandt van Rijn (1606–1669) and Giovanni Lorenzo Bernini (1598–1680).

Rembrandt was a Dutch Protestant, a devout man who read the Bible regularly. He painted both secular and religious subjects. His *Supper at Emmaus*, for example, portrays Jesus breaking bread with his disciples. The clearest evidence of Rembrandt's concern with religion and spirituality is the overwhelming use of drab colors like browns and dark reds in his work. He did not want his paintings to be so spectacular that they blinded viewers to the inner meaning of his art.

Bernini was an Italian sculptor, painter, and architect as well as a loyal Catholic. In fact, his most famous work was done at St. Peter's Basilica in Rome. It is the massive place of worship next to the papal residence. Michelangelo had designed the dome for St. Peter's, and Bernini added to Michelangelo's work. He built, on the inside, a large and elaborate bronze canopy above the central altar. On the outside, Bernini built two enormous colonnades that enclose a piazza in front of the Basilica. The piazza quickly became a gathering place for pilgrims and visitors coming to visit the Basilica and seek an audience with the pope.

Consequences of the Reformation

Some of the most important consequences of the Reformation era were the following:

1. Europe was split along religious lines. Much of northern Europe—northern Germany, the Scandinavian countries, Switzerland, parts of France, the Netherlands, England, and Scotland—became Protestant. Most of southern Europe—Spain, Italy, southern Germany, most of France, and Poland—remained Catholic.
2. The religious divisions led to numerous wars caused by both religious and political factors. During the sixteenth and seventeenth centuries, Protestants and Catholics fought each other and both persecuted the smaller religious sects. This had the further consequence of encouraging persecuted religious minorities to escape by emigrating to the Americas at the same time that, slowly, a desire grew for religious toleration, since most Protestants and Catholics eventually tired of trying to destroy each other.
3. Some old institutions and customs were abolished in Protestant areas; monasteries were disbanded and Protestant clergy were allowed to marry.
4. The phenomenon of witch-hunting was encouraged. Heightened religious tensions, added to the general chaos of the age, led in the sixteenth and seventeenth centuries to many women being accused of witchcraft. Europeans had believed in witches for a long time, but until the fourteenth century few people were actually identified as witches. After that, a growing number of single women who lived alone were accused of heresy, of worshipping the devil, or of bewitching people. Once an entire convent of nuns began to mew and purr like cats, and a woman was charged with casting a spell over them. By the sixteenth century, witchcraft trials were common in some parts of Europe. The bishop of Bamberg (Germany) had six hundred alleged witches burned in a

single year, and in Savoy (Italy) eight hundred were executed in one batch. In Salem, Massachusetts, twenty witches were killed in 1692. During the sixteenth and seventeenth centuries, more women were killed for witchcraft than for all other crimes combined. The exact number of women executed is unknown, but it was probably in the range of 60,000 to 80,000.

5. In some Protestant areas, the religious revolt helped increase the power of monarchs. Protestants no longer owed allegiance to an international institution—the papacy—and thus could be encouraged to focus their political loyalties on their kings or queens. Furthermore, Protestant monarchs often used religious reform as an excuse to confiscate property from the Catholic church.

THE EMERGENCE OF STRONG MONARCHICAL STATES

During the late Middle Ages, some European monarchs began to organize large states (see Chapter 8), but in most areas real political power continued to rest in the hands of the local feudal nobility. By the sixteenth century, monarchs in England, France, and Spain were building on the work of their predecessors, destroying the power of the local nobility and forming genuinely centralized kingdoms. England, after the chaos of the War of the Roses, experienced a succession of powerful monarchs—Henry VII (1485–1509), Henry VIII (1509–1547), and Elizabeth I (1558–1603). France, after driving out the English during the Hundred Years' War, received strong leadership from Louis XI (1461–1483) and Francis I (1515–1547). Spain was finally united in 1492 by Ferdinand (1479–1516) and Isabella (1474–1504), who were followed by Charles V (1519–1556) and Philip II (1556–1598).

The monarchs of England, France, and Spain used primarily four methods to strengthen their power. (1) They began to monopolize the use of force. Traditionally, the nobility was the backbone of royal armies, the result being that nobles had military training and power that could be used to enhance their political and social positions. By the sixteenth century, monarchs were hiring mercenaries to aid armies that used cannons and rifles. Thus, the new weapons made the armies more powerful and the paid mercenaries gave the monarch more control over military forces. (2) Monarchs began to build bureaucracies in which permanent officials collected taxes and applied royal law throughout the kingdom. Originally, these bureaucracies were small, but they gradually expanded and extended the power of centralized, royal government. (3) Monarchs began to justify their power in various ways. One way was through the theory of the divine right of kings, which held that rulers received their power from God. Monarchs also staged elaborate court ceremonials and public tours that were designed to build in the eyes of the populace an image of royal grandeur and majesty. (4) Finally, the monarchs sought to instill some cultural unity in their kingdoms by encouraging similarity of opinion among the members of the upper classes. In practice, this meant religious uniformity. Protestant monarchs tried to insist that all the leading members of society be Protestant, while Catholic monarchs demanded loyalty to Catholicism from their upper classes.

The emergence of large monarchical states in England, France, and Spain affected European history in several ways but two are most important. First, England and France in particular encouraged economic development and the growth of capitalism. This occurred in part because the governments were major customers for some products and in part because they provided the social stability and peace that allowed merchants to expand business and commerce. Second, England, France, and Spain fostered European expansion across the oceans. The monarchs wanted to increase their power and prestige and had the financial resources to sponsor oceanic voyages.

EUROPEAN WARS OF THE SIXTEENTH AND SEVENTEENTH CENTURIES

Many military conflicts occurred in Europe during the sixteenth and seventeenth centuries. Their causes were varied and intermixed. The religious hostilities between Protestants and Catholics contributed, as did the dynastic struggles over who would inherit the thrones in some countries. Another cause was the continuing struggle between monarchs, who sought to centralize political power, and nobles, who sought to decentralize power into their own hands. Further, some monarchs wanted to conquer more territory.

Spain and the Netherlands

Spain was in many ways the most powerful nation in Europe during the sixteenth century. Spanish *conquistadores* were gradually conquering a vast empire in the Americas, and the colonies were sending gold and silver back to Spain. Within Europe, the Holy Roman Emperor Charles V (reigned 1519–1556) ruled Spain as well as an extraordinary range of other territories. Charles was a member of the Hapsburg family, which had gradually acquired power in much of Europe. From his mother, the daughter of Ferdinand and Isabella of Spain, Charles inherited the throne of Spain (where he was known as Charles I). From his father, he inherited the territories of Burgundy (eastern France) and the Netherlands (present-day Holland and Belgium). And, from his paternal grandfather, the Holy Roman Emperor Maximilian I, he inherited the throne of

TECHNOLOGY
Weaponry

One reason for the political success of the European monarchs was the growing use of gunpowder and cannons. The Chinese discovered and used gunpowder as early as the eleventh century, but they never took the decisive step of inventing the cannon. The gunpowder discovery was passed on to the Arabs, and the Europeans probably learned about gunpowder from the Arabs in Spain. Early cannons were long wooden tubes. Stones inside the tube were propelled by a gunpowder explosion. Europeans first used cannons as siege guns in Spain during the thirteenth century. By the fourteenth century, the first portable rifles were in use in Europe.

The sixteenth century was the first great age of gunpowder in Europe. Cannons were mounted on wheels and thus became more mobile. Rifles were improved by the invention of the matchlock. The earliest rifles were just iron tubes in which the gunpowder had to be lit by hand, but the matchlock, operated by a trigger, made ignition of gunpowder easier and quicker.

Military forces armed with cannons and rifles were obviously much stronger than those equipped only with pikes and the weapons carried by soldiers on horseback. In particular, cannon fire could penetrate the walls of a noble's castle, so the availability of cannon weakened the power base of the nobility and thus strengthened the authority of many monarchs.

Cannons *A 1575 wood engraving of early cannons, which were mounted on mobile carriages. (The Granger Collection)*

Austria as well as the imperial throne of Germany. (Germany was politically divided—see Chapter 8—with real political power in the hands of the princes of the individual German states. However, there was a Holy Roman Empire to which the German states belonged, and the Holy Roman emperor exercised a nominal leadership in the Germanies.)

Ruling much of Europe as well as the Americas may have been more of a curse than a blessing to Charles V, for he spent much of his life planning and fighting wars. He fought the Ottoman Turks, who were asserting power in the Mediterranean, and he continually competed with France for control of Italy. (The Spanish-French wars in Italy helped destroy the economic prosperity that supported the Italian Renaissance.) Furthermore, as a loyal Catholic, Charles was embroiled for years in the religious wars in Germany and lived to see Catholicism lose much of its power and influence. Weary of his struggles, Charles abdicated his thrones in 1555 and 1556. His brother, Ferdinand I, received the Austrian and Holy Roman thrones, and his son, Philip II, became king of Spain and the overseas empire as well as ruler of Burgundy and the Netherlands.

Philip II (reigned 1556–1598) was also involved in several military conflicts. In France, Protestants and Catholics were struggling for power, and Philip's Spain intervened on the Catholic side. On the seas, the English and Dutch were attacking Spanish convoys from the Americas. Philip sent the Spanish Armada, a naval expedition, to punish the English in 1588, but it was defeated by a combination of English resistance and bad weather. Philip's longest struggle was with the Netherlands. In 1568, the Netherlands rebelled against Spanish rule. The rebellion was in part a war for political independence and in part a religious fight between the Protestant Dutch and the Catholic Spanish. The southern provinces of the Netherlands (present-day Belgium) eventually made peace with Spain, but the northern provinces (present-day Netherlands) continued fighting until they won independence in 1609. The Spanish later tried to reconquer them, but Dutch freedom was finally confirmed in 1648. (As in many other wars of the time, the fighting forced many people to leave their homes and migrate to other areas, as both Protestants and Catholics tried to escape the focus of the other side.)

Gaining independence stimulated Dutch energy and creativity, and the seventeenth century was a great age in Dutch history. The painter Rembrandt (1606–1669) was doing his greatest work then. The jurist Hugo Grotius (1583–1645) wrote an influential exposition of international law. Dutch scientists and artisans made important discoveries in the fields of human anatomy and optics. And, for a time, the leading Dutch city of Amsterdam was the world center of capitalism. The first stock exchange was created there, its function being to raise capital for large-scale enterprises. The largest banks and the largest collection of merchant vessels were also in Amsterdam. Dutch ships carried cargoes

The Resurrection of Jesus, (c. 1596–1600) by *El Greco* The Spanish painter El Greco (1541–1614) was originally from Greece; his birth name was Kyriakos Theotocopoulos. El Greco's style was gritty and dark. It represented a movement away from painting Jesus and other subjects as "glowing" and "perfect looking." (Gallery del Prado)

throughout the Baltic Sea as well as to and from Asia and the Americas. In the mid-seventeenth century, the Dutch seemed to be everywhere—in Russia building iron-smelting plants, in China buying silk, in Brazil organizing sugar plantations, in North America establishing New Amsterdam (now New York City). They were, for a time, the wealthiest people in Europe.

If the war of independence brought prosperity and power to the Dutch, it was for the Spanish one more step in a story of decline. As noted in Chapter 10, too many wars drained Spanish wealth and energy, and Spain was unable to build a permanently strong economy. Consequently, seventeenth-century Spain slowly lost power and wealth. At the same time, however, the Spanish enjoyed a cultural flowering. The artist El Greco (1541–1614) painted primarily religious subjects and expressed the spirit of the Catholic Reformation. The dramatist Lope de Vega (1562–1635) produced hundreds of plays and poems and helped found modern drama. And, Miguel de Cervantes (1547–1616) wrote *Don Quixote*, a masterpiece of world literature. In one sense, *Don Quixote* is a satire on the chivalric romances that appealed to many Spanish; in another sense, it is an inspiring examination of human idealism.

The Thirty Years' War in the Germanies

In the first half of the seventeenth century, the Germanies became enmeshed in a terrible struggle known as the *Thirty Years' War* (1618–1648). It was a conflict in which political and religious disputes were intermixed. As noted earlier, the Germanies were politically divided, with an emperor exercising nominal leadership over the whole but with real political power resting in the individual states. The Germanies were also religiously divided, with the north German states being predominantly Protestant and the south German states predominantly Catholic. The Thirty Years' War originated in a struggle between Protestant princes, defending both their religion and their political power, and the Catholic emperor, fighting to increase his imperial control over the Germanies and also to strengthen his church. As other nations intervened in the struggle, the conflict widened and became more intense. For the people of Germany, the war was a hideous nightmare. Many were killed, and some towns suffered so much destruction that they disappeared. When the fighting finally ended in 1648 with the Peace of Westphalia, the political decentralization of the Germanies was reaffirmed, and an exhausted German people began a slow recovery from the horrors of a long civil war.

Because several great powers intervened in the German struggle, the Thirty Years' War had a wide-ranging impact on European politics. France, for example, gained valuable parcels of land from the Peace of Westphalia. The small duchy of Brandenburg (northern Germany) captured some territories within Germany and began to grow and evolve into the state of Prussia (northeastern Europe, along the Baltic coast). Sweden tried to take several north German ports and thereby become the greatest power in the Baltic Sea area, but Swedish ambitions were finally contained by other nations. Muscovy (Russia) was also beginning to assert its power, while Poland was starting a long decline.

The English Civil War and the Glorious Revolution

The English civil war lasted through most of the seventeenth century. It was precipitated in part by a dispute between the English monarchs and Parliament. Because the expenses of armies and armaments were rapidly increasing, English monarchs continually tried to increase their tax revenues, often without the consent of Parliament. Many members of Parliament, particularly those representing the merchant class, interpreted the monarchical actions as attempts to impose tyranny on England.

Another cause of the English civil war was a religious quarrel between the monarchs, who headed the established Anglican church, and the Puritans, followers of Calvinism who wanted to "purify" Anglicanism. The Puritans objected in particular to the elaborate religious ceremonials and the complex administrative apparatus of the Anglican church, as they seemed similar to Roman Catholic practices. The Puritans favored simpler forms of religious worship that included a doctrine of spiritual equality in which believers could read and interpret the Bible themselves. To conservative Anglicans, the Puritan doctrine sounded like an invitation to religious chaos. The philosopher Thomas Hobbes wrote sarcastically: "Every man, nay, every boy and wench that could read English thought they spoke with God Almighty, and understood what he said."[3]

Serious disputes began during the reign of James I (1603–1625) and continued through the years of his son, Charles I (1625–1649). Both monarchs tried to increase taxes and impose Anglican church rules on all English, and neither was willing to compromise. The parliamentary opponents of taxation and the Puritan opponents of Anglicanism gradually became merged in a common front against monarchical policies. By the 1640s, the quarrel was increasingly tense and blunt, and fighting broke out in 1642.

On one side were the forces loyal to Charles I, sometimes called the *Cavaliers;* on the other was the parliamentary army led by the Puritan Oliver Cromwell, its members often called *Roundheads* (because their short hair marked them as socially inferior to the nobility). The parliamentary-Puritan army had an emotional advantage in that the Puritans were convinced they represented God's cause. Several years of fierce fighting led to the final defeat of the Cavaliers in 1646. (Not all Englishpeople knew or cared about what was happening. One farmer, told to get out of the way of a battle between royalist and parliamentary forces, did not know that "them two had fallen out."[4])

In 1649, Charles I was placed on trial and then executed by the Puritan-dominated Parliament, an extraordinary event in an age when monarchs were presumed to be God's representatives on earth. From 1649 to 1660, a Puritan republic first led by Oliver Cromwell (he died in

1658) governed England, but it gradually lost popularity. One reason was a war with the Dutch, which led to higher taxes in England and the disruption of English commerce. Another was that the Puritans tried to impose their strict moral precepts on the English. The Puritans prohibited gambling, profanity, and sometimes the playing of games. In one instance, a certain John Bishop was called to court for having "wilfully and in a violent and boisterous manner run to and fro" while kicking a football.[5]

After Cromwell's death in 1658, leading aristocrats invited Charles, son of Charles I, to become king. Charles II (reigned 1660–1685) ruled fairly effectively for a time, but his successor James II (reigned 1685–1688) resumed the uncompromising tax and religious policies of his predecessors. By 1688, James had little if any public support, and parliamentary leaders were able to force him out of the country in an essentially bloodless coup. Parliament then invited William and Mary of the Netherlands to become king and queen of England. Both were Protestants, and Mary was James II's daughter. This event became celebrated as the *Glorious Revolution* because in exchange for the throne William and Mary agreed to accept a Bill of Rights that limited the powers of the monarchy and guaranteed that monarchs would govern only with the consent of Parliament. The Glorious Revolution thus marked the end of the long English conflict. It was a victory for the upper classes, who being represented in Parliament would rule England in cooperation with the monarchs. The lower classes were not represented before or after the Glorious Revolution. During the 1640s, there had been some radical groups—the Levellers and the Diggers—who espoused egalitarian, democratic ideas, but they were suppressed by the Puritans.

These political and religious events in England stimulated a great deal of thought that influenced not only England but much of Western Europe and the future United States as well. In 1651, Thomas Hobbes wrote *Leviathan,* a defense of absolutist government that would continue to be read for centuries. (*Absolutism* refers to a type of government in which one person or group holds all power.) The theories of the Levellers and the Diggers had some impact on the founders of the United States. John Milton, the great poet of the Puritan cause, created *Paradise Lost* (1667), a prolonged meditation on the nature of divine justice and the sinfulness of humanity. And, John Locke, the philosophical defender of the Glorious Revolution, began to define what would later be known as *liberalism*.

The Wars of Louis XIV

France, like many other countries, endured civil strife during the sixteenth and seventeenth centuries. In the sixteenth century, Catholics and Protestants (often called *Huguenots* in France) fought so much that the stability of the French state was threatened. In the seventeenth century, a series of rebellions known as the *Fronde* (1649–1653) shook the country. The Fronde was launched by numerous aristocrats and townspeople who wanted to decentralize political power to the local level. French monarchs, however, were able to quash the rebellions and continue to centralize power in their own hands.

When Louis XIV (reigned 1643–1715) ascended the French throne, France began to assert its power on the international level even more forcefully than before. Louis saw himself as an absolute monarch, whose power was unrestricted in France. He sought, among other things, to control French industries and overseas trade and to enhance French culture by patronizing artists such as the dramatist Molière (1622–1673). But Louis's greatest passion was *la gloire*, "military glory," in order to enhance his and France's reputation. The result was a series of wars in which Louis sought to gain more territory for France. The War of Devolution (1667–1668) enabled Louis to annex part of the Spanish Netherlands (present-day Belgium). In the Dutch War (1672–1678), Louis sought to destroy Protestantism in the Netherlands (present-day Holland). He did not achieve that goal but did gain some more territory for France. The War of the League of Augsburg (1689–1697) resulted in some small annexations of German territory by France. Finally, the War of the Spanish Succession (1702–1713) was an unsuccessful attempt by Louis to ensure that one of his grandsons would inherit the Spanish throne. None of these wars was particularly deadly or involved large numbers of military forces, but together they did absorb much of France's wealth and therefore helped to weaken the French economy. Louis did acquire some small areas of land, but various coalitions of European powers always fought against him and prevented him from making large territorial gains. When Louis died in 1715, after several decades of warfare, France had relatively little to show for his ambitions.

CONCLUSION

Western Civilization experienced fundamental changes during the sixteenth and seventeenth centuries. The Reformation produced religious divisions that contributed to numerous wars. These wars were so destructive that they gradually produced among many people a desire for religious toleration in order to stop the killing. Another major change was the growth of monarchical power in some countries, as monarchs increased the authority of their centralized governments.

Also present in the sixteenth and seventeenth centuries were developments in capitalism, science, and overseas expansion that would become more significant in following centuries. As capitalism developed, it gradually produced more wealth and power for Europeans. Modern science gave people a deeper understanding of nature. And the expansion of European power overseas in the Americas and Asia would continue.

At the beginning of the eighteenth century, Western Civilization was still centered in Europe and continued to be dynamic and aggressive. That dynamism would be accentuated during the next three centuries.

THINGS YOU SHOULD KNOW

The Babylonian Captivity of the papacy and the Great Schism
The Protestant Reformation
Luther
Peace of Augsburg
Literalists
Anabaptists
Calvin and predestination
Henry VIII
The Catholic Reformation
Loyola
Council of Trent
Rembrandt

Bernini
Consequences of the Reformation era
Significance of new weaponry
Charles V
Philip II
Cervantes
Thirty Years' War
English civil war
Cromwell
Glorious Revolution
Louis XIV

SUGGESTED READINGS

Two good introductions to the Reformation era are Lewis W. Spitz, *The Protestant Reformation, 1517–1559* (New York: Harper & Row, 1986) and A. G. Dickens, *Reformation and Society in the Sixteenth Century* (New York: Harcourt Brace, 1966). On Martin Luther, see James Atkinson, *Martin Luther and the Birth of Protestantism* (Louisville, Ky.: Westminster/John Knox Press, 1981). Richard L. DeMolen (ed.), *Leaders of the Reformation* (Cranbury, N.J.: Susquehanna Univ. Press, 1984) offers good essays on Zwingli, Calvin, Loyola, and Cromwell.

A good text on the wars of the sixteenth and seventeenth centuries is Richard S. Dunn, *The Age of Religious Wars, 1559–1689* (New York: Norton, 1979). More specific works include Cicely V. Wedgwood, *The Thirty Years' War* (London: Routledge, Chapman, & Hall, 1981), which is very readable, and Christopher Hill, *The Century of Revolution, 1603–1714* (New York: Norton, 1961), a major interpretation of the English civil war emphasizing the radical groups that emerged in seventeenth-century England.

NOTES

[1] Quoted in George Huppert, *After the Black Death: A Social History of Early Modern Europe* (Bloomington: Indiana Univ. Press, 1986), p. 143.

[2] Quoted in John C. Olin, "The Catholic Reformation," in *The Meaning of the Renaissance and Reformation*, ed. Richard L. DeMolen (Boston: Houghton Mifflin, 1974), p. 274.

[3] Quoted in Christopher Hill, *The Century of Revolution, 1603–1714* (New York: Norton, 1961), p. 173.

[4] Quoted in Christopher Hibbert, *The English: A Social History* (New York: Norton, 1987), p. 254.

[5] Ibid., p. 260.

Index

Aachen, 149
Abbasid Caliphate, 134, 135
Abelard, Peter, 189
Abraham, 49–50, 52
Absolutism, 123, 264
Academy (Plate), 80
Acapulco, 242
Achilles, 65
Acropolis, 78
Act of Supremacy (1534), 253
A.D. (Anno Domini), 2*n*
Adam, 48
Adrianople, battle of, 120
Aeneas, 90
Aeneid (Virgil), 90, 98
Aeschylus, 76, 77
Agricultural Revolution, 145–48
Agriculture
    communal farming system in, 145, 208
    discovery of in Neolithic era, 7–8
    and enclosure movement, 208
    in Middle Ages, 145–48, 208
    role of, in development of civilization, 10
Ahriman, 39
Ahura-Mazda, 39
Aires, Buenos, 242
Akkadians, 15
Albert of Aix, 174
Albigensian Crusade, 178
Alchemy, 238
Alcuin of York, 149
Alexander the Great, 18, 60, 82, 94
Alexandria
    Christianity in, 108
    Hellenistic culture in, 84, 85
Alhambra Palace, 135
Alighieri, Dante, 229
Alphabet. *See* Writing
Americas, Spanish explorations in, 185, 242–43, 258
Amos, 58
Amsterdam, as center of capitalism, 260–61

Anabaptists, 251–52
Analects (Confucius), 30
Anatolia, 29
Anaxagoras, 69
Anaximenes, 69
Angleland, 121
Angles, 116, 121, 141, 175
Anglican church, 263
Animistic religion, 4–5
Anjou, 176
Anthony of Egypt, 111
Antigone (Sophocles), 77
Antigonid kingdom, 82
Antioch, Christianity in, 108
Anti-Semitism, 62, 174–75
Antony, Mark, 98
Aphrodite, 65, 69
Apollo, 65
Appian, 96
Appian Way, 101
Aqueduct, 92, 101
Aquitaine, 179, 185, 204–5
Arabesque art, 135
Arabs
    expansion of power, 116, 133–34
    as threat to Byzantine Empire, 127
Archbishops, 108
Archilochus, 68, 69
Archimedes, 85
Architecture
    Egyptian, 17–18
    Gothic, 171–74
    Romanesque, 171, 172
Archpoet, 187–88
Ares, 65
Arete, 65
Aristarchus, 84
Aristocracy, in Middle Ages, 209–11
Aristophanes, 79–80
Aristotle, 81–82, 184, 189, 190, 191
Armenia, 14
Art
    Arabesque, 135
    Byzantine, 126–27
    in Greece, 78–79

during the Reformation, 255–56
  Renaissance, 230–31
Arthur, King of England, 185
Art of Love (Ovid), 99
Aryans, 35–36
Ashurbanipal, 23
Aśoka, 38
Assyrians, 19, 23, 44–45, 56
Astrolabe, 241
Astrology, 236, 238
Athena, 66, 78
Athens, 71–74
  Persian threat to, 75
Augsburg, Peace of, 251
Augsburg, War of the League of (1689–1697), 265
Augustine, 111–12
Augustulus, Romulus, 121
Augustus, 98–99
Avars, 116, 127
Avicenna, 135
Axial period
  general characteristics of, 28–29
  religious influence of, 118, 120
  significance of, 41–43
Axial revolution, causes of, 29
Ayatollahs, 131
Aztecs, 22, 242

Babylon, 59
Babylonian captivity of the papacy, 248
Babylonian Empire, 15, 56
Bacon, Roger, 191
Baghdad, 135
Ball, John, 205
Baptism, 108
Barbary pirates, 228
Barraclough, Geoffrey, 181
Basil I, 128
Bath, B. H. Slicher van, 196
Baths, 101
Bavaria, 179, 181
B.C. ("before Christ"), 2*n*
Becket, 177
Becket, Thomas, 176
Bede, 143
Beggars, 215
Benedictine Rule, 142–44
Bernard of Clairvaux, 170
Bernini, Giovanni Lorenzo, 255, 256
Bill of Rights (English), 264
Biruni, al-, 135
Bishop, 108

Bishop, John, 264
Black Death, 202, 220–22
Boccaccio, Giovanni, 221–22, 229
Boeotia, 79
Boethius, 141
Boleyn, Anne, 253, 254
Botticelli, Sandro, 231
Bourgeois, 211, 213
Bowra, C. M., 65
Braehe, Tycho, 238
Brahman, 35
Brahmins, 36
Brandenburg, 262
Breasted, James, 17
Brown, Peter, 121–22
Brueghel, Pieter, 255
Buddha, 36–37, 42
Buddhism, 28, 29, 34, 36–37, 43, 118
  Mahayana, 38
  monasticism, 142
  spread of, 38
Bulgaria, 128
Bulgars, 128
Bull, 180–81
Byzantine Empire, 116
  Christianity in, 125–27
  end of, 128–29
  external and internal conflict, 127–28
  under Justinian, 102, 124–25, 140
Byzantium, 110

Cabral, Pedro Alvarez, 240
Cadmus, 69
Caesar, Julius, 97
Caesaropapism, 125
Calamities, 224
Caligula, 102–3, 103
Caliphs, 133
Calvin, John, 252–53
Calvinism, 253, 263
Canaan, 49, 56
Cannons, 259
Canon of Medicine (Avicenna), 135
Canton, 239
Capet, Hugh, 178
Capetian dynasty, 178
Cape Verde, 239
Capitalism, 168
  evolution of, 209, 220, 225–26
Caravel, 241
Cardinals, College of, 168
Carmelites, 254–55
Carolingian Renaissance, 149

Carolingian Empire, 149–51
Carthage, 94
Cartier, Jacques, 242–43
Cassiodorus, 141, 144
Caste system, 35–36, 38
Catherine of Aragon, 253
Catherine of Siena, 224
Catholic Inquisition, 169
Cavaliers, 263
Cervantes, Miguel de, 262
Chaldeans, 23
Champagne fairs, 167–68
Charlemagne, 149–51
Charles I (King of England), 263
Charles II (King of England), 264
Charles IV (King of Germany), 180
Charles V (Spain), 251, 257, 258, 260
Charles the Bald, 151
Children's Crusade, 183–84
Chimney, 212
China
  Chou dynasty in, 30
  Confucianism in, 30, 32–33
  Han dynasty in, 34, 117, 118
  impact of religion on, 34
  Shang civilization in, 21–22
  Sui dynasty in, 117, 118
  Sung dynasty in, 225
  T'ang dynasty in, 117, 118
  Taoism in, 33
Chou dynasty, 30
Christianity
  Byzantine, 125–27
  in the early Roman Empire, 108–9
  institutions in, 107–8
  message in, 107
  origins and growth of, 104–9
  and spiritual transformation of Roman Empire, 111–12
  teachings of Jesus in, 104
Christianization, 110
Cicero, 96–97, 98
Cistercians, 170
Citeaux, 170
City, life in, during Middle Ages, 211, 213–15
City of God (Augustine), 112
City-states
  Greek, 67
  Sumerian, 12
Civilization, development of, 9–10
Clark, Kenneth, 232
Claudius, 102–3
Cleisthenes, 72–73

Cleopatra, 98
Cluny, monastery at, 170
Codex Justinianus, 124
Coinage, early, 29
Colosseum, 95, 102
Columbus, Christopher, 185, 240
Common law, 176
Communal farming system, 145
Compass, 225
Confessions (Augustine), 112
Confucianism, 28, 30, 32–33, 34, 42–43, 118
Confucius, 28, 30, 32–33
Conquistadores, 185, 242, 258
Consolation of Philosophy (Boethius), 141
Constantine, 124
Constantinople, 110, 121, 124–25, 128, 135
  capture of, 129
  sieges of, 127
Copernicus, Nicolaus, 84, 238
Coronado, Francisco Vásquez, 242
Cortes, Hernando, 242
Cosmology, 5
Cosmos, 41, 42, 69
Council of Paris (1277), 190
Council of Trent (1545–1563), 255
Crassus, 97
Creation myth, 48–49, 51
Crete, Minoan civilization on, 20
Crime, in Middle Ages, 215–16
Cro-Magnon, 6
Cromwell, Oliver, 263–64
Crusades, 128–29, 156, 174, 176, 183–84
Cuba, 240
Cultural adaptation, 3
Cuneiform writing, 12, 31
Czechs, 128, 181

da Gama, Vasco, 239
Damascus, 133
Daniel, 60–61
Dark Ages, 140
Dating method, 2*n*
David, 54, 55
da Vinci, Leonardo, 232
Decameron (Boccaccio), 221, 229
Decline and Fall of the Roman Empire (Gibbon), 116
Defensor Pacis (Marsiglio), 229–30
Delian league, 79

INDEX

Delilah, 53
Democracy
  in Athens, 71–74
  definition of, 71
de Soto, Hernando, 242
Devolution, War of, 265
Diaspora, 174
Diggers, 264
Diocletian, 109–10, 157
Dionysus, 65
Divine Comedy (Dante), 229
Domesday Book, 175
Dominicans, 170
Domitian, 103
Donatello, 230
Don Quixote (Cervantes), 262
Dorian peoples, 64
Drama, in Greece, 76–77, 79–80
Duby, Georges, 140
Dutch War (1672–1678), 265

Earth, age of, 2
Eckhart, Meister, 224
Edict of Milan, 110
Education, monastic schools, 144
Egypt
  Arab seizure of, 133
  Hebrews in, 50
Egyptian civilization, 16–19
  Late Period, 18–19
  Middle Kingdom, 18
  New Kingdom, 18–19
  Old Kingdom, 16–18
Eleanor of Aquitaine, 176, 186
Elements of Geometry (Euclid), 84
El Greco, 262
Eliot, T. S., 236
Elizabeth I (Queen of England), 254, 257
Empedocles, 69
Enclosure movement, 208
England
  attempts to convert Angles and Saxons in, 141–44
  civil war in, 263–64
  enclosure movement in, 208
  Glorious Revolution in, 264
  and Hundred Years' War, 205, 222–23
  monarchy in, 175–77, 257–58
  Peasants' Revolt of 1381 in, 205
  reformation in, 253–54
  and Spanish Armada, 260
  War of the Roses in, 223

Enki, 14
Epic, 15
Epic of Gilgamesh, 15–16, 18
Epicureanism, 83
Epicurus, 83
Erasmus, Desiderius, 234
Erastosthenes, 84
Eriksson, Leif, 152
Essays (Montaigne), 234–35
Etruscans, 90
Eucharist, 108
Euclid, 84
Euphrates River, 13–14
Eurasia, nomad invaders of, 116–18, 120
Euripides, 79
Eve, 48
Exchequer, 176
Exiguus, Dionysius, 104
Exodus, 50

Fairs, 167
Famine, in Middle Ages, 202–4
Faust, Dr., 238
Ferdinand I (Holy Roman Emperor), 257, 258, 260
Ferdinand of Aragon, 184–85, 257, 258
Feudalism, 154
  feudal relationships, 154–57
  manorialism, 157
  serfdom, 157
Ficino, Marsilio, 230
Flagellation, 224
Flavian dynasty, 103
Florence, 225, 228
France
  Huguenots in, 265
  and Hundred Years' War, 205, 222–23
  Jacquerie rebellion in, 205
  under Louis XIV, 264–65
  monarchy in, 178–79, 257–58
Franciscans, 170, 191
Francis I (King of France), 257
Francis of Assisi, 170
Franconia, 179
Frankland, 121, 149
Franks, 116, 121
Frederick Barbarossa, 180, 183
Fronde, 265
Frost, Frank, 65
Fulcher of Chartres, 183

Gaius Gracchus, 96
Galen, 125
Galileans, 105
Galilei, Galileo, 238
Gandhi, Mohandas, 37–38
Gaul, 121, 149
Genesis, 48–49, 51, 144
Genghis Khan, 224
Genoa, 166
Gentiles, 105
Germanic tribes, 109
  invasions by, 120–21, 122–24
  origin of, 120
Germany
  Peasants' War of 1525 in, 205
  Thirty Years' War in, 262
  use of national monarchy in, 179–81
Ghettoes, 174
Ghiberti, Lorenzo, 230–31
Gibbon, Edward, 116
Giotto di Bondone, 230
Gladiators, 102
Glorious Revolution, 264
Goa, 239
God, Judaeo-Christian perception of, 146
Golden Bull of 1356, 180–81
Goliath, 53
Goths, 116
Grain mills, 146
Granada, Spain, 135
Great Pyramid of Gizeh, 17
Great Schism, 249
Greco-Roman heritage, importance of preserving, 141
Greek civilization, 64
  Athenian, 71–82
  Dark Ages, 64–66
  Hellenistic era, 82–84
  Homeric age of, 64–66
  intellectual and artistic creativity, 75–78
  Ionic age of, 66–69
  law, 67–68
  Peloponnesian War, 79–80
  Persian threat to, 75
  philosophy, 41, 68–69
  position of women and slaves, 74–75
  religion, 65–66
  slaves in, 69–70
  society, 78–79
  Sparta, 69–71

Greek Orthodox Church, 128
Greenland, 152
Gregory of Tours, 123
Gregory the Great, Pope, 141
Gregory VII, Pope, 168–69, 179
Grosseteste, Robert, 191
Grotius, Hugo, 260
Gunpowder, 225, 259
Gupta dynasty, 117
Gutenberg, Johannes, 227

Hades, 65
Hadith, 131
Hadrian, 103
Hammurabi, 15
Hammurabi's code, 15
Han dynasty, 34, 117, 118
Hanging gardens of Babylon, 23
Hannibal, 94
Hanseatic League, 166–67
Hardy, Thomas, 200
Hastings, battle of, 175
Hebrew religion, origins of, 49–50, 52
Hebrews, 39, 40–41, 42
Hebrew state, establishment of, 41–56
Hecataeus, 69
Hegel, G. W. F., 17
Hegira, 130
Hellenes, 111
Hellenistic Age of Greece, 82–84
Hellenistic inventions, 85–86
Heloise, 189
Helots, 69–70
Henry II (King of England), 176
Henry IV, (King of Germany), 179–80
Henry VII (King of England), 223, 257
Henry VIII (King of England), 253–54, 257
Henry the Navigator, 239
Hera, 65
Heraclitus, 69
Heraclius, 127
Herjolfsson, Bjarni, 152
Herlihy, David, 186
Herlinda of Eika, 141
Hero, 85
Herodotus, 77
Herophilus, 84
Hesiod, 65
Hetairai, 74
Hieroglyphics, 31

High Middle Ages, 162
  See also Middle Ages
Hilda of Whitby, 141
Hindu-Arabic system of numbers, 119
Hinduism, 28, 35–36, 118
Hippocrates, 84
Hispaniola, 240
Hittites, 19, 23
Hobbes, Thomas, 2, 263, 264
Holbein, Hans, 255
Hollister, C. Warren, 123, 156
Holocaust, 62
Holy Roman Empire, 179, 258, 260
Homer, 64, 65
Homeric age, in Greece, 64–66
Hood, Robin, 177
Horace, 99
Horatius, 90–91
Hormuz, 239
Horse, 22
  and invention of stirrup, 154–55
  use of, in agriculture, 145–46
Hortensian Law, 92
Hosea, 58
Huguenots, 265
Humanism, 234
Humanitas, 100
Humans, early, 2–3
Hundred Years' War (1338–1453), 179, 205, 222–23, 257
Huns, 116, 117, 120–21, 127
Hunting
  in Neolithic era, 6–7
  in Paleolithic era, 3
Hus, John, 249
Hyksos, 18, 19, 23, 50

Ice ages, 6
Iceland, 152
Icon, 125
Iconoclasm, 127–28
Iliad (Homer), 64, 65
Imans, 131
Inca Empire, 22
Index, 255
India
  Buddhism in, 36–37
  castes in, 35–36
  early civilization in, 19–20, 34–35
  Gupta period in, 117
  Hindu-Arabic system of numbers, 119
  Hinduism in, 35–36
  Hun invasions of, 117

Jainism in, 37–38
literature in, 117
numerical system in, 117
impact of religion on, 38–39
Individualism, growth of, 187–88
Indulgences, sale of, 250
Indus valley civilization, 19–20
Innocent III, Pope, 169, 178
Institutes of the Christian Religion (Calvin), 252
Investiture controversy, 169, 179–80
Ionia, 66–69
Ireland, Monks in, 141
Iron Age, 22
Irrigation, early, 11
Isaac, 49
Isabella of Castile, 185, 257, 258
Isaiah, Second, 59–60
Islam, 28, 116, 118, 129
  expansion of, 133–34
  Islamic faith, 130–33
  Muhammad, 130
  political unity of, 135
  Shiite, 133
  society and culture, 134–36
  Sunni, 133
  weakening of, 135
Israel, 41–56
Israelites, 52
Italy
  Renaissance in, 226, 228–34
  Roman conquest of, 93–94

Jacob, 49, 50
Jacquerie, 205, 224
Jainism, 37–38
Jamaica, 240
James I (King of England), 263
James II (King of England), 264
Jaspers, Karl, 28, 42
Jeremiah, 58
Jesuits, 255
Jesus, 130
  followers of, 105–7
  teachings of, 104–5
Jews, 59, 174–75
Jihad, 133
Job, 59
John (King of England), 177, 178
John the Baptist, 104, 105
Journeymen, 213
Judah, 56, 59
Judaism, 28, 29, 40–41, 130
  after the prophets, 60–61

Judaism, *continued*
  impact of, on western civilization, 61–62
Julio-Claudian emperors, 102–3
Julius II, Pope, 232
Jury, 176
Justinian, 102, 124–25, 140
Jutinian's Code, 188
Jutes, 121, 175

Karma, 35, 36
Kassites, 23
Kepler, Johannes, 238
Kiev, Byzantine influence on, 128
Koran, 130–31, 131
Kshatriya, 36
Kublai Khan, 224

Lais (of Corinth), 74
Lancasters, 223
Langland, Williams, 212
Language, origin of, 3–4
Languedoc, 178, 202
Lao-tzu, 28, 33
Lateen sail, 241
Lateran Coucil, Fourth, 169
Latins, 90
Law
  Babylonian, 15
  feudal, 156
  Ionian, 67–68
  under Justinian, 124
  in Rome, 92–93, 100, 102
Lechfeld, battle of, 179
Leo, Emperor of Byzantium, 127
Lepidus, 98
Lesbos, 68
Levellers, 264
Leviathan (Hobbes), 264
Liberalism, 264
Libyans, 19
Liege, 155
Lindisfarne, 152
Lion in Winter, 177
Literalists, 251
Literature
  Babylonian, 15–16
  Greek, 64–65
  Indian, 117
  in Middle Ages, 187–88
  Nouvelles, 197
  in the Renaissance, 229–30, 234, 236
Locke, John, 264

Lombards, 116
Lothair, 151
Louis IX (St. Louis), (King of France), 178
Louis XI (King of France), 257
Louis XIV (King of France), 264–65
Louis the German, 151
Love, "courtly" or "romantic", 185–86
Loyola, Ignatius, 255
Luke, 105
Luther, Martin, 249–52
Lutheran church, 251
Lycurgus, 69
Lydians, 29
Lyons, 149
Lyric poetry, 68
Lysistrata (Aristophanes), 80

Macao, 239
Macedonia, 82, 94
Macedonian dynasty (Byzantine Empire), 128
Machiavelli, 232–34
Magellan, Ferdinand, 240
Magna Carta, 177
Magnetic compass, 241
Magyars, 151, 179
Mahayana Buddhism, 38
Malacca, 239
Malmesbury, Eilmer of, 164
Malmesbury Abbey, 164
Manetti, Gianozzo, 230
Manorialism, 154, 157
  decline of, 207–8
Manzikert, battle of, 183
Marcus Aurelius, 103
Marathon, battle of, 75
Marie of Chapagne, 186
Marius, Gaius, 96
Mark, 105
Marriage, in Middle Ages, 200–1
Marsiglio of Padau, 229–30
Martel, Charles, 133, 149
Mary II (of Orange), 264
Matthew, 104
Maximilian I, 258
Mayan civilization, 22
Mecca, 130
Medici family, 228
Medici, Cosimo de, 230
Medina, 130
Mendoza, Pedro de, 242
Mesoamerica, 7, 22
Mesopotamian civilizations, 22, 12–16

INDEX

Messiah, 61
Mexico City, 243
Michelangelo, 232, 256
Middle Ages, 140–41
  agricultural revolution in, 145–48
  architecture in, 171–74
  aristocracy in, 209–11
  Black Death in, 202–3, 220–22
  Carolingian Empire, 149–51
  Church in, 168–74
  contributions of monks and nuns, 141–44
  crime and punishment in, 215–16
  crusades in, 183–85
  famines in, 202–4, 220
  feudalism in, 154–57
  guilds in, 213
  Hundred Years' War in, 222–23
  Jews in, 174–75
  Magyar invasions of, 151
  manorialism in, 154, 157, 207–8
  peasants in, 197–202, 204–9, 215
  rise of national monarchies in, 175–82
  scholasticism in, 188–92
  serfdom in, 157, 207–8
  social changes in, 185–88
  technology in, 164–66, 212
  towns in, 163–64, 211, 213–15
  trade in, 166–68
  university in, 188–89
  Viking invasions, 151–54
Milan, 225, 228
Miletus, 69, 72
Militarization, 109
Milton, John, 264
Minoan civilization, 20, 23, 64
Minotaur, 20
Mirandola, Pico della, 230
Mithraism, 109
Mithras, 109
Moksha, 35, 36
Moldboard plow, 145, 147
Moliére, 265
Monarchies, 12
  in Eastern Europe, 181
  in England, 175–77, 257–58
  in France, 178–79, 257–58
  in Germany, 179–81
  in Spain, 257–58
Monasticism, 111, 170
Mongols, 135, 224
Monolatry, 48
Monotheism, 48, 129
Montaigne, Michel de, 234

Monte Cassino, Italy, 142
Montpellier, 202
Moravia, 128
More, Sir Thomas, 234
Moses, 50, 52
Muawiya, 133
Muhammad, 130
Muller, Herbert J., 28
Muslims, 129, 130, 133. See also Islam
Mycenaean civilization, 64
Myron, 79
Myth, 5

Nagasaki, 239
Naples, 211
Native Americans, 242–43
Navigation, improvements in, 241
Nebuchadnezzar, 23
Needham, Joseph, 225
Neolithic era, 6–8
  impact of, 9
  religion in, 8
  tools in, 4
Nero, 102–3, 103
Nerva, 103
Netherlands
  art in, 260
  growth of capitalism, 260–61
  independence of, 260
  and Spain, 258, 260–62
New Amsterdam, 261
New stone age. See Neolithic era
New Testament, 104–5
Nirvana, 37, 42
Nomad invasions, 22–23
  consequences of the, 118, 120
Norman Conquest, 175
North America, Viking explorations of, 152
Northern renaissance, 234–36
Nostradamus, 236
Notre Dame, 172
Nouvelles, 197
Number system, in India, 117, 119

Octavian, 98
Odysseus, 65
Odyssey (Homer), 64, 65
Old stone age. See Paleolithic era
Old Testament, 54–55
Olmecs, 22
Olympia, 67
Olympic games, 67, 86

On the Dignity and Excellence of Man (Manetti), 230
On the Fabric of the Human Body (Vesalius), 238
On the Revolutions of the Celestial Bodies (Copernicus), 238
Optimates, 96
Orlinsky, Harry, 61
Ostracism, 73
Ostrogoths, 121, 141
Otto I, the Great, 179
Ottoman Turks, 129, 260
Otto the Great, 179
Ovid, 99
Oxford, 190
Oxford, University of, 188

Paleolithic era, 2–3
  human thought and religion during, 3–6
  last millennia of, 6
  tools in, 4
Palestine, 104
Panama, 240
Pandora, 77
Papacy, 168–69
Papism, 125
Paracelsus, 238
Paradise Lost (Milton), 264
Pariahs, 36
Paris, 211
Paris, University of, 188–89
Parliaments, 177
Parthenon, 73, 78
Patricians, 91
Paul, 105–6, 144
Pax Mongolica, 220, 224–26
Pax Romana, 98
Peasants, 197
  customs and attitudes, 200–2
  decline of manorial system, 207–8
  expansion of, in Eastern Europe, 208–9
  material conditions of, 197–98
  rebellions, 204–5, 251
  standard of living, 206–7
  village life of, 198–200
Peasants' Revolt of 1381, 205
Peasants' War of 1525, 251
Peloponnesian War, 79–80
Pepin the Short, 149
Pericles, 79
Perioeci, 70
Persia, threat of, to Athens, 75

Persian Empire, 23
  nomad attacks on, 117–18
Persians, 39, 59, 75
Peter, 105, 108
Petrarca, Francesco, 229
Pharoah, 17
Pheidippides, 75
Phidias, 79
Philip Augustus II, (King of France), 177, 178
Philip II (King of Spain), 257, 260
Philip of Macedon, 82
Philip the Good, 164
Philistines, 53
Philosophy
  Greek, 68–69, 80–82
  Hellenistic, 83–84
  humanism, 230, 234
  liberalism, 264
  platonism, 230
  scholasticism, 189–92
Phoenician alphabet, 23, 29, 31
Phoenicians, 20–21, 53
Piers the Plowman, 212
Pindar, 86
Pisa, 225
Pius, Antoninus, 103
Pizarro, Francisco, 242
Plato, 80–81, 189
Platonism, 230
Plebeians, 91
Plow, 10
Poitiers, 133, 149
Poland, 128, 181
Polo, Marco, 225
Polytheism, 5
Pompey, 97
Poor
  in Middle Ages, 215
  See also Peasants
Pope, 108
Populares, 96
Pornai, 74
Portugual, exploration of, 239–40
Poseidon, 65
Praise of Folly (Erasmus), 234
Praxiteles, 79
Predestination, 252–53
Priests, 108
Prince (Machiavelli), 233
Printing press, 225, 227
Procopius of Caesarea, 124
Prometheus, 77
Prophet, 56

INDEX

Prophetic movement, 56–60
Protestant reformation, 249–52
Prussia, 184, 262
Ptolemaic kingdom, 82
Ptolemy, 84
Punic Wars, 94
Puritans, 263
Pyramids, Egyptian, 17
Pythagoras, 69
Pytheas of Massalia, 85

Quadrant, 241

Race, origin of, 3
Raphael, 232
Reconquista, 184
Reeve, 175
Reformation
　art during, 255–56
　Catholic, 254–55
　consequences of, 256–57
　in England, 253–54
　Protestant, 248–53
Religion
　Buddhism, 36–37, 118
　Confucianism, 30, 32–33, 118
　Greek, 65–66
　Hinduism, 35–36
　impact of, on Chinese history, 34
　impact of, on Indian history, 38–39
　Jainism, 37–38
　Judaism, 40–41, 48–61
　neolithic, 8
　origin and growth of Christianity, 104–9
　Paleolithic, 4–6
　Roman, 94
　Sumerian, 14
　Taoism, 33
　Zoroastrianism, 39, 118
Rembrandt van Rijn, 255–56, 260
Remus, 90
Renaissance, 220
　in Italy, 226, 228–34
　Northern Renaissance, 234–36
　science and magic during, 236, 238
Republic (Plato), 80–81
Rich, Lord, 210
Richard the Lionhearted, 183
Roads, Roman, 101
Roman Catholic Church, 128, 168
　abuses in, leading to reformation, 250–51
　anticlericalism in, 249

Avignon papacy, 248–49
and the Babylonian captivity, 248
for the common people, 170–71
contributions of monks and nuns, 141–44
and the Council of Trent, 255
and the Crusades, 183–84
in England, 176
and the Great Schism, 249
and investiture controversy, 179–80
monasticism, 170
papacy, 168–69
and the *Pax Ecclesiae*, 156–57
and reactions to calamities, 224
and the Reformation, 254–55
Romanesque and Gothic architecture, 171–74
significance of medieval political history, 182
and status of women, 186
Rome
　Christianity in, 104–9, 110
　conquest of Italy, 93–94
　decline of empire, 116
　early history of, 90–91
　empire, 98–110, 102–4
　end of the republic, 96–98
　first-century emperors, 102–3
　five good emperors, 103–4
　grandeur and degradation of Roman society, 100–102
　impact of Roman conquests on, 94–96
　laws in, 100, 102
　Pax Romana in, 98
　philosophy in, 94
　political transformation of Empire, 109–10
　Punic Wars, 94
　religion in, 94
　republic, 91–94
　roads, 101
　slaves in, 102
　spiritual transformation of the Empire, 111–12
　Western Europe after fall of, 121–23
　women in, 100
Romulus, 90
Romulus Augustulus, 121
Roundheads, 263
Rubens, Peter Paul, 255
Runneymede, 177

St. Benedict of Nursia, 142
St. Dominic, 170
St. Francis, 170, 191
St. John of the Cross, 255
St. Patrick, 141
St. Peter's Basilica, 232, 256
St. Teresa, 254, 255
St. Thomas Aquinas, 190
Sakyamuni, Siddārtha Gautama, 36
Salamanca, University of, 188
Salamis, battle of, 75
Salerno, University of, 188
Samaria, 56
Samson, 53
Sancta Sophia, Church of, 124–25
Sappho, 68–69
Sardinia, 94
Sargon I, 15
Sassanian Persia, 117–18, 127, 133
Saul, 54
Savonarola, Girolamo, 231
Saxons, 116, 121, 141, 175
Saxony, 179, 181
Scholasticism, 189–92
Schwartz, Benjamin, 42
Science
  in Hellenistic Greece, 84, 85–86
  in Renaissance, 236, 238
  See also Technology
Scotus, John Duns, 190
Sea Peoples, 19, 23
Secularization, 169
Seleucid Kingdom, 82
Seljuk Turks, 128, 183
Senate, 91
Serfdom, 157, 207–8
  expansion of, in Eastern Europe, 208–9
Serfs, legal status of, 207–8
Seymour, Jane, 253
Shakespeare, William, 223, 236, 237
Shang civilization, 21–22, 23, 29
Sheba, Queen of, 54
Sheriff, 175
Shiite Muslims, 133
Shires, 175
Sic et Non (Abelard), 189
Sicily, 94
Simeon the Stylite, 111
Sistine Chapel, 232
Sixtus IV, Pope, 232
Slavery
  in Greece, 69–70, 74–75
  in Rome, 91–92, 102

Slavs, 116, 128, 181
  as threat to Byzantine Empire, 127
Slovaks, 128
Social history, 196
Socrates, 80
Sodom, 50
Solomon, 55, 56
Solon, 72
Sophists, 77–78
Sophocles, 77
Spain
  in Americas, 240, 242–43, 258
  and Holy Roman Empire, 258, 260
  monarchy in, 257–58
  and the Netherlands, 258, 260–62
  Reconquista in, 184
Spanish Armada, 260
Spanish Succession, War of (1702–1713), 265
Sparta, 69–71, 72, 79
Sphinxes, 17–18
Spiritualization, 42
Stirrup, invention of, 154–55
Stoicism, 84, 94
Subinfeudation, 155
Sudra, 36
Suger, the Abbot of Saint-Denis, 171
Sui dynasty, 117, 118
Sumerian civilization, 12–15
Summa Theologica (Aquinas), 190
Sung dynasty, 225
Sunni Muslims, 133
Sweden, 262
Syphilis, 243

T'ang dynasty, 117, 118
Taoism, 28, 33, 34, 42, 43
Technology
  as cause of Axial revolution, 29
  in Hellenistic Age, 85–86
  improvements in navigation, 241
  medieval, 164–66
  in Middle Ages, 212, 225
  printing press, 227
  role of, in develoment of civilization, 10, 11
  weaponry, 259
Tell, William, 204
Ten Commandments, 52
Tetzel, Johann, 250
Teutonic Knights, 184
Thales of Miletus, 68–69
Theocracy, 12

INDEX

Theodora, Empress of Byzantium, 124
Theodoric, 122
Theodosius I, 110, 120
Theogony, 65
Thermopylae, battle at, 75
Thirty Years' War, 262
Thomism, 190
Thucydides, 79
Thuringians, 123
Tiberius Gracchus, 96, 102–103
Tigris River, 13–14
Titus, 103
Toledo, 184
Toltec, 22
Topkapi Palace, 135
Toulouse, 178
Tours, 133
Towns, medieval, 163–64
Trade
  medieval, 166–68
  Phoenician, 20–21
  role of, in development of civilization, 10
Trajan, 103
Trial by ordeal, 123
Tribal Assembly, 92
Trojan War, 64, 65
Trojan Women (Euripides), 79
Troyes, Chretien de, 185
Twelve Tables, 100
Tyler, Wat, 205

Ulema, 130–31
Umayyad dynasty, 133, 134
University, 188–89
Upanishads, 35
Utopia (More), 234

Vaisya, 36
Vandals, 116, 121
Van Eyck, Jan, 234
Vassals, 155
Vedas, 35
Vega, Lope de, 262
Venice, 166, 225, 228
Ventadorn, Bernart de, 186
Verdun, Treaty of, 151
Vesalius, Andreas, 238
Vespucci, Amerigo, 240

Via Appia, 101
Vikings, 151–54, 175
Villages, in Middle Ages, 198–200
Virgil, 90, 98
Visigoths, 120, 121

War of the Roses, 223, 257
Water mill, 164, 165
Weaponry, 259
Western Europe, after the fall of Rome, 121–23
Westphalia, Peace of, 262
White, Lynn, Jr., 166
William III (King of England), 264
William IX, duke of Aquitaine, 186
William of Occam, 190–91
William the Conqueror, 175–76, 177
Windmill, 164, 165
Witch-hunting, 256–57
Women
  in Athens, 74–75
  in Carolingian Empire, 151
  in Middle Ages, 186–87, 201–2, 213–15
  Muslim, 132–33
  in Neolithic era, 7
  in Paleothic era, 3
  in Rome, 100
Worms, 180
Writing
  Egyptian, 31
  Mesopotanian, 31
  Phoenician, 23, 29, 31
  Sumerian, 12

Yahweh, 50, 56
Yathrib, 130
Yehweh, 52
Yemen, 129
Yorks, 223

Zarathustra, 39
Zeno of Citium, 84
Zeus, 65–66, 77, 94
Zimmern, Alfred, 78
Zoroaster, 28, 39
Zoroastrianism, 28, 29, 39, 42, 60, 118
Zwingli, Huldrych, 252